BASED ON DAVE ELLIS' BECOMING A MASTER STUDENT

THE ESSENTIAL GUIDE TO
Becoming a
Master Student

Second Edition

Doug Toft

Contributing Editor

WADSWORTH
CENGAGE Learning

Australia • Brazil • Canada • Mexico • Singapore • Spain • United Kingdom • United States

WADSWORTH
CENGAGE Learning™

The Essential Guide to Becoming a Master Student
Second Edition
Ellis

Senior Sponsoring Editor: Shani Fisher

Development Editor: Daisuke Yasutake

Media Editor: Amy Gibbons

Senior Marketing Manager: Kirsten Stoller

Marketing Coordinator: Ryan Ahern

Marketing Communications Manager:
Courtney Morris

Content Project Manager: Jessica Rasile

Senior Art Director: Pam Galbreath

Print Buyer: Julio Esperas

Senior Rights Acquisition Specialist, Images:
Jennifer Meyer Dare

Senior Rights Acquisition Specialist, Text:
Katie Huha

Text Designer: Susan Gilday

Cover Designer: Yvo Riezebos

Cover Image: Ted Humble-Smith/RF/Getty

Project Management/Composition:
MPS Limited, a Macmillan Company

Library of Congress Control Number: 2010930871
ISBN-13: 978-0-495-91371-9
ISBN-10: 0-495-91371-5

Wadsworth
20 Channel Center Street
Boston, MA 02210
USA

Cengage Learning is a leading provider of customized learning solutions with office locations around the globe, including Singapore, the United Kingdom, Australia, Mexico, Brazil and Japan. Locate your local office at **international.cengage.com/region**

Cengage Learning products are represented in Canada by Nelson Education, Ltd.

For your course and learning solutions, visit **www.cengage.com**.

Purchase any of our products at your local college store or at our preferred online store **www.cengagebrain.com**.

Printed in the United States of America
1 2 3 4 5 6 7 14 13 12 11

THE ESSENTIAL GUIDE TO
Becoming a Master Student

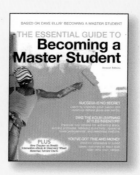

ADVISORY BOARD

Andrew Alt, *Bowling Green State University*

Eva S. Berg, *Edison State College*

Jay Christensen, *California State University, Northridge*

Cathy Clay, *Pellissippi State Technical Community College*

Karen Costa, *Mount Wachusett Community College*

Rachael Cragle, *Pellissippi State Technical Community College*

Susan Dutch, *Westfield State College*

Lorraine Fedrizzi, *Niagara Community College*

Doroteo Franco, *El Paso Community College*

Tracy Gottlieb, *Seton Hall University*

Patricia Gottschalk, *United States Air Force Academy*

Ryan K. Guth, *Lambuth University*

Nancy S. Hoefer, *Central Carolina Technical College*

Taryn Hutchins, *Spokane Falls Community College*

CoCo Hutchison, *Valencia Community College*

Joyce Kevetos, *Palm Beach Community College*

Joseph Kornoski, *Montgomery County Community College*

Edith T. Lang, *Brunswick Community College*

Charlene Latimer, *Daytona Beach Community College*

Mia Pierre, *Valencia Community College*

Paula M. Plageman, *Kutztown University*

Patty Santoianni, *Sinclair Community College*

Jennifer Scalzi, *American River College*

Sherri Singer, *Alamance Community College*

Bruce Skolnick, *Edinboro University of Pennsylvania*

Kathleen Speed, *Texas A&M University*

Lester Tanaka, *Community College of Southern Nevada*

John Timmons, *Winthrop University*

Mary Tolejko, *Erie Community College*

Oscar R. Velasquez, *El Paso Community College*

Jodi Webb, *Bowling Green State University*

Brief Contents

Contents

9 Choosing Greater Health

10 Choosing Your Major and Planning Your Career

Getting Started and Getting Involved

Making the transition to higher education: *Five things you can do now*

You share one ng in common with every other student at your school: Entering higher education represents a major change in your life. You've joined a new culture with its own set of rules, both spoken and unspoken. Feelings of anxiety, isolation, and homesickness are common among students. To master the transition, keep the following strategies in mind.

1. Plug into resources. These include people, campus clubs and organizations, and school and community services. Of all resources, people are the most important. You can isolate yourself, study hard, and get a good education. But when you establish relationships with teachers, staff members, fellow students, and employers, you can get a *great* education. Build a network of people who will personally support your success in school.

2. Meet with your academic advisor. Your academic advisor can help you access resources that will ease your transition. Meet with this person regularly. Advisors generally know about course requirements, options for declaring majors, and the resources available to you. Peer advisors might also be available.

3. Show up for class. Showing up for class occurs on two levels. The most visible level is being physically present in the classroom. Just as important is showing up mentally—taking detailed notes, asking questions, and contributing to discussions.

4. Take the initiative in meeting new people. Introduce yourself to classmates and instructors before or after class. Most of the people in this new world of higher education are waiting to be welcomed. You can help them and yourself at the same time.

5. Admit your feelings—whatever they are. Simply admitting the truth about how you feel—to yourself and to someone else—can help you cope with tough emotions. No matter how you feel, you can almost always do something constructive—such as going to class and completing assignments—in the present moment. If negative feelings make it hard for you to carry out the tasks of daily life, then gettalk with a professional, such as a counselor at the student health service. The act of seeking help can make a difference.

You're One Click Away . . .
from more strategies for mastering the art of transition.

Discover what YOU WANT from this chapter

Start becoming a master student this moment by doing a five-minute chapter preview. The goal is for you to get the big picture of what this chapter includes. This can help you understand and recall the details later.

Here's how to do the preview: Look at every page in this chapter. Move quickly. Scan headlines. Look at pictures. Notice any forms, charts, and diagrams. Then complete the following sentences.

Three things that I can do right away to promote my success in school are . . .

_____

_____

_____

_____

_____

_____

_____

_____

_____

_____

What I want most from this course and this chapter is . . .

_____

_____

_____

_____

_____

_____

_____

When you see 🖥 *You're One Click Away . . ., remember to go to this book's College Success CourseMate for additional content. And for a summary of this chapter, see the Master Student Review Cards at the end of this book.*

Start with the *Discovery Wheel*

The Discovery Wheel is an opportunity to tell the truth about the kind of person you are—and the kind of person you want to become.

This tool is based on a fundamental idea: Success in any area of life starts with telling the truth about what is working—and what *isn't*—in our lives right now. When we acknowledge our strengths, we gain an accurate picture of what we can accomplish. When we admit that we have a problem, we free up energy to find a solution.

It's that simple. The Discovery Wheel gives you an opportunity to sit back for a few minutes and think about yourself. This is not a test. There are no trick questions. There are no grades. The answers you provide will have meaning only for you.

HOW THE DISCOVERY WHEEL WORKS

The purpose of the Discovery Wheel is to gain awareness of your current behaviors—especially the kind of behaviors that affect your success in school. With this knowledge, you can choose new behaviors and start to enjoy new results in your life.

During this exercise, you will fill in a circle similar to the one on this page. The closer the shading comes to the outer edge of the circle, the higher the evaluation of a specific skill. In the example below, the student has rated her reading skills low and her note-taking skills high.

The terms *high* and *low* are not positive or negative judgments. When doing the Discovery Wheel, you are just making observations about yourself. You're like a scientist running an experiment—you are just collecting data and recording the facts. You're not evaluating yourself as good or bad.

Also remember that the Discovery Wheel is not a permanent picture of who you are. It is a snapshot in time—a picture of what you're doing right now. You'll do this exercise again, near the end of this book and at the end of the course. That means you will have a chance to measure your progress. So be honest about where you are right now.

To succeed at this exercise, tell the truth about your strengths. This is no time for modesty! Also, lighten up and be willing to laugh at yourself. A little humor can make it easier to tell the truth about your areas for improvement.

To begin this exercise, read the following statements and give yourself points for each one. Use the point system described below. Then add up your point total for each category and shade the Discovery Wheel on page 4 to the appropriate level.

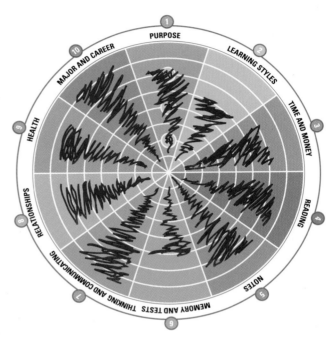

5 points
This statement is always or almost always true of me.

4 points
This statement is often true of me.

3 points
This statement is true of me about half the time.

2 points
This statement is seldom true of me.

1 point
This statement is never or almost never true of me.

1. _____ I can clearly state my overall purpose in life.
2. _____ I can explain how school relates to what I plan to do after I graduate.
3. _____ I capture key insights in writing and clarify exactly how I intend to act on them.
4. _____ I am skilled at making transitions.
5. _____ I seek out and use resources to support my success.

_____ Total score (1) **Purpose**

1. _____ I enjoy learning.
2. _____ I make a habit of assessing my personal strengths and areas for improvement.
3. _____ I monitor my understanding of a topic and change learning strategies if I get confused.
4. _____ I use my knowledge of various learning styles to support my success in school.
5. _____ I am open to different points of view on almost any topic.

_____ Total score (2) *Learning Styles*

1. _____ I can clearly describe what I want to experience in major areas of my life, including career, relationships, financial well-being, and health.
2. _____ I set goals and periodically review them.
3. _____ I plan each day and often accomplish what I plan.
4. _____ I will have enough money to complete my education.
5. _____ I monitor my income, keep track of my expenses, and live within my means.

_____ Total score (3) *Time and Money*

1. _____ I ask myself questions about the material that I am reading.
2. _____ I preview and review reading assignments.
3. _____ I relate what I read to my life.
4. _____ I select strategies to fit the type of material I'm reading.
5. _____ When I don't understand what I'm reading, I note my questions and find answers.

_____ Total score (4) *Reading*

1. _____ When I am in class, I focus my attention.
2. _____ I take notes in class.
3. _____ I can explain various methods for taking notes, and I choose those that work best for me.
4. _____ I distinguish key points from supporting examples.
5. _____ I put important concepts into my own words.

_____ Total score (5) *Notes*

1. _____ The way that I talk about my value as a person is independent of my grades.
2. _____ I often succeed at predicting test questions.
3. _____ I review for tests throughout the term.
4. _____ I manage my time during tests.
5. _____ I use techniques to remember key facts and ideas.

_____ Total score (6) *Memory and Tests*

1. _____ I use brainstorming to generate solutions to problems.
2. _____ I can detect common errors in logic and gaps in evidence.
3. _____ When researching, I find relevant facts and properly credit their sources.

4. _____ I edit my writing for clarity, accuracy, and coherence.
5. _____ I prepare and deliver effective presentations.

_____ Total score (7) *Thinking and Communicating*

1. _____ Other people tell me that I am a good listener.
2. _____ I communicate my upsets without blaming others.
3. _____ I build rewarding relationships with people from other backgrounds.
4. _____ I effectively resolve conflict.
5. _____ I participate effectively in teams and take on leadership roles.

_____ Total score (8) *Relationships*

1. _____ I have enough energy to study, attend classes, and enjoy other areas of my life.
2. _____ The way I eat supports my long-term health.
3. _____ I exercise regularly.
4. _____ I can cope effectively with stress.
5. _____ I am in control of any alcohol or other drugs I put into my body.

_____ Total score (9) *Health*

1. _____ I have a detailed list of my skills.
2. _____ I have a written career plan and update it regularly.
3. _____ I use the career-planning services offered by my school.
4. _____ I participate in internships, extracurricular activities, information interviews, and on-the-job experiences to test and refine my career plan.
5. _____ I have declared a major related to my interests, skills, and core values.

_____ Total score (10) *Major and Career*

Using the total score from each category above, shade in each section of the blank Discovery Wheel on the next page. If you want, use different colors. For example, you could use green for areas you want to work on.

REFLECT ON YOUR DISCOVERY WHEEL

Now that you have completed your Discovery Wheel, spend a few minutes with it. Get a sense of its weight, shape, and balance. How would it sound if it rolled down a hill?

Next, complete the following sentences in the space below. Just write down whatever comes to mind. Remember, this is not a test.

The two areas in which I am strongest are . . .

_____

_____

The two areas in which I most want to improve are . . .

_____

_____

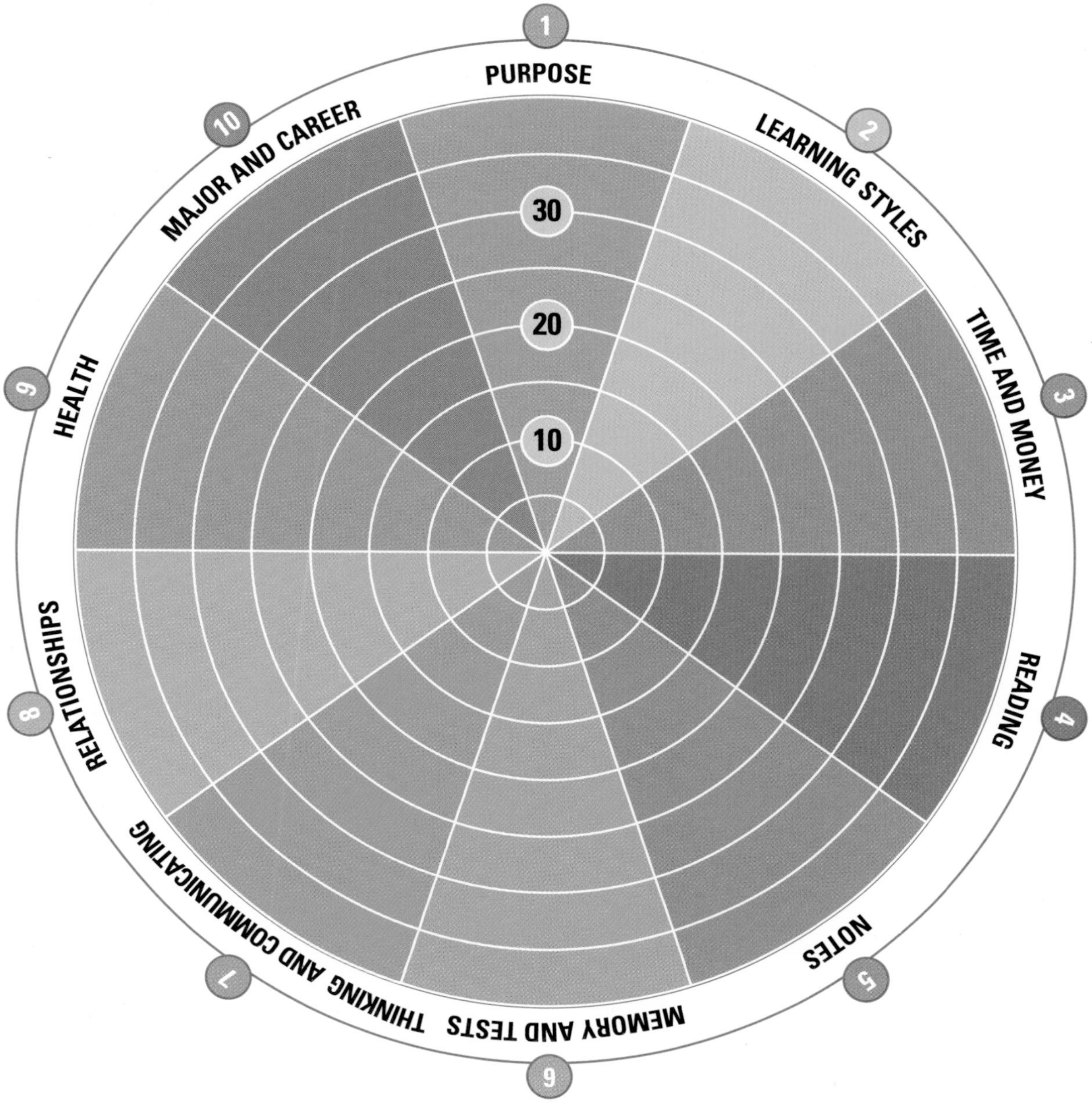
1
PURPOSE
2
LEARNING STYLES
3
TIME AND MONEY
4
READING
5
NOTES
6
MEMORY AND TESTS
7
THINKING AND COMMUNICATING
8
RELATIONSHIPS
9
HEALTH
10
MAJOR AND CAREER
30
20
10

Finally, take about 15 minutes to do a "textbook reconnaissance," much like the preview you did for this chapter. First, scan the table of contents for the entire book. Next, look at every page in the book. Move quickly. Skim the words in bold print. Glance at pictures. You'll see pages with ideas that might help you with the areas in your life you want to improve. Find five such ideas that look especially interesting to you. Write the page number and a short description of each idea in the space below.

Page number	Description

You're One Click Away . . .
from doing this exercise online.

The essentials OF
MASTERY

In 1482, Leonardo da Vinci wrote a letter to a wealthy baron, applying for work. In excerpted form, he wrote,

"I can contrive various and endless means of offense and defense. . . . I have all sorts of extremely light and strong bridges adapted to be most easily carried. . . . I have methods for destroying every turret or fortress. . . . I will make covered chariots, safe and unassailable. . . . In case of need I will make big guns, mortars, and light ordnance of fine and useful forms out of the common type." And then he added, almost as an afterthought, "In times of peace I believe I can give perfect satisfaction and to the equal of any other in architecture . . . can carry out sculpture . . . and also I can do in painting whatever may be done."[1]

The Mona Lisa, for example.

This book is about something that cannot be taught. It's about becoming a master student.

Mastery means attaining a level of skill that goes beyond technique. For a master, methods and procedures are automatic responses to the task at hand. The master carpenter is so familiar with her tools, they are part of her. To a master chef, utensils are old friends. Because these masters don't have to think about the details of the process, their work seems to happen by itself.

Mastery can lead to flashy results—an incredible painting, for example, or a gem of a short story. In basketball, mastery might result in an unbelievable shot at the buzzer. For a musician, it might be the performance of a lifetime, the moment when everything comes together.

The master student is in all of us. By design, human beings are learning machines. We have an innate ability to learn, and all of us have room to grow and improve. The unknown does not frighten the master student. In fact, he welcomes it—even the unknown in himself. The master student is open to changes in her environment and in himself.

One sign of mastery is a sense of profound satisfaction. Distractions fade. Time stops. Work becomes play. After hours of patient practice, after setting clear goals and getting precise feedback, the master has learned to be fully in control. At the same time, she lets go of control. Results happen without effort, struggle, or worry.

Of course, those statements make no sense. Mastery, in fact, doesn't make sense. It defies analysis. It cannot be explained. But it can be experienced. You could call it "flow" or being "in the zone." Or—*mastery.*

As you meet and read about people during your stay in higher education, look for those who excel at learning. You will find endless diversity among these master students. They are old and young, male and female. They exist in every period of history. And they come from every culture, race, and ethnic group. The master student is not a vague or remote ideal. Rather, master students move freely among us.

In fact, there's one living inside your skin. No matter what your past experiences, the master student within survives.

The Essential Guide to Becoming a Master Student offers many strategies for success in school and life. Use these strategies to discover the master student in you.

 You're One Click Away . . .
from more qualities of a master student.

Success
in *three words*

Success is no mystery. Successful people have left clues—*many* clues, in fact. There are thousands of articles and books that give tools, tips, techniques, and strategies for success. Do a Google search on *success* and you'll get over 300 million results.

If that sounds overwhelming, don't worry. Success is simply the process of setting and achieving goals. And the essentials of that process can be described in 10 words or less.

Actually, those essentials can be described in three words: *Discovery. Intention. Action.* Success is really that simple. It's not always easy, but there are no secrets about the process. If you did the Discovery Wheel on page 2, then you already got a taste of it.

Continue the process. Throughout this book are exercises labeled Commit to Action. These exercises are your chance to experience the essentials of success in three stages.

1. WRITE DISCOVERY STATEMENTS

The first stage is a Discovery Statement. These often begin with a prompt, such as, "I discovered that. . . ." Here is an opportunity to reflect on "where you are." Discovery Statements describe your current strengths and areas for improvement. Discovery Statements can also be descriptions of your feelings, thoughts, and behavior. Whenever you get an "aha!" moment—a flash of insight or a sudden solution to a problem—put it in a Discovery Statement. To write effective Discovery Statements, remember the following.

Record specifics. If you spent 90 minutes chatting online with a friend instead of reading your anatomy text, write about it. Include the details, such as when you did it, where you did it, and how it felt. Record your observations quickly, as soon as you make them.

Suspend judgment. When you are discovering yourself, be gentle. Suspend self-judgment. If you continually judge your behaviors as "bad" or "stupid," your mind will quit making discoveries. For your own benefit, be kind.

Be truthful. Suspending judgment helps you tell the truth about yourself. "The truth will set you free" is a saying that endures for a reason. The closer you get to the truth, the more powerful your Discovery Statements will be. And if you notice that you are avoiding the truth, don't blame yourself. Just tell the truth about it.

2. WRITE INTENTION STATEMENTS

Intention Statements can be used to alter your course. They are statements of your commitment to do a specific task or achieve a longer-range goal. Whereas Discovery Statements promote awareness, Intention Statements are blueprints for action. The two processes reinforce each other.

Make intentions positive. The purpose of writing intentions is to focus on what you want rather than what you don't want.

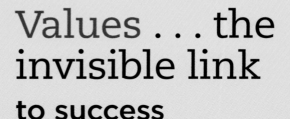

Values . . . the invisible link
to success

Values are the things in life that you want for their own sake. Even though they are invisible, values shape your attitudes, direct your goals, and guide your moment-by-moment choices. Your values define who you are and who you want to be. Success is about taking action that aligns with your values.

This book is based on a specific set of values. You live these values when you demonstrate:

- Focused attention—living fully and mindfully in the present moment.

- Self-responsibility—seeing your own thinking and behavior as the major factor in your success.

- Integrity—making and keeping agreements and staying true to your word.

- Risk taking—stretching yourself to accomplish larger goals, even if you fail occasionally.

- Contribution—taking action to reduce human suffering and promote the happiness of other people.

You're One Click Away . . .
from more information about defining your values and aligning your actions.

Instead of writing "I will not fall asleep while studying accounting," write "I intend to stay awake when studying accounting."

Make intentions observable. Rather than writing "I intend to work harder on my history assignments," write "I intend to review my class notes and write summary sheets of my reading." Writing summary sheets is a visible, physical action. There's no fooling yourself about whether you get it done.

Make intentions achievable. Give yourself opportunities to succeed. Break large goals into small, specific tasks that can be accomplished quickly. Timelines can help. For example, if you are assigned to write a paper, break the assignment into small tasks and set a precise due date for each one. You might write: "I intend to select a topic for my paper by 9 a.m. Wednesday."

3. ACT NOW!

Carefully crafted Discovery Statements are a beauty to behold. Precise Intention Statements can inspire awe. But neither will be of much use until you put them into action.

Life responds to what you *do*. Successful people are those who consistently produce the results that they want. And results follow from specific, consistent behaviors. If you want new results in your life, then adopt new behaviors.

Even simple changes in behavior can produce results. If you feel like procrastinating, then tackle just one small, specific task related to your intention. Find something you can complete in five minutes or less and do it *now*. For example, access just one Web site related to the topic of your next assigned paper.

Changing your behavior might lead to feelings of discomfort. Instead of reverting back to your old behaviors, befriend the yucky feelings. Tell yourself you can handle the discomfort just a little bit longer. Act on your intention. You will be rewarded.

REPEAT THE CYCLE

The process of discovery, intention, and action is a cycle. First, you write Discovery Statements about where you are now. Next, you write Intention Statements about where you want to be and the specific steps you will take to get there. Follow up with action—the sooner, the better.

Then start the cycle again. Write Discovery Statements about whether you act on your Intention Statements—and what you learn in the process. Follow up with more Intention Statements about what you will do differently in the future. Then move into action and describe what happens next.

This process never ends. Each time you repeat the cycle, you get new results. It's all about getting what you want and becoming more effective in everything you do. This is the path of mastery, a path that you can travel for the rest of your life.

 You're One Click Away . . .
from more suggestions for Discovery, Intention, and Action Statements.

Get the most *from* this *book*

Y ou can do several things to receive full value for the money you invested in this book.

Do this book. This book is unusual in that you will create much of it. The Critical Thinking Experiments and Commit to Action exercises call on you to reflect, write, and take action. Fill these pages with your own ideas.

If it works, use it. If it doesn't, lose it. If some sections of this book don't apply to you at all, skip them unless they are assigned. In that case, see if you can gain value from those sections anyway. When you are committed to getting value from this book, even an idea that seems irrelevant or ineffective at first can trun out to be a powerful tool.

Skip around. You can use this book in several different ways. You might read it straight through. Or pick it up, turn to any page, and find an idea you can use. Look for ideas you can use right now.

Claim your power. At the end of each chapter in this book, you'll find a *Power Process*. Each offers a suggestion for shifting your perspective or changing your behavior. The results can apply to any area of your life. Students consistently point to these short, offbeat, and occasionally outrageous articles as especially useful parts of the text. To test your understanding of the Power Processes, see whether you can take each one apply it to *any* topic in this book.

Go online for added content. Look for a recurring feature titled 🖥 "You're One Click Away. . . ." These are reminders to go online to **this text's College Success CourseMate** for useful ideas that didn't fit into the book.

Get key points at a glance. Turn to the back of this book for chapter summaries that you can tear out and review when you're on the go. There's also a one-page summary of the entire book and a complete list of "You're One Click Away. . . ." features.

CAMPUS RESOURCES—
You paid for them, so use them

A supercharger increases the air supply to an internal combustion engine. The resulting difference in power can be dramatic.

You can make just as powerful a difference in your education if you supercharge it by using all of the resources available to students. In this case, your "air supply" includes people, campus clubs and organizations, and school and community services.

Think about all the services and resources that your tuition money buys: academic advising to help you choose classes and select a major; access to the student health center and counseling services; a career planning office that you can visit even after you graduate; athletic, arts, and entertainment events at a central location; and much more.

If you live on campus, you also get a place to stay with meals provided, all for less than the cost of an average hotel room.

And, by the way, you also get to attend classes.

Name a challenge that you're facing right now: finding money to pay for classes, resolving conflicts with a teacher, lining up a job after graduation. Chances are that a resource on campus can help.

Following are a few examples of services available on many campuses. Check your school's catalog for even more.

Academic advisors can help you with selecting courses, choosing majors, career planning, and adjusting in general to the culture of higher education.

Alumni organizations can be good sources of information about the pitfalls and benefits of being a student at your school.

Arts organizations can include concert halls, museums, art galleries, observatories, and special libraries.

Athletic centers and gymnasiums often open weight rooms, swimming pools, indoor tracks, and athletic courts for students.

Churches, synagogues, mosques, and temples have members who are happy to welcome fellow worshippers who are away from home.

Childcare is sometimes provided at a reasonable cost through the early-childhood education department.

Computer labs, where students can go 24 hours a day to work on projects and use the Internet, are often free.

Counseling centers help students deal with the emotional pressures of school life, usually for free or at a low cost.

Financial aid offices help students with loans, scholarships, grants, and work-study programs.

Job placement and career-planning offices can help you find part-time employment while you are in school and a job after you graduate.

Libraries are a treasure chest on campus and employ people who are happy to help you locate information.

Newspapers published on campus list events and services that are free or inexpensive.

Registrars handle information about transcripts, grades, changing majors, transferring credits, and dropping or adding classes.

School media—including campus newspapers, radio stations, Web sites, and instructional television services—provide information about school policies and activities.

School security employees provide information about parking, bicycle regulations, and traffic rules. Some school security agencies provide safe escort at night for students.

Student government can assist you in developing skills in leadership and teamwork. Many employers value this kind of experience.

Student health clinics often provide free or inexpensive treatment of minor problems. Many counseling and student health centers target certain services to people with disabilities.

Student organizations offer you an opportunity to explore fraternities, sororities, service clubs, veterans' organizations, religious groups, sports clubs, political groups, and programs for special populations. The latter include women's centers, multicultural student centers, and organizations for international students, disabled students, and gay and lesbian students.

Student unions are hubs for social activities, special programs, and free entertainment.

Tutoring programs can help even if you think you are hopelessly stuck in a course—usually for free. Student athletes and those who speak English as a second language can often get help here.

Note: Community resources—those located off-campus—can range from credit counseling and chemical dependency treatment to public health clinics and churches. Check the city Web site.

You're One Click Away . . .
from more resources that can save you time and money.

Why are you in school?

In each chapter of this book is at least one Critical Thinking Experiment. These exercises offer you a chance to apply a model for thinking that's explained more thoroughly in Chapter 7: "Thinking." This model has two basic parts. The first part is creative thinking, which opens up many possible ideas about any topic and many possible solutions to any problem. The second part is critical thinking, which narrows down your initial ideas and solutions to those that are most workable and supported by logic and evidence.

This first experiment asks you to do both kinds of thinking. You will begin by creating ideas and then follow up by refining them.

Part 1

Select a time and place when you know you will not be disturbed for at least 20 minutes. Relax for two or three minutes, clearing your mind. Then complete the following sentences with any ideas that enter your mind. Continue on additional paper as needed.

What I want from my education is . . .

_____

_____

_____

When I complete my education, I want to be able to . . .

_____

_____

_____

I also want . . .

_____

_____

_____

_____

Part 2

After completing Part 1, take a short break. Reward yourself by doing something that you enjoy. Then review the above list of things that you want from your education. See whether you can summarize them in a one-sentence, polished statement. This will become a statement of your purpose for taking part in higher education.

Write several drafts of this purpose statement, and review it periodically as you continue your education. With each draft, see whether you can capture the essence of what you want from higher education—and from your life. Craft a statement that you can easily memorize, one that sparks your enthusiasm and makes you want to get up in the morning.

You might find it difficult to express your purpose statement in one sentence. If so, write a paragraph or more. Then look for the sentence that seems most charged with energy for you.

Following are some sample purpose statements:

- My purpose for being in school is to gain skills that I can use to contribute to others.

- My purpose for being in school is to live an abundant life that is filled with happiness, health, love, and wealth.

- My purpose for being in school is to enjoy myself by making lasting friendships and following the lead of my interests.

Write at least one draft of your purpose statement below:

_____

_____

_____

_____

_____

You're One Click Away . . .
from more sample purpose statements.

Master Students in Action

The master student is not a vague or remote ideal. Master students move freely among us. Consider the following examples of people who have found success in their own way.

JENNIE LONG

College: Seminole Community College, Sanford, FL
Major: Nursing
Goals: My goals are to become a registered nurse, to be a mentor to other adult learners, and to strive to learn something new every day. Every day I wake up determined to stay on track toward my goals. I am attending classes and studying to obtain my nursing degree, and I keep abreast of new medical discoveries. Also, I try to encourage someone else each day to pursue his or her goals.

Advice: It is important to keep a positive attitude and have an open mind while in college. Be willing to learn about new ideas and concepts and then apply this knowledge every day.

JENNIFER JARDING

College: Kilian Community College, Sioux Falls, SD
Major: Chemical Dependency Counseling
Goals: My goals in life today are simple really; I want to be the best me I can be. I have set an educational goal to finish my associate's degree in chemical dependency counseling. I have a financial goal to become debt free. I have set personal goals to have better relationships with my family. I aspire to be a more spiritually grateful and giving person as well.

Advice: My advice to new college students is to follow your dreams and don't underestimate yourself. Be aware of the reality of the study time that goes along with the classes you take. Sit in the front row. Ask questions. Participate often. Remember that you are paying for this, so you want to get as much out of it as possible. Not every class you take will be fun, but the satisfaction that comes from achieving definitely is.

ALEX DENIZARD

College: Technical Career Institute—College of Technology, New York, NY
Major: Networking Technology
View of Success: The feeling of accomplishment is a feeling like no other. To know what it is like to finish what you started and what it took to get there . . . I believe that success is not about what you have gained, but what you have gone through to achieve success.

Advice: Look ahead and never give up on yourself. Know that you are worth something and that no one can tell you any differently. Think about all you have been through. Think about what it took to get you thus far in your life. Don't think of being in college as a burden; on the contrary, think of it as just one more step toward your many other goals.

LIZ MURRAY

Liz Murray's life is about setting outrageous goals and meeting them. This is true even though she grew up in a household where both parents were addicted to cocaine and money was scarce. By age 16, Liz was living on the streets of New York City and had lost her mother to AIDS. Liz sensed that her life was now in her own hands. She vowed that she would create a new future for herself.

Though she had poor grades, Liz entered the Humanities Preparatory Academy in Manhattan at age 17. Because she was homeless, she spent long hours studying in a stairwell at school. The hard work paid off: She graduated in just two years.

After hearing about a college scholarship offered by the *New York Times* to needy students, Liz decided to apply. It worked. The *Times* awarded her a scholarship, and with that financial support Liz set a goal to attend Harvard University. She succeeded, enrolling there in the fall of 2000. After taking time off to care for her father, she eventually returned to Harvard to complete her degree. Today she works as an inspirational speaker.

CESAR CHAVEZ

Cesar Chavez dedicated his life to improving conditions for migrant workers in the United States. Chavez knew those conditions well. He, along with his four siblings and parents, entered the ranks of migrant workers during the Great Depression after his family lost their farm.

When Chavez was 12, his father and uncle joined a union, part of the Congress of Industrial Organizations, that was organizing fruit workers. Chavez learned firsthand about strikes, boycotts, fasts, and other nonviolent means of creating social change.

He never forgot those lessons. After serving in the United States Navy, Chavez returned to the fields as a community organizer. Despite the fact that he'd attended 65 elementary schools and never graduated from high school, Chavez cofounded and led the United Farm Workers (UFW) until his death in 1993. The UFW gained a national profile in 1968 after organizing a successful grape boycott that led to new contracts for migrant workers. Today the UFW is the largest union of its kind, with members in ten states.

SAMPSON DAVIS

"Determination is simply fixing your mind on a desired outcome, and I believe it is the first step to a successful end in practically any situation," wrote Sampson Davis, coauthor of *The Pact: Three Young Men Make a Promise and Fulfill a Dream.*

The pact referred to in that title is one that Davis made with two friends who grew up in a rough section of Newark, New Jersey. At age 17, they vowed to "beat the streets," get a college education, and become physicians.

To become a physician, Sampson had to take a state board exam. The first time he took the exam, Sampson failed it. Instead of giving up, he got help. He started seeing a counselor. He also asked for support from George Jenkins and Rameck Hunt, the friends with whom he'd made "the pact." He took the exam again and passed.

Today Davis is a board-certified emergency physician at St. Michael's Medical Center in Newark. Along with Jenkins and Hunt, he directs The Three Doctors Foundation, which offers mentoring, educational programs, and health services to kids from inner-city communities.

 You're One Click Away . . .
from more personal profiles in the Master Student Hall of Fame.

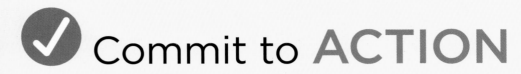

Commit to ACTION

Whom are you bringing with you?

You've succeeded in entering higher education. Congratulations. Behind you stand networks of people and services that support your success in school. Take some time now to discover the details about that network. Then commit to using it.

Discovery Statement

Reflect on all the people who helped you get this far in your educational journey. These people might include valued teachers, family members, fellow students, and friends. Think of those who helped you at a crucial point in your schooling and encouraged you to continue your education. These are the people who stand with you as you begin your freshman year. List their names in the space below, and use additional paper as needed.

I discovered that the people who've made a special contribution to my life so far include . . .

_____

_____

_____

_____

_____

_____

Intention Statement

Next, create an intention to use campus services. Examples include academic advising, counseling, tutoring, and services from the housing, financial aid, and health offices at your school. For ideas, see your school catalog and Web site. Use the space below to list specific services that interest you.

To support my success in school, I intend to . . .

_____

_____

_____

_____

_____

Action Statement

Finally, prepare to follow up with people on both of the lists that you've just created. List contact information (name, address, phone number, Web site address, and email address) for the people included in your Discovery Statement. Plan to thank them for supporting you. Keep them updated on how you're doing in school.

Also list contact information for the services included in your Intention Statement, and schedule a time to see someone from each office. Begin writing in the space below and continue on additional paper.

_____

_____

_____

_____

_____

_____

_____

_____

_____

_____

_____

_____

_____

_____

_____

_____

_____

_____

_____

_____

_____

_____

POWER process

Discover what you want

This chapter is all about getting what you want out of school. The point is this: Discovering what you want makes it more likely that you will attain it.

In all areas of life, knowing where you want to go increases the probability that you will arrive at your destination. Once your goals are defined precisely, your brain reorients your thinking and behavior. You're well on the way to actually *getting* what you want.

Suppose that you ask someone what she wants from her education and you get this answer: "I plan to get a degree in journalism with double minors in earth science and Portuguese so that I can work as a reporter covering the environment in Brazil." Chances are you've found a master student. The details of a person's vision offer clues to her mastery.

Discovering what you want greatly enhances your odds of succeeding in higher education. Students might invest years of their lives and thousands of dollars with only a hazy idea of their destination in life. Some quit school simply because they are unsure of their goals.

If you know what you want, you can constantly look for connections between your passions and your coursework. The more connections you discover, the more likely you'll stay in school—and succeed.

To move into action, use this book. It's filled with activities—including the Discovery Wheel and Commit to Action exercises—that encourage you to discover what you want to have, do, and be. Fill up those pages. Then turn your discoveries into immediate action. Every day, do one thing—no matter how simple or small—that takes you one step closer to your goals. Watch your dreams evolve from fuzzy ideals into everyday realities.

 You're One Click Away . . .
from more ideas about discovering what you want.

2

Using Your Learning Styles

Learning styles:
Discovering how you learn

R ight now, you are investing substantial amounts of time, money, and energy in your education. What you get in return for this investment depends on how well you understand the process of learning and use it to your advantage.

We learn by perceiving and processing When we learn well, says psychologist David Kolb, two things happen.[1] First, we *perceive*, that is, we notice events and take in new experiences. Second, we *process*, or deal with, experiences in a way that helps us make sense of them.

Some people especially enjoy perceiving through *concrete experience*. They like to absorb information through their five senses. They learn by getting directly involved in new experiences. When solving problems, they rely on intuition as much as intellect. These people typically function well in unstructured classes that allow them to take initiative.

Other people favor perceiving by *abstract conceptualization*. They take in information best when they can think about it as a subject separate from themselves. They analyze, intellectualize, and create theories. Often these people take a scientific approach to problem solving and excel in traditional classrooms.

People also process experiences differently. Some people favor processing information by *reflective observation*. They prefer to stand back, watch what is going on, and think about it. They consider several points of view as they attempt to make sense of things and generate many ideas about how something happens. They value patience, good judgment, and a thorough approach to learning.

Other people like to process experience by *active experimentation*. They prefer to jump in and start doing things immediately. These people do not mind taking risks as they attempt to make sense of things; this helps them learn. They are results oriented and look for practical ways to apply what they have learned.

Discover what
YOU WANT
from this chapter

T he Discovery Wheel on page 2 includes a section titled *Learning Styles.* Take some time right now to go beyond your responses to that section. Think about times in the past when you felt successful at learning. Were you in a highly structured setting, with a lot of directions about what to do and feedback on how well you did at each step? Were you free to learn at your own pace and in your own way? Were you part of a small group, or did you work alone in a quiet place? In the space below, describe any patterns in the way you prefer to learn.

_____

_____

_____

_____

_____

_____

_____

_____

_____

Next, spend five minutes skimming this chapter. Then complete the following sentence:

The topics in this chapter that interest me most are . . .

_____

_____

_____

_____

_____

_____

_____

When you see 🖱 *You're One Click Away . . ., remember to go to this book's College Success CourseMate for additional content. And for a summary of this chapter, see the Master Student Review Cards at the end of this book.*

Directions for completing the
LEARNING STYLE INVENTORY

To help you become more aware of learning styles, Kolb developed the Learning Style Inventory (LSI). This inventory is included on the next page. Responding to the items in the LSI can help you discover a lot about ways you learn.

The LSI is not a test. There are no right or wrong answers. Your goal is simply to develop a profile of your current learning style. So, take the LSI quickly. You might find it useful to recall a recent time when you learned something new at school, at home, or at work. However, do not agonize over your responses.

Note that the LSI consists of 12 sentences, each with four different endings. You will read each sentence, and then write a "4" next to the ending that best describes the way you currently learn. Then you will continue ranking the other endings with a "3," "2," or "1," with "1" representing the ending that least describes you. You must rank each ending. *Do not leave any endings blank.* Use each number only once for each question.

Following are more specific directions:

1 Read the instructions at the top of page LSI-1. When you understand example A, you are ready to begin.

2 Before you write on page LSI-1, remove the sheet of paper following page LSI-2.

3 While writing on page LSI-1, *press firmly* so that your answers will show up on page LSI-3.

4 After you complete the 12 items on page LSI-1, go to page LSI-3.

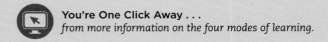

You're One Click Away . . .
from more information on the four modes of learning.

Perceiving and processing—an example

Suppose that you get a new cell phone. It has more features than any phone you've used before. You have many options for learning how to use it. For example, you could do any of the following:

- Just get your hands on the phone right away, press some buttons, and see whether you can dial a number or send a text message.
- Read the instruction manual and view help screens on the phone before you try to make a call.
- Recall experiences you've had with phones in the past and what you've learned by watching other people use their cell phones.
- Ask a friend who owns the same type of phone to coach you as you experiment with making calls and sending messages.

These actions illustrate the different ways of perceiving and processing:

- Getting your hands on the phone right away and seeing whether you can make it work is an example of learning through concrete experience.
- Reading the manual and help screens before you use the phone is an example of learning through abstract conceptualization.
- Recalling what you've experienced in the past is an example of learning through reflective observation.
- Asking a friend to coach you through a hands-on activity with the phone is an example of learning through active experimentation.

Four modes of learning and four questions

A learning style is a unique blending of the possible ways of perceiving and processing experience. Learning styles can be described in many ways. To keep things simple, just think in terms of four *modes* of learning.

Mode 1 learners are concrete and reflective. They seek a purpose for new information and a personal connection with the content. They want to know that a course matters and how it challenges or fits in with what they already know. These learners embrace new ideas that relate directly to their current interests and career plans. In summary, Mode 1 learners ask, *Why learn this?*

Mode 2 learners are abstract and reflective. They crave information. When learning something, they want to know the main facts, ideas, and procedures. They seek a theory to explain events and are interested in what experts have to say. Often these learners like ideas that are presented in a logical, organized way. They break a subject down into its key elements or steps and master each one in a systematic way. Mode 2 learners ask, *What is the content?*

Mode 3 learners are abstract and active. They hunger for an opportunity to try out what they're studying. They want to take theories and test them by putting them into practice. These learners thrive when they have well-defined tasks, guided practice, and frequent feedback. Mode 3 learners ask, *How does this work?*

Mode 4 learners are concrete and active. They get excited about going beyond classroom assignments. They apply what they're learning in various situations and use theories to solve real problems. Mode 4 learners ask, *What if I tried this in a different setting?*

Learning Style Inventory

Before completing the items, remove the sheet of paper following this page. While writing, press firmly.

1. When I learn: _____ I like to deal with my feelings. _____ I like to think about ideas. _____ I like to be doing things. _____ I like to watch and listen.

2. I learn best when: _____ I listen and watch carefully. _____ I rely on logical thinking. _____ I trust my hunches and feelings. _____ I work hard to get things done.

3. When I am learning: _____ I tend to reason things out. _____ I am responsible about things. _____ I am quiet and reserved. _____ I have strong feelings and reactions.

4. I learn by: _____ feeling. _____ doing. _____ watching. _____ thinking.

5. When I learn: _____ I am open to new experiences. _____ I look at all sides of issues. _____ I like to analyze things, break them down into their parts. _____ I like to try things out.

6. When I am learning: _____ I am an observing person. _____ I am an active person. _____ I am an intuitive person. _____ I am a logical person.

7. I learn best from: _____ observation. _____ personal relationships. _____ rational theories. _____ a chance to try out and practice.

8. When I learn: _____ I like to see results from my work. _____ I like ideas and theories. _____ I take my time before acting. _____ I feel personally involved in things.

9. I learn best when: _____ I rely on my observations. _____ I rely on my feelings. _____ I can try things out for myself. _____ I rely on my ideas.

10. When I am learning: _____ I am a reserved person. _____ I am an accepting person. _____ I am a responsible person. _____ I am a rational person.

11. When I learn: _____ I get involved. _____ I like to observe. _____ I evaluate things. _____ I like to be active.

12. I learn best when: _____ I analyze ideas. _____ I am receptive and open-minded. _____ I am careful. _____ I am practical.

Critical Thinking Experiment: Take a snapshot of your learning styles

This page and the Commit to Action on page LSI-6 are intended to be culminating exercises. Before you do these exercises, complete the Learning Styles Inventory and read the rest of this chapter.

Any inventory of your learning styles is just a snapshot that gives a picture of who you are today. Your answers are not right or wrong. Your score does not dictate who you can become in the future. The key questions are simply "How do I currently learn?" and "How can I become a more successful learner?"

Take a few minutes right now to complete the following sentences describing your latest insights into the ways you currently prefer to learn.

If someone asked me, "What do you mean by learning styles, and can you give me an example?" I'd say . . .

When learning well, I tend to . . .

I would describe my current learning style(s) as . . .

When I study or work with people whose learning styles differ from mine, I usually respond by . . .

Remove this sheet before completing the Learning Style Inventory.

This page is inserted to ensure that the other writing you do in this book doesn't show through on page LSI-3.

Remove this sheet before completing the Learning Style Inventory.

This page is inserted to ensure that the other writing you do in this book doesn't show through on page LSI-3.

Scoring your Inventory

Now that you have taken the Learning Style Inventory, it's time to fill out the Learning Style Graph (page LSI-5) and interpret your results. To do this, please follow the next steps.

1 First, add up all of the numbers you gave to the items marked with brown F letters. Then write down that total to the right in the blank next to "**Brown F**." Next, add up all of the numbers for "**Teal W**,"

"**Purple T**," and "**Orange D**," and also write down those totals in the blanks to the right.

2 Add the four totals to arrive at a GRAND TOTAL and write down that figure in the blank to the right. (Note: The grand total should equal 120. If you have a different amount, go back and re-add the colored letters; it was probably just an addition error.) Now remove this page and continue with Step 3 on page LSI-5.

Scorecard

Brown F   total _____

Teal W   total _____

Purple T   total _____

Orange D   total _____

GRAND TOTAL   _____

F	T	D	W
W	T	F	D
T	D	W	F
F	D	W	T
F	W	T	D
W	D	F	T
W	F	T	D
D	T	W	F
W	F	D	T
W	F	D	T
F	W	T	D
T	F	W	D

Remove this sheet after you have completed Steps 1 and 2 on page LSI-3. Then continue with Step 3 on page LSI-5.

Learning Style Graph

3 Remove the sheet of paper that follows this page. Then transfer your totals from Step 1 on page LSI-3 to the lines on the Learning Style Graph below. On the brown (F) line, find the number that corresponds to your "**Brown F**" total from page LSI-3. Then write an X on this number. Do the same for your "**Teal W**," "**Purple T**," and "**Orange D**" totals. The graph on this page is yours to keep and to refer to, and the graph on page LSI-7 is for you to turn in to your professor if he or she requires it.

4 Now, pressing firmly, draw four straight lines to connect the four X's and shade in the area to form a kite. (For an example, see the illustration to the right.) This is your learning style profile. Each X that you placed on these lines indicates your preference for a different aspect of learning:

Concrete experience ("Feeling"). The number where you put your X on this line indicates your preference for learning things that have personal meaning and have connections to experiences in your life. The higher your score on this line, the more you like to learn things that you feel are important and relevant to yourself.

Reflective observation ("Watching"). Your number on this line indicates how important it is for you to reflect on the things you are learning. If your score is high on this line, you probably find it important to watch others as they learn about an assignment and then report on it to the class. You probably like to plan things out and take the time to make sure that you fully understand a topic.

Abstract conceptualization ("Thinking"). Your number on this line indicates your preference for learning ideas, facts, and figures. If your score is high on this line, you probably like to absorb many concepts and gather lots of information on a new topic.

Active experimentation ("Doing"). Your number on this line indicates your preference for applying ideas, using trial and error, and practicing what you learn. If your score is high on this line, you probably enjoy hands-on activities that allow you to test out ideas to see what works.

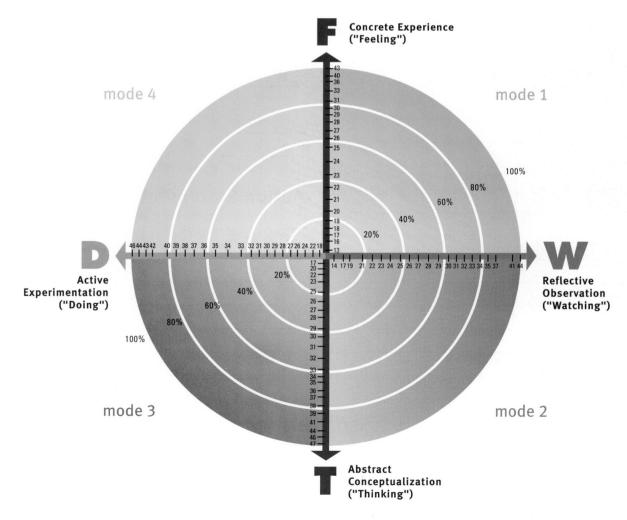

Commit to Action: Create value from learning styles

This page and the Critical Thinking Experiment on page LSI-2 are intended to be culminating exercises. Before you do these exercises, complete the Learning Styles Inventory and read the rest of this chapter.

The concept of learning styles is controversial. As you talk to students and instructors, you may find some who believe that teachers should provide a variety of activities to engage students with different learning styles. Other people might deny that matching teaching styles and learning styles makes much difference.

As you think critically about these different viewpoints, remember that you don't have to believe in any of them. (See the Power Process: "Ideas are tools" on page 43.) Just reflect on the insights you've gained from this chapter and test them for yourself. See whether you can *use* these insights to become more successful in school and the workplace.

Discovery Statement

After reading and doing this chapter, my ideas about learning styles have changed in the following ways . . .

_____

_____

_____

_____

_____

_____

_____

_____

_____

_____

_____

_____

_____

_____

_____

Intention Statement

To effectively use my preferred learning styles, I intend to . . .

_____

_____

_____

_____

_____

_____

_____

_____

_____

_____

To explore other learning styles, I intend to . . .

_____

_____

_____

_____

_____

_____

_____

_____

_____

Action Statement

To act on the above intentions, I will . . .

_____

_____

_____

_____

_____

_____

Remove this sheet before completing the Learning Style Graph

This page is inserted to ensure that the other writing you do in this book does not show through on page LSI-7.

Remove this sheet before completing the Learning Style Graph

This page is inserted to ensure that the other writing you do in this book does not show through on page LSI-7.

Using your learning style profile to succeed

Each mode of learning highlighted in the Learning Styles Inventory represents a unique blend of concrete experience, reflective observation, abstract conceptualization, and active experimentation. Remember that any idea about learning styles will make a difference in your life only when it leads to changes in your behavior:

- *To develop Mode 1,* ask questions that help you understand *why* it is important for you to learn about a specific topic. You might want to form a study group or join an online or campus-based community where you can debate and discuss topics from your course.

- *To develop Mode 2,* ask questions that help you understand *what* the main points and key facts are. Also, learn a new subject in stages. For example, divide a large reading assignment into sections and then read each section carefully before moving on to the next one.

- *To develop Mode 3,* ask questions about *how* a theory relates to daily life. Also, allow time to practice what you learn. You can do experiments, conduct interviews, create presentations, find a relevant work or internship experience, or even write a song that summarizes key concepts. Learn through hands-on practice.

- *To develop Mode 4,* ask questions about ways to use what you have just learned in several different situations (*what if?*) Also, seek opportunities to demonstrate your understanding. You could coach a classmate about what you have learned, present findings from your research, explain how your project works, or perform your song.

The main point is this: Even when teachers don't promote all four modes of learning, you can take charge of the way you learn. In the process, you take charge of your education and create new options for success.

You're One Click Away . . .
More ways to use your current learning styles and develop new ones.

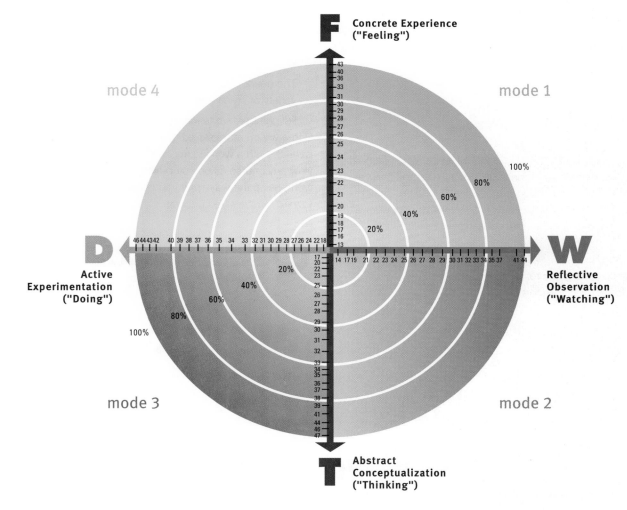

More views of learning styles

There are many theories of learning styles, and any of them can support your success in school. In addition to David Kolb's ideas about experiential learning, for example, you might hear about the VAK system. This theory focuses on preferences related to

- Seeing, or *visual* learning.
- Hearing, or *auditory* learning.
- Movement, or *kinesthetic* learning.

Howard Gardner of Harvard University developed the theory that no single measure of intelligence can tell us how smart we are. In his theory of multiple intelligences, Gardner describes:[2]

Verbal/linguistic intelligence—learning through speaking, writing, reading, and listening.

Mathematical/logical intelligence—skill at working with numbers, logic, problem solving, patterns, relationships, and categories.

Visual/spatial intelligence—a preference for learning through images, including charts, graphs, maps, mazes, tables, illustrations, art, models, puzzles, and costumes.

Bodily/kinesthetic intelligence—learning through physical activity such as role playing, games, and model building.

Musical/rhythmic intelligence—a preference for expression through songs and rhythms.

Intrapersonal intelligence—self-motivation combined with a deep awareness of personal feelings and values.

Interpersonal intelligence—skill at cooperative learning and awareness of the feelings of others.

Naturalist intelligence—a love of the outdoors and skill at observing nature.

To prevent confusion, remember that there is one big idea behind theories about learning styles. They all promote *metacognition* (pronounced "metta-cog-NI-shun"). *Meta* means "beyond" or "above." *Cognition* refers to everything that goes on inside your brain—perceiving, thinking, feeling, and urges to act. So, metacognition refers to your ability to view your thoughts, emotions, and behaviors from beyond—that is, to take an objective viewpoint and accurately observe the ways you learn. With that perspective, you can choose to think and act in new ways. Metacognition is one of the main benefits of higher education.

In addition, theories about learning styles share the following insights:

- People differ in important ways.
- We can see differences as strengths—not deficits.
- Relationships improve when we take differences into account.
- Learning is continuous—a *process,* as well as a series of outcomes.
- We *create* knowledge rather than simply absorbing it.
- We have our own preferences for learning.
- We can often succeed by matching our activities with our preferences.
- Our preferences can expand as we experiment with new learning strategies.
- The deepest learning takes place when we embrace a variety of styles and strategies.

Remember that teachers in your life will come and go. Some will be more skilled than others. None of them will be perfect. With a working knowledge of learning styles, you can view any course as one step along a path to learning what you want, using the ways that *you* choose to learn. On this path toward mastery, you become your own best teacher.

You're One Click Away . . .
More information on multiple intelligences and VAK learning styles

POWER process

Risk being a fool

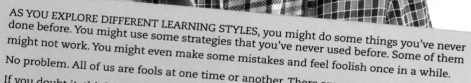

AS YOU EXPLORE DIFFERENT LEARNING STYLES, you might do some things you've never done before. You might use some strategies that you've never used before. Some of them might not work. You might even make some mistakes and feel foolish once in a while.

No problem. All of us are fools at one time or another. There are no exceptions.

If you doubt it, think back to that stupid thing you did just a few days ago. You know the one. Yes . . . *that* one. It was embarrassing, and you tried to hide it. You pretended you weren't a fool. This happens to everyone.

We are all fallible human beings. Most of us, however, spend too much time and energy trying to hide our foolhood. No one is really tricked by this—not even ourselves. And whenever we pretend to be something we're not, we miss part of life.

This Power Process comes with a warning label: Taking risks does not mean escaping responsibility for our actions. "Risk being a fool" is not a suggestion to get drunk at a party and make a fool of yourself. It is not a suggestion to act the fool by disrupting class. It is not a suggestion to be foolhardy or to "fool around."

"Risk being a fool" means that foolishness—along with courage and cowardice, grace and clumsiness—is a human characteristic. We all share it. You might as well risk being a fool because you already are one, and nothing in the world can change that. Why not enjoy it once in a while?

There's one sure-fire way to avoid any risk of being a fool, and that's to avoid life. The writer who never finishes a book will never have to worry about getting negative reviews. The center fielder who sits out every game is safe from making any errors. And the comedian who never performs in front of an audience is certain to avoid telling jokes that fall flat.

For a student, the willingness to take risks means releasing your pictures about how you're "supposed" to learn. Be willing to appear the fool as you experiment with new learning styles. The rewards can include more creativity, more self-expression, and more joy.

You're One Click Away . . .
from more ways to take creative risks.

3

Taking Charge of Your Time and Money

You've got *the time—and the money*

The words *time management* may call forth images of restriction and control. You might visualize a prune-faced Scrooge hunched over your shoulder, stopwatch in hand, telling you what to do every minute. Bad news.

Here's some good news: You do have enough time for the things you want to do. All it takes is thinking about the possibilities and making conscious choices.

Time is an equal opportunity resource. All of us, regardless of gender, race, creed, or national origin, have exactly the same number of hours in a week. No matter how famous we are, no matter how rich or poor, we get 168 hours to spend each week—no more, no less.

Approach time as if you were in control. Sometimes it may seem that your friends control your time, that your boss controls your time, that your teachers or your parents or your kids or somebody else controls your time. Maybe that is not true, though. When you say you don't have enough time, you might really be saying that you are not spending the time you *do* have in the way that you want.

The same idea applies to money. When you say you don't have enough money, the real issue might be that you are not spending the money you *do* have in the way that you want.

Most money problems result from spending more than is available. It's that simple, even though we often do everything we can to make the problem much more complicated. The solution also is simple: Don't spend more than you have. If you are spending more than you have, then increase your income, decrease your spending, or do both.

Again, you are in control of what you spend. This idea has never won a Nobel Prize in economics, but you won't go broke applying it.

Everything written about time and money management boils down to two ideas. One is knowing exactly *what* you want. The other is knowing *how* to get what you want. State your wants as written goals. Then choose actions that will help you meet those goals.

Strategies for managing time and money are not complicated. In fact, they're not even new. These strategies are all based on the cycle of discovery, intention, and action that you're already practicing in this book. Throw in the ability to add and subtract, and you have everything you need to manage your time and your money.

You can learn to spend time and money in ways that align with your values. That's the purpose of this chapter.

Discover what **YOU WANT** from this chapter

The Discovery Wheel on page 2 includes a section titled *Time and Money*. Take some time to go beyond your initial responses to that section. First, spend five minutes skimming this chapter. Then complete the following sentences honestly and without self-judgment.

The most important goal for me to accomplish this school year is . . .

_____

_____

_____

_____

_____

_____

Right now my biggest challenge in managing money is . . .

_____

_____

_____

_____

_____

Ideas from this chapter that I want to use include. . .

_____

_____

_____

_____

_____

_____

When you see 🔘 *You're One Click Away . . ., remember to go to this book's College Success CourseMate for additional content. And for a summary of this chapter, see the Master Student Review Cards at the end of this book.*

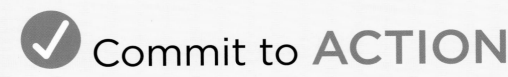

Commit to ACTION

Give your goals some teeth

Many of us have notions about what we want out of life. They are warm, fuzzy ideals such as "I want to be a good person," "I want to be financially secure," or "I want to be happy." Left in such vague terms, however, these notions will seldom lead to any results.

Another option is to translate your ideals into goals. Find out what a goal looks like. Listen to what it sounds like. Pick it up and feel it. Make your goal as real as the teeth on a chain saw.

The key is to state your goals as specific outcomes. Think in detail about how things will be different once your goals are attained. List the changes in what you'll see, feel, touch, hear, do, or have. Whenever possible, state this outcome as a result that you can measure.

Perhaps one of your desires is to get a good education and graduate on time. Translate that into: "Graduate with a B.S. degree in engineering, with honors, by 2014."

Suppose that you want to improve your health. You might translate that into "lose 10 pounds over the next 10 months."

Likewise, a desire to improve your personal finances could translate into "pay off my car loan in 24 months" or "reduce my monthly expenses by 10 percent."

Next, use a process of brainstorming and evaluation to break down each goal into short-term actions. When you analyze a goal down to this level, you're well on the way to meeting it.

You're about to experience the process of setting a goal for yourself. Gather a pen, extra paper, and a watch with a second hand. To get the most benefit, follow the stated time limits. The entire exercise takes about 30 minutes.

Discovery Statement

For 10 minutes write down everything that you want in your life. Write as fast as you can and write whatever comes into your head. Leave no thought out. Don't worry about accuracy. The object of a brainstorm is to generate as many ideas as possible. Begin your list in the space below and continue on additional paper as needed. Simply brainstorm as many answers as possible to the following sentence:

I discovered that I want . . .

_____

_____

_____

_____

_____

_____

_____

_____

_____

_____

_____

_____

_____

_____

_____

_____

_____

_____

_____

_____

_____

_____

_____

_____

_____

_____

_____

_____

_____

_____

_____

_____

Intention Statement

After you have finished brainstorming, spend the next five minutes looking over your list. Analyze what you wrote. Read the list out loud. If something is missing, add it.

Then look for *one* thing on the list that's important to you right now, even if it's something that might take many years and many steps to achieve. State this as a goal—a specific outcome or result to achieve by a certain date.

Write your goal in the following space.

I intend to . . .

_____

_____

_____

_____

_____

_____

_____

_____

_____

_____

_____

_____

_____

_____

_____

_____

Action Statement

Now spend 10 minutes writing a list of specific actions that you will take to produce the outcome or result you listed above. Be specific. The idea is to list actions that you can include on a daily to-do list or write down on a calendar. For example, a goal to graduate by a certain date could call for actions such as "call the financial aid office to ask about student loans" or "ask my academic advisor about course requirements for my major."

In your list, include actions that you will take only once as well as habits—things that you will do on a regular basis. For example, a goal to graduate with honors can include a habit such as, "I will study two hours for every hour I'm in class."

Create your list of actions in the space below and use separate paper as needed.

_____

_____

_____

_____

_____

_____

_____

_____

_____

_____

_____

_____

_____

_____

_____

_____

For five minutes, review your brainstormed list of actions. Are they specific? Can you see yourself actually *doing* each of them? If anything on your list is vague or fuzzy, go back and revise it.

Congratulations! Take one more minute to savor the feeling that comes with getting clarity about your deepest values and heartfelt desires. You can take the process you just used and apply it to getting *anything* you want in life. The essential steps are the same in each case: State your desire as a specific outcome. Then translate the goal into a list of concrete actions.

 You're One Click Away . . .
from an online goal-setting exercise.

Seven ways
to take back
your time

The truth about time management is that it doesn't exist. Think about it: Time cannot be managed. Every human being gets exactly the same allotment of hours: 24 per day, 168 per week.

However, we can manage our *behavior* so that we become more productive during the fixed number of hours that we all have.

You might know people who seem efficient and yet relaxed. These people do not have more time than you do. They simply manage their behavior in productive ways.

Experiment with the following behaviors. Each of them is a strategy for using the time of your life in the way that you choose. Select one strategy to apply right away. When it becomes a habit, come back to this article and choose another one. Repeat this process as often as you like, and reap the rewards.

1. DO IT NOW

Postponing decisions and procrastinating are major sources of stress. An alternative is to handle the task or decision immediately. Answer that e-mail now. Make that phone call as soon as it occurs to you.

Also use waiting time. Five minutes waiting for a subway, 20 minutes waiting for the dentist, 10 minutes between classes—all that time adds up fast. Have short study tasks ready to do during these periods. For example, you can carry 3 × 5 cards with facts, formulas, or definitions and pull them out anywhere.

2. DELEGATE

Asking for help can free up extra hours you need for studying. Instead of doing all the housework or cooking yourself, assign some of the tasks to family members or roommates. Instead of driving across town to deliver a package, hire a delivery service to do it.

It's neither practical nor ethical to delegate certain study tasks, such as writing term papers or completing reading assignments. However, you can still draw on the ideas of other people in completing such tasks. For instance, form a writing group to edit and critique papers, brainstorm topics or titles, and develop lists of sources.

3. SAY NO

Suppose that someone asks you to volunteer for a project and you realize immediately that you don't want to do it. Save time by graciously telling the truth up front. Saying "I'll think about it and get back to you" just postpones the conversation until later, when it will take more time.

Saying no graciously and up front can be a huge timesaver. Many people think that it is rude to refuse a request. But saying no can be done effectively and courteously. When you tell people that you're saying no to a new commitment because you are busy educating yourself, most of them will understand.

Saying no includes logging off e-mail and instant messaging when appropriate. The Internet is the ultimate interrupter. In today's world, responses to e-mails or instant messages are expected almost immediately. To avoid distraction set an "away" alert for instant messages and set specific times during the day to check your e-mail.

Also experiment with doing less. Planning is as much about dropping worthless activities as about adding new ones. See whether you can reduce or eliminate activities that contribute little to your values or goals.

4. USE A CALENDAR

Use a calendar to remind yourself about commitments that will take place on a certain date or at a certain time—classes, meetings, appointments, and the like. You can also schedule due dates for assignments, reviewing sessions for tests, and any other events you want to remember.

Many students use a paper-based calendar that they can carry along with their textbooks and class notes. Other people favor online calendars such as those offered by Google and Yahoo! Experiment with both and see what works best for you.

When using any kind of calendar, schedule fixed blocks of time first. Start with class time and work time, for instance. These time periods are usually determined in advance. Other activities are scheduled around them.

As an alternative to entering class times in your calendar each week, you can simply print out your class schedule and consult it as needed. As a general guideline, schedule about two hours of study time each week for every hour that you spend in class.

Tasks often expand to fill the time we allot for them, so use your calendar to set clear starting and stopping times. Plan a certain amount of time for that reading assignment, set a timer, and stick to it. Feeling rushed or sacrificing quality is not the aim here. The point is to push yourself a little and discover what your time requirements really are.

Avoid scheduling marathon study sessions, however. When possible, study in shorter sessions. Three 3-hour sessions are usually far more productive than one 9-hour session.

Recognize that unexpected things will happen, and leave some holes in your schedule. Build in blocks of unplanned time, and mark these in your calendar as "flex time" or "open time."

5. WRITE REMINDERS

Almost every book about personal productivity mentions a to-do list. This is a list of specific actions—phone calls to make, errands to run, assignments to complete. Also include actions that are directly related to your goals. (See Commit to Action: "Give your goals some teeth" on page 20.)

Save your to-do list for actions that do *not* have to be completed on a certain date or at a certain time. Complete your to-do items at times between the scheduled events in your day. Delete items on your list when you complete them, and add new items as you think of them.

You can record your to-do items on sheets of paper. Another option is to put each to-do item on its own 3 × 5 card. This allows for easy sorting into categories. Also, you'll never have to recopy your to-do list. Whenever you complete a to-do item, simply throw away or recycle the card.

Computers offer similar flexibility. Just open up a file and key in all your to-do items. In a single window on your screen, you'll be able to see at least a dozen to-do items at a glance. As with 3 × 5 cards, you can delete and rearrange to your heart's content.

6. DISCOVER YOUR PERSONAL RHYTHMS

Many people learn best during daylight hours. If this is true for you, then schedule study time for your most difficult subjects when the sun is up.

When you're in a time crunch, get up a little early or stay up late. If the time crunch is chronic, experiment with getting up 15 minutes earlier or going to bed 15 minutes later each day on a more permanent basis. Over the course of one year, either choice will yield 91 extra hours of waking activity.

7. GO FOR THE LONG TERM

Experiment with longer-term planning. Thinking beyond today and the current week can help you see how your daily activities relate to longer-range goals. On your calendar, include *any* key dates for the upcoming quarter, semester, or year. These dates can relate to any area of life—academic, career, or family events. Here are some examples:

- Test dates
- Lab sessions
- Due dates for assignments
- Days when classes will be canceled
- Interim due dates, such as when you plan to complete the first draft of a term paper
- Birthdays, anniversaries, and other special occasions
- Medical and dental checkups
- Application due dates for internships
- Concerts and plays
- Due dates for major bills—insurance, taxes, car registration, credit card and installment loan payments, medical expenses, interest charges, and charitable contributions
- Trips, vacations, and holidays

You're One Click Away . . .
from additional ways to become more productive.

Forget about time management— *just get things done*

David Allen, author of *Getting Things Done: The Art of Stress-Free Productivity,* says that a lack of time is not the real issue for the people he coaches. Instead, the problem is having only a vague idea of our desired outcomes and the specific actions needed to produce them. Allen offers the following suggestions.

3

1. Collect. To begin, make a note about every unfinished project, incomplete task, misplaced object—or anything else that's nagging you. List each of these items on a separate 3 × 5 card or piece of paper and dump it into an in-basket.

2. Process. Pick up each note in your in-basket, one at a time, and ask, "Do I truly want or need to do something about this?" If the answer is no, then trash the item. If the answer is yes, then choose immediately how to respond: Do it now, write a reminder to do it later, or file the item away for future reference. The goal is to *empty* your in-basket at least once each week.

3. Organize. Now group your reminders into appropriate categories. Allen recommends using a calendar for scheduled events, a list of current projects, and a list of next actions to take on each project.

4. Review. Every week, collect any new projects or tasks that are on your mind. Also update your calendar and lists. Ask yourself, "What are all my current projects? And what is the *very next physical action* (such as a phone call or errand) that I can take to move each project forward?"

5. Do. Every day, review your calendar and lists. Based on this information and on your intuition, make moment-to-moment choices about how to spend your time.

David Allen, *Getting Things Done: The Art of Stress-Free Productivity* (New York: Penguin, 2001).

Commit to ACTION

Discover where your time goes

Do you ever hear yourself saying, "Where did my morning go?" Many people have little idea where their time really goes. But with some heightened awareness and minimal record keeping, you can discover exactly how you spend your time. With this knowledge you can diagnose productivity problems with pinpoint accuracy. You can delete the time-killers and the life-drainers—activities that consume hours yet deliver the least in results or satisfaction. This frees up more time for the activities that you truly value.

If you think you already have a good idea of how you spend time, then predict how many hours you devote each week to sleeping, studying, working, attending classes, and socializing. Use this exercise to monitor your time for one week. Then notice how accurate your predictions were. You'll quickly see the value of collecting accurate data about the way you use time.

Following is a series of steps for monitoring your use of time. To get the most benefit from this exercise, proceed like a scientist. Adopt the hypothesis that you can manage your time in more optimal ways. Then see whether you can confirm or refute that hypothesis by collecting precise data in the laboratory—the laboratory in this case being your life.

1. Choose a specific period to monitor

To get the most benefit from monitoring your time, do it for at least one day. You can extend this practice over several days, a week, or even a month. Monitoring your time over greater intervals can reveal broader patterns in your behavior. You'll get more insight into the way that you spend your most precious resource—you.

2. Plan how to record your data

The key to this exercise is to record the times that you start and stop each activity over a period of 24 hours: sleeping, eating, studying, travelling to and from class, working, watching television, listening to music, sitting in lectures, taking care of the kids, running errands. To promote accuracy and accumulate useful data, track your activity in 30-minute intervals. Tracking 15-minute intervals can be even more useful.

You can record this data in any way that works. Consider these options:

- **Carry a 3 x 5 card** with you each day for recording your activities. Every time that you start a new activity, describe it in a word or two and write down the time you started.

- **Use a daily calendar** that includes slots for scheduling appointments at each hour of the day. Instead of scheduling events ahead of time, simply note how you actually spend each hour.

- **Use time-tracking software.** For the latest products, key the words *time tracking* into a search engine.

- **Create your own system for time monitoring.** For example, before you go to bed, review your day and write down your activities along with starting and stopping times. (See the illustration on this page.)

Sample Time Monitor		
Activity	Start	Stop
Sleep	11:00 pm	6:00 am
Jog/Stretch	6:00 am	7:00 am
Shower/Dress	7:00 am	7:30 am
Breakfast	7:30 am	8:00 am
Travel to Campus	8:30 am	9:00 am
History	9:00 am	10:20 am
Check Email	10:30 am	11:00 am
English Lit	11:00 am	12:00 pm
Lunch/Review for Psych test	12:00 pm	1:00 pm
Work-Study Job	1:00 pm	4:00 pm
Run Errands	4:00 pm	5:00 pm
Travel Home	5:00 pm	5:30 pm
Watch TV/Relax	5:30 pm	6:30 pm
Dinner/Socialize	6:30 pm	8:00 pm
Read Chapter 4/English	8:00 pm	9:00 pm
Make Flashcards for Psych test	9:00 pm	10:00 pm
Review notes from today's History/English Lectures	10:00 pm	11:00 pm

Note: Keep this exercise in perspective. No one says that you have to keep track of the rest of your life in 15-minute intervals. Eventually you can monitor selected activities in your life and keep track of them only for as long as you choose.

3. Record your data

Now put your plan into action. For a minimum of one day, collect data about how much time you spend on each activity.

4. List how much time you spent on each activity

At the end of the day or week, add up the total hours you devoted to each activity. Examples might include eight hours for sleeping, two hours for watching a movie, three hours of class, and six hours for studying. Make sure the grand total of all activities is 24 hours per day or 168 hours per week.

5. Group your activities into major categories

After you've monitored your time for at least one week, group your activities together into broader categories. Examples are *sleep*, *class*, *study*, and *meals*. Another category, *grooming*, might include showering, putting on makeup, brushing your teeth, and getting dressed. *Travel* can include walking, driving, taking the bus, and riding your bike. Other categories might be *exercise*, *entertainment*, *work*, *television*, *domestic*, and *children*. Use categories that make sense for you.

6. Summarize your data

Use the blank two-column chart on this page to summarize the results of the previous steps. Include each

category of activity and the number of hours for each category. First, look at the sample chart. Then, using the blank chart provided, fill in your own information.

Categories Of Activity	Hours Spent On Each Activity
Total_____	

Also consider using a pie chart to represent your categories of activity. This can be useful for two reasons. First, a circle is a fixed shape, reinforcing the idea that you have only a fixed amount of time to work with: 24 hours a day, 168 hours per week. Second, seeing your life represented on a pie chart tempts you to adjust the sizes of the slices—each slice being a category of activity. You make this adjustment by consciously choosing to devote more or less time to each category. Look at the sample chart below and then fill in your own pie chart using the information from your chart on page 26.

Categories Of Activity	Hours Spent On Each Activity
Class	
Study/Reading for Classes	
Meals (including cooking)	
Free Time	
Exercise	
Clean Apartment	
Laundry	
Call Family	
Work	
Personal Maintenance	
Sleep	
Total	

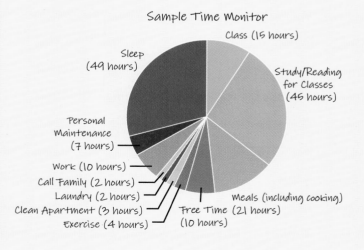

Sample Time Monitor

Class (15 hours)
Study/Reading for Classes (45 hours)
Meals (including cooking)
Free Time (21 hours)
Exercise (4 hours)
Clean Apartment (3 hours)
Laundry (2 hours)
Call Family (2 hours)
Work (10 hours)
Personal Maintenance (7 hours)
Sleep (49 hours)

7. Reflect on your time monitor

Complete the following sentences.

After monitoring my time, I discovered that . . .

_____

_____

_____

_____

I was surprised that I spent so much time on . . .

_____

_____

_____

I was surprised that I spent so little time on . . .

_____

_____

_____

_____

I intend to spend more time on . . .

_____

_____

_____

_____

_____

_____

_____

I intend to spend less time on . . .

_____

_____

_____

_____

_____

You're One Click Away . . .
from an online version of this exercise.

Procrastination unplugged

The terms *self-discipline*, *willpower*, and *motivation* are often used to describe something missing in ourselves. Time after time, we invoke these words to explain another person's success—or our own shortcomings: "If I were more motivated, I'd get more involved in school." "Of course she got an A. She has self-discipline." "If I had more willpower, I'd lose weight."

It seems that certain people are born with lots of motivation, whereas others miss out on it.

An alternative way of thinking is to stop assuming that motivation is mysterious, determined at birth, or hard to come by. In fact, perhaps the whole concept of motivation is just a myth. Maybe what we call motivation is something that you already possess—the ability to do a task even when you don't feel like it.

We don't need the concept of motivation to change our behavior. Rather, immediate action can flow from genuine commitment. With that idea in mind, test the following suggestions.

CHECK FOR ATTITUDES THAT PROMOTE PROCRASTINATION

Certain attitudes fuel procrastination and keep you from experiencing the rewards in life that you deserve. In their book *Procrastination: Why You Do It and What to Do About It*, psychologists Jane Burka and Lenora Yuen list these examples:

> I must be perfect.
> Everything I do should go easily and without effort.
> It's safer to do nothing than to take a risk and fail.
> If it's not done right, it's not worth doing at all.
> If I do well this time, I must always do well.
> If I succeed, someone will get hurt.[1]

If you find such beliefs running through your mind, write them down. Getting a belief out of your head and on to paper can rob that belief of its power. Also write a more effective belief that you

10 things *you can do in* 10 minutes (or less)

3

- Preview a textbook chapter.
- Write a Discovery or an Intention Statement.
- Reread an article in this book.
- Do an exercise (or part of an exercise) in this book.
- Create your weekly budget.
- Take a brisk walk or climb several flights of stairs for exercise.
- Do a spiritual practice, such as meditation or prayer.
- Write and use an affirmation.
- Write a goal or action plan. Review your calendar or to-do list. (Refer to Commit to Action: "Give your goals some teeth.")
- Nothing. Just chill. Stare out the window. Breathe deeply and notice how good it feels.

want to adopt. For example: "Even if I don't complete this task perfectly, it's good enough for now, and I can still learn from my mistakes."

ACCEPT YOUR FEELINGS OF RESISTANCE—THEN TAKE ACTION

If you wait to exercise until you feel energetic, you might wait for months. Instead, get moving now and watch your feelings change. After five minutes of brisk walking, you might be in the mood for a 20-minute run. Don't wait to feel "motivated" before you take action. Instead, apply the principle that action *creates* motivation.

This principle can be applied to any task you've been putting off. You can move into action no matter how you feel about a task. Simply notice your feelings of resistance, accept them, and then do one small task related to your goal. Then do one more task, and another. Keep at it, one task at a time, and watch procrastination disappear.

 You're One Click Away . . .
from more ways to prevent procrastination.

Put an end
to money worries

"I can't afford it" is a common reason that students give for dropping out of school. "I don't know how to pay for it" or "I don't think it's worth it" are probably more accurate ways to state the problem. No matter what the money problem, the solution usually includes two actions. First, discover the facts about how much money you have and how much you spend. Second, commit to live within your means—that is, spend no more than you have.

DISCOVER THE FACTS

Money likes to escape when no one is looking. And usually no one *is* looking. That's why the simple act of noticing the details about money can be so useful—even if this is the only idea from this chapter that you ever apply.

To discover the facts, record all the money you receive and spend over the course of each month. This sounds like a big task. But if you use a simple system, you can turn it into a habit.

One option is to carry 3 × 5 cards. Every time you receive money, write the date, the source of income, and the amount on a card. Be sure to use a separate card for each amount. Do the same for money that you spend. On separate cards, list the date, the amount you spent, and what you paid for.

At the end of the month, sort your cards into income and expense categories and then total the amounts for each category. There's a payoff for this action. When you know how much money you really earn, you'll know how much you really have to spend. And if you know what your biggest expenses are, you'll know where to start cutting back if you overspend.

Of course, 3 × 5 cards are just one option. You can also use computer software and online banking services. Or carefully file all your receipts and paycheck stubs and use them to tally up your monthly income and expenses. Whatever tools you choose, start using them today.

LIVE WITHIN YOUR MEANS

There are three broad strategies for living within your means: increase your income, decrease your expenses, or do both.

Increase income. If you work while you're in school, you'll gain experience, establish references, and expand your contacts for getting a new job or making a career change. And regular income in any amount can make a difference in your monthly cash flow. Talk to someone in the financial aid office who helps students find work. In addition, check into career-planning services.

Once you graduate and land a job in your chosen field, continue your education. Gain additional skills and certifications that lead to higher earnings. Once you get a job, also excel as an employee. Be as productive as possible. Look for ways to boost sales, increase quality, or accomplish tasks in less time. These achievements can help you earn a raise. A positive work experience can pay off for years by leading to a raise, recommendations, and contacts for a new job.

Decrease expenses. When you look for places to cut expenses, start with the items that cost the most. Consider housing, for example. Sometimes a place a little farther from campus, or a smaller house or apartment, will be much less expensive. You can also keep your housing costs down by finding a roommate.

Another high-ticket item is a car. You might find that it makes more sense to use public transportation.

Also cook for yourself. This single suggestion could save many a sinking budget.

These are only a few suggestions. You can create many more strategies. The bottom line is this: Before you spend money on anything, ask whether you could get the same benefit from another source for free or for a lower cost.

Use credit with *care*

A good credit rating will serve you for a lifetime. With this asset, you'll be able to borrow money any time you need it.

A poor credit rating, however, can keep you from getting a car or a house in the future. You might also have to pay higher insurance rates, and you could even be turned down for a job.

To take charge of your credit, borrow money only when truly necessary. If you do borrow, then make all of your payments, and make them on time. This is especially important for managing credit cards and student loans.

USE CREDIT CARDS WITH CAUTION

An unpaid credit card balance is a sure sign that you are spending more money than you have. To avoid this outcome, keep track of how much you spend with credit cards each month. Pay off the card balance each month, on time, and avoid finance or late charges.

If you do accumulate a large credit card balance, go to your bank and ask about ways to get a loan with a lower interest rate. Use this loan to pay off your credit cards. Then promise yourself never to accumulate credit card debt again.

To simplify your financial life and take charge of your credit, consider using only one card. Choose one with no annual fee and the lowest interest rate.

As of February 22, 2010, credit card companies must comply with new regulations designed to protect consumers. In most cases, for example, a company cannot raise interest rates within the first year of a new account. And if you are under age 21, you will need to show that you can make credit card payments, or get a cosigner. For more information, go online to **www.federalreserve.gov** and search on *new credit card rules*.

MANAGE STUDENT LOANS

A college degree is one of the best investments you can make. But you don't have to go broke to get that education. Make this investment with the lowest debt possible.

The surest way to manage debt is to avoid it altogether. If you do take out loans, borrow only the amount that you cannot get from other sources—scholarships, grants, employment, gifts from relatives, and personal savings.

Also set a target date for graduation, and stick to it. The fewer years you go to school, the lower your debt.

If you transfer to another school, consider costs carefully. In addition to choosing schools on the basis of reputation, consider tuition, fees, housing, and financial aid packages.

When borrowing money for school, shop carefully. Go to the financial aid office and ask whether you can get a Stafford loan. These are fixed-rate, low-interest loans from the federal government.

If your parents are helping to pay for your education, they can apply for a PLUS loan. There is no income limit, and parents can borrow up to the total cost of their children's education.

Some lenders will forgive part of a student loan if you agree to take a certain job for a few years, such as teaching in a public school in a low-income neighborhood or working as a nurse in a rural community. This arrangement is called an *income-based repayment plan*. Ask someone in the financial aid office whether it is an option for you.

If you take out student loans, find out exactly when the first payment is due on each of them. Don't assume that you can wait to start repayment until you find a job. Any bill payments that you miss will hammer your credit score.

Also ask your financial aid office about whether you can consolidate your loans. This means that you lump them all together and owe just one payment every month. Loan consolidation makes it easier to stay on top of your payments and protect your credit score.

3

CRITICAL THINKING
experiment

Reflect on your spending

Review the article "Put an end to money worries" on page 28. Then use the suggestions in that article to actually keep track of your income and expenses for one month.

If doing this for an entire month seems like too much work, then commit to keeping these records for just one week or even a few days. As you gain experience with monitoring the details of your money life, you can gradually extend the period to one month.

Next, reflect on what you're learning. To start creating a new future with money, complete the following statements.

After monitoring my income and expenses, I was surprised to discover that . . .

_____

_____

_____

_____

When it comes to money, I am skilled at . . .

_____

_____

_____

When it comes to money, I am *not* so skilled at . . .

_____

_____

_____

_____

I could increase my income by . . .

_____

_____

_____

_____

_____

I could spend less money on . . .

_____

_____

_____

_____

_____

The most powerful step I can take right now to take charge of my money is . . .

_____

_____

_____

_____

_____

Finally, take a moment to congratulate yourself for completing this exercise. No matter how the numbers add up, you are learning to take conscious control of your money. Repeat this exercise every month. It will keep you on a steady path to financial freedom.

Be here now

TO **"BE HERE NOW"** means to pay full attention to what you're doing—right here, right now. This is such a simple idea. It seems obvious. Where else can you be but where you are?

The answer is that you can be somewhere else at any time—in your head. It's common for our thoughts to distract us. Instead of paying attention to reading this page, for example, your mind might drift to what you're having for dinner. During class, your thoughts might take you to the beach or the party you're planning to attend on Saturday night.

When we develop a habit of getting distracted, we lose the benefits of focusing our attention on what's important to us in the present moment. While studying, we waste time. During class, we miss important points. During dinner, we forget to really taste what we're eating. And when attending a party, we don't really hear what our friends are saying.

Many distractions result from a voice in our head that rarely shuts up. If you don't believe it, try this: Close your eyes for 10 seconds and pay attention to what is going on in your head. Do this right now.

Notice something? Perhaps your voice was saying, "Forget it. I'm in a hurry." Or, "I wonder when 10 seconds is up?" Or, "What little voice? I don't hear any little voice."

That's the voice.

Instead of trying to force the voice out of your head—which is futile—simply notice it. Accept it. Tell yourself, "There's that thought again." Then gently return your attention to the task at hand. That thought, or another, will come back. Your mind will drift. Simply notice again where your thoughts take you, and gently bring yourself back to the here and now.

Another way to return to the here and now is to notice your physical sensations. Notice the way the room looks or smells. Notice the temperature and how the chair feels. Once you've regained control of your attention by becoming aware of your physical surroundings, you can more easily take the next step and bring your full attention back to your present task.

The idea behind this Power Process is simple. When you listen to a lecture, listen to a lecture. When you read this book, read this book. And when you choose to daydream, daydream.

Students consistently report that focusing attention on the here and now—no matter what they're doing—is one of the most powerful tools in this book.

Do what you're doing when you're doing it.

Be where you are when you're there.

Be here now . . . and now . . . and now.

 You're One Click Away . . .
from more ways to be here now.

4

Achieving Your Purpose for Reading

Reading

essentials

Picture yourself sitting at a desk, a book in your hands. Your eyes are open and it looks as if you're reading. Suddenly your head jerks up. You blink. You realize your eyes have been scanning the page for 10 minutes, and you can't remember a single thing you have read.

Or picture this: You woke up at 6 a.m. to get the kids ready for school. A coworker called in sick and work was busy. You picked up the kids, then had to shop for dinner. Dinner was late and the kids were grumpy. Finally, you get to your books at 8 p.m. You begin a reading assignment on something called "the equity method of accounting." "I am preparing for the future," you tell yourself, as you plod through two paragraphs and begin the third.

Suddenly, everything in the room looks different. Your head is resting on your elbow. The clock reads 11:00 p.m. Say good bye to three hours.

Sometimes the only difference between a sleeping pill and a textbook is that the textbook doesn't have a warning label.

Contrast this scenario with the image of an active reader who

- Stays alert, poses questions about what she reads, and searches for the answers.
- Recognizes levels of information within the text, separating the main points and general principles from supporting details.
- Quizzes herself about material, makes written notes, and lists unanswered questions.
- Instantly spots key terms and takes the time to find the definitions of unfamiliar words.
- Thinks critically about the ideas in the text and looks for ways to apply them.

That sounds like a lot to do. Yet skilled readers routinely accomplish all these things and more—while enjoying reading.

To experience this kind of success, approach reading with a system in mind. You can avoid mental minivacations and unscheduled naps, even after a hard day.

This chapter presents a three-phase technique to extract the ideas and information you want from your reading assignment:

1. Question your text
2. Read for answers
3. Review the answers

Discover what YOU WANT from this chapter

The Discovery Wheel on page 2 includes a section titled *Reading*. Take some time to go beyond your initial responses to that section. Spend five minutes skimming this chapter. Then complete the following sentences:

4

The thing about my experience of reading that I would most like to change is . . .

_____

_____

_____

_____

_____

_____

_____

Some ideas from this chapter that can help me make that change are . . .

_____

_____

_____

_____

_____

_____

_____

When you see 🖱 **You're One Click Away . . .**, *remember to go to this book's College Success CourseMate for additional content. And for a summary of this chapter, see the Master Student Review Cards at the end of this book.*

This system may take some effort to learn, but keep with it. Mastery comes with time and practice. Once you learn this system, you might actually spend less time on your reading and get more out of it. Effective reading is an active, energy-consuming, sit-on-the-edge-of-your-seat business.

Question your text

Powerful reading starts with powerful questions. Questions open up inquiries. Questions focus your attention and prompt you to become an active learner. Questions help you get your money's worth from your textbooks.

To frame questions about your reading, first do a preview. Also create an informal outline to discover how the material is organized.

PREVIEW

Before you start reading, preview the entire assignment. You don't have to memorize what you preview to get value from this step. Previewing sets the stage for incoming information by warming up a space in your mental storage area.

The preview step can significantly increase your comprehension of reading material. Previewing is also an easy way to get started when an assignment looks too big to handle. It is an easy way to step into the material.

When you preview, look for the following:

- Your book's front matter such as the copyright page, preface, dedication, introduction, and contents

- Sectional or chapter contents, chapter previews, summaries, abstracts, and lists of review questions.

- Graphically highlighted material—anything underlined or printed in large, bold, italic, or color type.

- Visuals, including boxes, charts, tables, diagrams, illustrations, and photographs.

- Your book's back matter such as a glossary, bibliography, list of references or works cited, and index.

Keep the preview short. If the entire reading assignment will take less than an hour, your preview might take five minutes.

When previewing, look for familiar concepts, facts, or ideas. Read all chapter headings and subheadings. Like the headlines in a newspaper, these items are usually printed in large, bold type. They can help link new information to previously learned material.

Keep an eye out for summary statements. If the assignment is long or complex, read the summary first. Many textbooks have summaries in the introduction or at the end of each chapter. Often headings are brief summaries in themselves.

Also look for ideas that spark your imagination or curiosity. Ask yourself how the material can relate to your long-term goals.

Finally, consider your purpose for reading the material. Are you reading just to get to the main points? Key supporting details? Additional details? All of the above? Your answers will guide what you do with each phase of the reading process.

Note: When you face a long reading assignment, break it into manageable chunks and preview each one. Textbooks are usually divided into chapters—a logical chunk. However, if the chapter is long or difficult, feel free to tackle it in smaller sections with study breaks between each section.

OUTLINE

With complex material, take time to understand the structure of what you are about to read. Outlining actively organizes your thoughts about the assignment, and it can make complex information easier to understand. If your textbook provides chapter outlines, spend some time studying them.

When an outline is not provided, sketch a brief one in the margin of your book or at the beginning of your notes on a separate sheet of paper. Use headings in the text as the major and minor entries in your outline. Later, as you read and take notes, you can add to your outline.

Stick with a simple, informal outline. Capture each topic in a single word or phrase. List topics in the order that they're mentioned in the text. You can create this outline in pencil in the margins of a book or article.

For added precision, copy your outline on separate paper and edit it after reading. Or open a computer file and create your outline there.

The amount of time you spend on outlining can vary. For some assignments (fiction and poetry, for example), skip this step. For other assignments, a 10-second mental outline is enough.

LIST QUESTIONS

Before you begin a careful reading, determine what information you want to get from an assignment. Write a list of questions to answer.

Have fun with this technique. Make the questions playful or creative. You don't need an answer to every question that you ask. The purpose of making up questions is to get your brain involved in the assignment.

Questions can come from previewing and outlining. For example:

- Brainstorm a list of topics covered in a chapter. Then write a question about each topic.

- Turn chapter headings and subheadings into questions. For example, if a heading is *Transference and Suggestion,* ask yourself, "What are transference and suggestion? How does transference relate to suggestion?" Make up a quiz as if you were teaching this subject to your classmates.

- If there are no headings, look for key sentences and turn them into questions. These sentences usually show up at the beginnings or ends of paragraphs and sections.

- Have an imaginary dialogue with your teacher, or with the author of the book. List the questions you would ask.

- If you do not understand a concept, write specific questions about it. The more detailed your questions, the more powerful this technique becomes.

Another option is to use the six journalist questions: *Who? What? When? Where? Why? How?* Reporters ask these questions when researching a story. You can use the same strategy to dig out the news from your reading assignments. For example:

- *Ask, "Who?"* Who wrote this, and what qualifications or special experience does this author bring to bear on the subject? Who is the publisher, and has this organization published other useful texts on the same subject?

- *Ask, "What?"* What are the key terms in this material, and what is the definition for each one? What are the major topics covered in this text? What do I already know about these topics? What are the main points the author makes about each topic? Can I give an example of each major concept? What points will the author make next?

- *Ask, "When?"* When was this material published, and does it matter? (For scientific and technical topics, you may want the most current information that's available.)

- *Ask, "Where?"* Where can I use the ideas and information contained in this text? Where can I find out more about the topics covered?

- *Ask, "Why?"* Why did my teacher assign this reading? Why does this material matter to me?

Create outlines from *headings*

Headings in a chapter or article can serve as major and minor entries in your outline. For added clarity, distinguish major headings from minor headings. Using the headings from the previous article, for example, you can create the following outline:

ACHIEVING YOUR PURPOSE FOR READING (chapter heading on page 32)

    QUESTION YOUR TEXT (major heading on page 34)

    Preview (minor heading on page 34)

    Outline (minor heading on page 34)

    List questions (minor heading on page 34)

Note: Feel free to rewrite headings so that they are more meaningful to you. Substitute complete sentences for headings that consist of just a single word or phrase. In addition, you can write a sentence or two after each heading to include some more details about the topic.

4

- *Ask, "How?"* How can I explain this material to someone else? How can I organize or visualize this information to make it more vivid? How can I remember these ideas? How can I relate this material to something I already know? How will I be tested or otherwise evaluated on this material? How can learning this material benefit me in this course, in another course, or in my life outside the classroom?

Note: These six kinds of questions will lead you to common test items.

Keep track of your questions. Write them on 3 × 5 cards, one question per card. Or open a word processing file on your computer and key in your questions. Take your unanswered questions to class, where they can be springboards for class discussion.

You're One Click Away . . .
from more strategies for powerful previewing.

Read
for
answers

At last! You have previewed the reading assignment, organized it in your mind, and formulated questions. Now you're ready to inspect the text in greater detail.

READ WITH FOCUSED ATTENTION

Before you dive into the first paragraph, take a few moments to reflect on what you already know about the subject. Do this even if you think you know nothing. This technique prepares your brain to accept the information that follows.

As you read, be conscious of where you are and what you are doing. When you notice your attention wandering, gently bring it back to the present. It's easy to fool yourself about reading. Just having an open book in your hand and moving your eyes across a page doesn't mean you are reading effectively. Reading textbooks takes energy, even if you do it sitting down.

One way to stay focused is to avoid marathon reading sessions. Schedule breaks and set a reasonable goal for the entire session. For every hour or two of work, reward yourself with an enjoyable 5 to 10 minute activity.

For difficult reading, set shorter goals. Read for a half hour and then take a break. Most students find that shorter periods of reading distributed throughout the day and week can be more effective than long reading sessions.

You can use the following techniques to stay focused during these sessions:

- **Visualize the material.** Form mental pictures of the concepts as they are presented. Get a "feel" for the subject. If you read that a voucher system can help control cash disbursements, picture a voucher handing out dollar bills. If you are reading about the microorganism called a paramecium, imagine what it would feel like to run your finger around the long, cigar-shaped body of the organism.

- **Read it out loud.** This is especially useful for complicated material. Some of us remember better and understand more quickly when we hear an idea.

- **Get off the couch.** Read at a desk or table and sit up, on the edge of your chair, with your feet flat on the floor. If you're feeling adventurous, read standing up.

- **Get moving.** Make reading a physical as well as an intellectual experience. As you read out loud, get up and pace around the room. Read important passages slowly and emphatically, and add appropriate gestures.

MAKE MULTIPLE PASSES THROUGH THE TEXT

Somehow, students get the idea that reading means opening a book and dutifully slogging through the text—line by line, page by page—moving in a straight line from the first word until the last. Actually, this can be an inflexible and ineffective way to interact with reading material.

Feel free to shake up your routine. Make several passes through any reading material. During a preview, for example, just scan the text to look for key words and highlighted text.

Next, skim the entire chapter or article again, spending a little more time and taking in more than you did during your preview.

Finally, read in more depth, proceeding word by word through some or all of the text. Save this type of close reading for the most important material—usually the sections that directly answer the questions you raised while previewing and outlining.

Underlining and highlighting the text can be part of this step. Deface your books. Have fun writing in them. Indulge yourself as you never could with your grade-school books.

The purpose of making marks in a text is to call out important concepts or information that you will need to review later. Be aware, though, that underlining a text with a pen can make underlined sections—the important parts—harder to read. As an alternative, many students underline in pencil or use colored highlighters to flag key words and sentences.

Underlining offers a secondary benefit. When you read with a highlighter, pen, or pencil in your hand, you involve your kinesthetic senses of touch and motion. Being physical with your books can help build strong neural pathways in your memory.

Avoid underlining too soon. Wait until you complete a chapter or section to make sure you know the key points. Then mark up the text. Sometimes, underlining after you read each paragraph works best.

Underline sparingly—usually less than 10 percent of the text. If you mark up too much on a page, you defeat the purpose—to flag the most important material for review.

ANSWER YOUR QUESTIONS

As you read, look for the answers to the questions you raised earlier. Create an image of yourself as a detective, watching for every clue, sitting erect in your straight-back chair, demanding that your textbook give you the answers you seek. Write those answers down. Also revise and expand your initial outline.

If you listed your questions on 3 × 5 cards, write an answer on the back of each card. If you entered your questions in a computer file, then open the file again and add answers. Either way, you'll instantly have useful review materials on hand.

Note when you don't get the answers you wanted to find, and write down any new questions that occur to you while you're reading. Bring these questions to class, or see your instructor personally.

 You're One Click Away . . .
from more strategies for reading to answer your questions.

Nine ways to
overcome confusion

Active readers monitor their understanding of a text. When they get confused, they use strategies such as the following.

1. Collect data. When you feel stuck, pause and diagnose the situation. Mark an S for "stuck" in the page margin. If you see a pattern over several pages, it might indicate a question you want to answer or a reading habit you'd like to change.

2. Look for essential words. Mentally cross out all the adjectives and adverbs and read the sentence without them. The most important words will usually be verbs and nouns.

4

3. Read it again. Difficult material is often easier the second or third time around.

4. Skip around. Jump to the end of the passage. You may have lost the big picture, and sometimes seeing the conclusion or summary helps you put the details in context. Retrace the steps in a chain of ideas and look for examples. Absorb facts and ideas in whatever order works for you.

5. Summarize. Pause briefly to summarize what you have read. Stop at the end of a paragraph and recite the main points in your own words. Jot down some notes or create a short outline.

6. Ask for help. Make an appointment with your instructor. Most teachers are happy to work individually with students. Point out the paragraph that you found toughest to understand. Be specific.

7. Find a tutor. Many schools provide free tutoring services. You can also ask for help from a student who has completed the course.

8. Pretend you understand, then explain it. We often understand more than we think we do. Pretend that the topic is as clear as a bell, and explain it to another person. Write your explanation down. To go even further, volunteer to teach the topic to a study group.

9. Stop reading. If all else fails, admit your confusion and take a break. Take a walk, study another subject, or sleep. The concepts you've absorbed may mesh at a subconscious level while you pursue other tasks. Give it some time. When you return to the reading, see it with fresh eyes.

REVIEW
the answers

Also review the outline you created while previewing, and review it for accuracy. Ask yourself how each chapter or section of the material relates to the rest. Aim to see how the whole book, chapter, or article is organized. Understanding the overall organization gives you a context for the details, making individual facts easier to remember.

RECITE THE ANSWERS

To understand the reasons for reciting, briefly review the way that your memory works:

- The process starts with sense perception, such as words and images printed on a page or displayed on a screen.
- Your brain translates these perceptions into ideas and places them in your short-term memory.
- However, the content of short-term memory quickly fades—unless you actively rehearse it.

Reciting offers one means of rehearsal. The benefits are enormous. Reciting helps to move information into your long-term memory.

What's more, reciting instantly focuses your attention and turns you into an active learner. If you recite the key points from a chapter by explaining them to someone, you engage your sense of hearing as well as seeing. If you recite by writing a summary of what you've read, you move your fingers and engage additional senses. In each way, your reading experience becomes more vivid.

When you recite, you also get important feedback about your learning. If there are any gaps in your understanding of the material, they'll become obvious as you speak or write. Reciting forces you to put ideas in your own words and avoid the pitfalls of rote memorization.

Besides being useful, reciting can be fun. Experiment with any of the following techniques.

This stage of reading completes the process that you begin when previewing, outlining, and posing questions. After digging into the text to uncover answers, take your understanding of them to a deeper level.

REFLECT ON THE ANSWERS

Reading has been defined as borrowing the thoughts of others just long enough to stimulate your own thinking. To get lasting pleasure and benefit from reading, use it as fuel for insights and *aha!* moments of your own.

Review the answers you uncovered by reading. Mull them over, ponder them, wonder about them, question them, modify them, make them your own.

Begin by testing your understanding of the author's ideas. See whether you can think of your own examples to illustrate the main points. Convert text into visual forms, such as charts, diagrams, and maps.

Just speak. Talk informally about what you've read. Stop after reading a chapter or section and just speak off the cuff. Summarize the key points or events from your reading.

Pretend that you've been asked to give an impromptu speech about the book or article. Talk about what you found significant or surprising in the material. Talk about what you intend to remember. Also talk about how you felt about the reading and whether you agree or disagree with the author.

To make this technique more effective, do it in front of a mirror. It might seem silly, but the benefits can be enormous. Reap them at exam time.

Classmates are even better than mirrors. Form a group, and practice teaching one another what you have read. One of the best ways to learn anything is to teach it to someone else.

In addition, talk about your reading whenever you can. Tell friends and family members what you're learning from your textbooks.

Just write. Stop at any point in your reading and write freely. Don't worry about following a particular format or creating a complete summary. Just note the points that emerge with the most clarity and force from your reading, along with your responses to them.

Structure your reciting. Find a chapter title or heading in the text. Then close your book and summarize the text that follows that heading.

When you're done, go back to the text and check your recitation for accuracy. Go on to the next heading and do the same. If you underlined or highlighted any main points in the text, use these as cues to recite. Note what you marked, then put the book down and start talking out loud. Explain as much as you can about that particular point.

Another option is to summarize the material in topic-point format. To practice this skill, pick one chapter (or one section of one chapter) from any of your textbooks. State the main topic covered in this chapter (or section of the chapter). Then state the main points that the author makes about this topic.

For even more structure, put your recitation in writing by using one of the note-taking formats explained in Chapter 5.

REVIEW REGULARLY

Plan to do your first complete review within 24 hours of reading the material. Sound the trumpets! This point is critical: A review within 24 hours moves information from your short-term memory to your long-term memory.

Review within one day. If you read it on Wednesday, review it on Thursday.

During this review, look over your notes and clear up anything you don't understand. Recite some of the main points again.

This review can be short. You might spend as little as 15 minutes reviewing a difficult two-hour reading assignment. Investing that time now can save you hours later when studying for exams.

The final step is the weekly or monthly review. This can be very short—perhaps only four or five minutes per assignment. Simply go over your notes. Read the highlighted parts of your text. Recite one or two of the more complicated points.

Sometimes longer review periods are appropriate. For example, if you found an assignment difficult, consider rereading it. Start over, as if you had never seen the material before. Sometimes a second reading will provide you with surprising insights.

You're One Click Away . . .
from more strategies for powerful reviewing.

Five ways to read with *children underfoot*

It is possible to combine effective study time and quality time with children by following these tips:

1. Attend to your children first.
Spend 10 minutes with your children before you settle in to study. If your children are infants or toddlers, schedule sessions of concentrated study for when they are asleep.

2. Use "pockets" of time.
Look for an extra 15 minutes in your day that you could spend on your reading assignments. You may find extra time at the doctor's office, waiting for the bus, or while your children are warming up for soccer or dance. Also look for opportunities to study between classes.

3. Plan special activities for your child while you're studying.
Find a regular playmate for your child. Some children can pair off with close friends and safely retreat to their rooms for hours of private play. You can check on them occasionally and still get lots of reading done.

4. Find community activities and services.
Ask whether your school provides a day care service. In some cases, these services are available to students at a reduced cost. Community agencies such as the YMCA might offer similar programs.

5. When you can't read everything, just read something.
It's okay to realize that you can't get all the reading done in one sitting. Just get something done with the time you have. (*Caution:* Supplement this strategy with others so you can stay on top of your work.)

4

experiment

"Dear author—I don't necessarily agree"

Two cornerstones of critical thinking are the abilities to test logic and examine evidence. Some strategies for doing both are explained in Chapter 7: "Thinking Clearly and Communicating Your Ideas." You can start testing logic right now by asking the following questions about what you read:

- Does the author define her key terms?

- Do any of the author's main points contradict each other?

- Has the author clearly stated her assumptions (the points that she simply accepts as true without trying to prove them)?

- Is the author's material free of logical fallacies, such as jumping to conclusions or making personal attacks?

Choose a current reading assignment—a nonfiction piece rather than a novel, short story, or poem. Focus on a particular chapter or section of this assignment and test it by asking the above questions. If you answered no to any of the above questions, then explain your reasons for doing so in the space below:

_____

_____

_____

_____

_____

_____

_____

_____

_____

_____

_____

_____

_____

Now review the same chapter or section and examine evidence. In the space below, list the author's main points. Did she present enough facts, examples, or expert testimony to support each one? If you answered no to this question, then explain your reasons for doing so in the space below:

_____

_____

_____

_____

_____

_____

_____

_____

_____

_____

_____

_____

_____

_____

_____

_____

_____

_____

You're One Click Away . . .
from more ways to think critically about your reading.

Decoding the deadly textbook

It's no secret: Some textbooks are deadly—dry, disorganized, and long. Skilled readers actually create benefit from such books by using them to practice high-level reading skills.

MAKE CHOICES ABOUT WHAT TO READ

Flexible readers constantly make choices about what to read—and what *not* to read. They realize that some texts are more valuable for their purposes than others, and that some passages within a single text are more crucial than the rest. When reading, they instantly ask: What's most important here?

The answer to this question varies from assignment to assignment, and even from page to page within a single assignment. Pose this question each time that you read, and look for clues to the answers. Pay special attention to the following:

- Parts of the text that directly answer the questions you generated while previewing.
- Any part of the text that's emphasized graphically—for example, headings, subheadings, lists, charts, graphs, and passages printed in bold or italic.
- Summary paragraphs (usually found at the beginning or end of a chapter or section).
- Any passage that provokes a strong response from you or raises a question that you cannot answer.

ADJUST YOUR READING PACE

Another key aspect of flexible reading is choosing your pace. Most people can read faster simply by making a conscious effort to do so.

Experiment with this idea right now. Read the rest of this chapter as fast as you can. After you finish, come back and reread the material at your usual rate. Notice how much you remembered from your first sprint through. You might be surprised to find how well you comprehend material even at dramatically increased speeds.

Following are more strategies for adjusting your reading pace.

Set a time limit. When you read, use a clock or a digital watch with a built-in stopwatch to time yourself. The objective is not to set speed records, so be realistic.

For example, set a goal to read a chapter in an hour. If that works, set a goal of 50 minutes to read a similar chapter. Test your limits. The idea is to give yourself a gentle push, increasing your reading speed without sacrificing comprehension.

Notice and release tension. It's not only possible to read fast when you're relaxed, it's easier. Relaxation promotes concentration. And remember, relaxation is not the same thing as sleep. You can be relaxed and alert at the same time.

Before you read, take a minute to close your eyes, notice your breathing, and clear your mind. Let go of all concerns other than the reading material that's in front of you. Then slowly open your eyes and ease into the text.

Notice and release regressions. Ineffective readers and inexperienced readers make many regressions. That is, they back up and reread words.

You can reduce the number of regressions by paying attention to them. Use a 3 × 5 card to cover words and lines you have read. This activity can reveal how often you stop and move the card back.

Don't be discouraged if you stop often at first. Being aware of it helps you naturally begin to regress less frequently.

Notice and release vocalizing. Obviously, you're more likely to read faster if you don't read aloud or move your lips. You can also increase your speed if you don't subvocalize—that is, if you don't mentally "hear" the words as you read them. To stop vocalizing, just be aware of it.

Remember that speed isn't everything. Skilled readers vary their reading rate according to their purpose and the nature of the material. An advanced text in analytic geometry usually calls for a different reading rate than the Sunday comics.

You also can use different reading rates on the same material. For example, you might sprint through an assignment looking for the key words and ideas, then return to the difficult parts for a slower and more thorough reading.

 You're One Click Away . . . *from more ways to master challenging reading material.*

Commit to ACTION

Experiment with active reading

Recall a time when you encountered problems with reading, such as words you didn't understand or paragraphs you paused to reread more than once. Perhaps you remember a time when you were totally confused by a reading assignment and had no idea how to overcome that confusion.

In either case, sum up the experience and how you felt about it by completing the following statement.

Discovery Statement

I discovered that I . . .

_____

_____

_____

_____

_____

_____

_____

Next, list the three most useful suggestions for reading that you gained from this chapter.

_____

_____

_____

_____

_____

_____

_____

Intention Statement

Describe how you will apply a suggestion from this chapter to a current reading assignment.

I intend to . . .

_____

_____

_____

_____

_____

_____

_____

Action Statement

After acting on your intention, consider how you might adapt or modify the suggestion to make it more useful to you.

I intend to . . .

_____

_____

_____

_____

_____

_____

_____

_____

POWER process

Ideas are tools

If you develop a lifelong habit of reading, you'll open yourself to thousands of new ideas. When you first encounter these ideas, don't believe any of them. Instead, think of ideas as tools.

To understand this Power Process, think about how you use a hammer. This tool exists for a purpose—to drive a nail. When you use a new hammer, you might notice its shape, its weight, and its balance. You don't try to figure out whether the hammer is "right." You just use it. If it works, you use it again. If it doesn't work, you get a different hammer.

This is not the attitude most people adopt when they encounter new ideas. The first thing most people do with new ideas is to measure them against old ones. If a new idea conflicts with an old one, the new one is likely to be rejected.

People have plenty of room in their lives for different kinds of hammers, but they tend to limit their capacity for different kinds of ideas. A new idea, at some level, is a threat to their very being—unlike a new hammer, which is simply a new hammer.

This book is a toolbox, and tools are meant to be used. If you read about a tool in this book that doesn't sound "right" or one that sounds a little goofy, remember that the ideas here are for using, not necessarily for believing. Suspend your judgment. Test the idea for yourself. If it works, use it. If it doesn't, don't.

To stay open-minded and discover useful intellectual tools, develop a habit of asking the following questions whenever you encounter a new idea: What if this is true? Even if it's not true all the time, could it be true *some* of the time? How could I use this idea? What benefit could I gain?

A word of caution: A master mechanic carries a variety of tools because no single tool works for all jobs. If you throw a tool away because it doesn't work in one situation, you won't be able to pull it out later when it's just what you need.

So if an idea doesn't work for you and you are satisfied that you gave it a fair chance, don't throw it away. File it away. The idea might come in handy sooner than you think.

 You're One Click Away . . .
from more ways to see ideas as tools.

5

Participating in Class and Taking Notes

Note-taking
essentials

You enter a lecture hall filled with students. For the next hour, one person standing at the front of the room will do most of the talking. Everyone else is seated and silent, taking notes. The lecturer seems to be doing all the work.

Don't be deceived. Look closely and you'll see students taking notes in a way that radiates energy. They're awake and alert. They're writing, a physical activity that expresses mental engagement. They listen for levels of information, make choices about what to record, and create effective materials to review later.

While in school, you may spend hundreds of hours taking notes. Experimenting with ways to make those notes more effective is a direct investment in your success. Think of your notes as a textbook that *you* create—one that's more in tune with your learning preferences than any textbook you could buy.

Legible and speedy handwriting, knowledge about outlining, a nifty pen, a new notebook, and a laptop computer are all great note-taking devices. But they're worthless if you don't take notes in a way that helps you *think* about what you're reading and experiencing in class. Effective note taking consists of a series of activities. You observe an "event"—a statement by an instructor, a slide show, or a chapter of required reading. Then you record your observations of that event—that is, you "take notes." Then you review what you have recorded and reflect on it more deeply.

Each phase of note taking is essential, and each depends on the others. Your observations determine what you record. What you record determines what you review. And the quality of your review can determine how effective your next observations will be.

Use the suggestions in this chapter to complete each phase of note taking more effectively. Here are the main strategies:

- Set the stage.
- Show up for class.
- Listen for key points.
- Capture key words.
- Predict test questions.
- Play with formats.
- Mine your notes for more value.

If you put these ideas into practice, you can turn even the most disorganized chicken scratches into tools for learning.

Discover what YOU WANT from this chapter

The Discovery Wheel on page 2 includes a section titled *Notes*. Take some time to go beyond your initial responses to that section. Spend five minutes skimming this chapter. Then complete the following sentences.

If asked to evaluate the overall quality of the notes that I've taken in the last week, I would say that . . .

_____
_____
_____
_____
_____
_____
_____
_____
_____
_____

Some ideas from this chapter that look especially useful for my note taking are . . .

_____
_____
_____
_____
_____
_____
_____
_____
_____
_____
_____

When you see 🖱 *You're One Click Away . . . , remember to go to this College Success CourseMate for additional content. And for a summary of this chapter, see the Master Student Review Cards at the end of this book.*

5

Set the stage
for *note taking*

The process of note taking begins well before you enter a classroom or crack open a book. Promote your success by "psyching up"—setting the physical and mental stage to receive what your teachers have to offer.

COMPLETE REQUIRED READING

Instructors usually assume that students complete reading assignments, and they construct their lectures accordingly. The more familiar you are with a subject, the easier it will be to understand in class.

PACK MATERIALS

A good pen does not make you a good observer, but the lack of a pen or a notebook can disrupt your concentration. Make sure you have any materials you will need, including your textbook.

ARRIVE EARLY TO PUT YOUR BRAIN IN GEAR

Arriving at class late or with only seconds to spare can add a level of stress that interferes with listening. Avoid that interference by arriving at least five minutes before class begins. Use this spare time to review notes from the previous class session.

SIT IN THE FRONT OF THE CLASSROOM

The closer you sit to the front, the fewer the distractions. Also, material on the board is easier to read from up front, and the instructor can see you more easily when you have a question.

TAKE CARE OF HOUSEKEEPING DETAILS

Write your name and phone number in each notebook in case you lose it. Class notes become more valuable as a term proceeds.

Develop the habit of labeling and dating your notes at the beginning of each class. Number the pages too.

Devote a specific section of your notebook to listing assignments for each course. Keep all details about test dates here also, along with a course syllabus. You're less likely to forget assignments if you compile them in one place where you can review them all at a glance.

Leave blank space. Notes tightly crammed on the page are hard to read and difficult to review. Leave plenty of space on the page. Later, when you review, you can use the blank space to clarify points, write questions, or add other material.

Use a three-ring binder. Three-ring binders give you several benefits. First, pages can be removed and spread out when you review. Second, the three-ring-binder format will allow you to insert handouts right into your notes easily. Third, you can insert your own out-of-class notes in the correct order.

Use only one side of a piece of paper. When you use one side of a page, you can review and organize all your notes by spreading them out side by side.

 You're One Click Away . . .
from more ways to set the stage for note taking.

Take effective notes for *online learning*

Courses that take place online can pose challenges for note taking. When there are no in-person class meetings, find ways to actively engage with online course material:

- Talk to classmates about what you're learning (and consider running a voice recorder at the same time).

- Organize a study group with other members of your online class.

- Write summaries of online articles and chat room sessions.

- Save online materials in a word processing file on your computer and add your own notes.

- Keep a personal journal to capture key insights from the course and ways you plan to apply them outside the class.

- Print out online materials and treat them like a textbook, applying the suggestions for reading explained in Chapter 4: "Achieving Your Purpose for Reading."

Show up *for* class

Your ability to take notes in any course can instantly improve when you truly show up for class. That means taking a seat in the room *and* focusing your attention while you're there. Use the following suggestions to meet both goals.

LIMIT DISTRACTIONS

Listening well can be defined as the process of overcoming distraction. In the classroom, you may have to deal with external distractions—noises from the next room, other students' conversations, or a lecturer who speaks softly. Internal distractions can be even more potent—for example, stress, memories about last night's party, or daydreams about what you'll do after class.

When the distraction is external, the solution may be obvious. Move closer to the front of the room, ask the lecturer to speak up, or politely ask classmates to keep quiet. Internal distractions can be trickier. Some solutions follow:

- Flood your mind with sensory data. Notice the shape of your pen. Feel the surface of your desk. Bring yourself back to class by paying attention to the temperature or the quality of light in the room.

- Notice and release daydreams. If your attention wanders, don't grit your teeth and try to stay focused. Just notice when your attention has wandered and gently bring it back.

- Pause for a few seconds and write distracting thoughts down. If you're thinking about the errands you want to run later, list them on a 3 × 5 card. Once your distractions are out of your mind and safely stored on paper, you can gently return your attention to taking notes.

Let go of judgments about lecture styles. Human beings are judgment machines. We evaluate everything, especially other people. We notice the way someone looks or speaks and we instantly make up a story about her. We do this so quickly that we don't even realize it. Don't let your attitude about an instructor's lecture style, habits, or appearance get in the way of your education. You can decrease the power of your judgments if you pay attention to them and let them go.

You can even let go of judgments about rambling, unorganized lectures. Take the initiative and organize the material yourself. While taking notes, separate the key points from the examples and supporting evidence. Note the places where you got confused and make a list of questions to ask.

Participate in class activities. Ask questions. Volunteer for demonstrations. Join in class discussions. Be willing to take a risk or look foolish if that's what it takes for you to learn. Chances are, the question you think is "dumb" is also on the minds of several of your classmates.

Relate the class to your goals. If you have trouble staying awake in a particular class, write at the top of your notes how that class relates to a specific goal. Identify the payoff for reaching that goal.

REMEMBER THAT YOU CAN LISTEN AND DISAGREE

When you hear something you disagree with, notice your disagreement and let it go. If your disagreement is persistent and strong, make note of this and then move on. Internal debate can prevent you from receiving new information. Just absorb it with a mental tag: "I don't agree, but my instructor says. . . ."

When you review your notes later, think critically about the instructor's ideas. List questions or note your disagreements.

Also, avoid "listening with your answer running," which refers to the habit of forming your response to people's ideas *before* they've finished speaking. Let the speaker have his say, even when you're sure you'll disagree.

GIVE THE SPEAKER FEEDBACK

Speakers thrive on attention. Give lecturers verbal and nonverbal feedback—everything from simple eye contact to insightful comments and questions. Such feedback can raise an instructor's energy level and improve the class.

BRACKET EXTRA MATERIAL

Bracketing refers to separating your own thoughts from the lecturer's as you take notes. This is useful in several circumstances:

- Bracket your own opinions. For the most part, avoid making editorial comments in your lecture notes. The danger is that when you return to your notes, you may mistake your own ideas for those of the speaker. Clearly label your own comments, such as questions to ask later or strong disagreements. Pick a symbol, like brackets, and use consistently.

- Bracket material that confuses you. Invent your own signal for getting lost during a lecture. For example, write a circled question mark in the margin of the paper. Or simply leave

5

Cope with fast-talking teachers

Ask the instructor to slow down. This obvious suggestion is easily forgotten. If asking him to slow down doesn't work, ask him to repeat what you missed. Also experiment with the following suggestions.

Take more time to prepare for class.
Familiarity with a subject increases your ability to pick out key points. Before class, take detailed notes on your reading and leave plenty of blank space. Take these notes with you to class and simply add your lecture notes to them.

Be willing to make choices.
Focus your attention on key points. Instead of trying to write everything down, choose what you think is important. Occasionally you will make a wrong choice and neglect an important point. Worse things could happen.

Exchange photocopies of notes with classmates.
Your fellow students might write down something you missed. At the same time, your notes might help them.

Leave empty spaces in your notes.
Allow plenty of room for filling in information you missed. Use a symbol that signals you've missed something, so you can remember to come back to it.

See the instructor after class.
Take your class notes with you and show the instructor what you missed.

Learn shorthand.
Some note-taking systems, known as shorthand, are specifically designed for getting ideas down fast. Books and courses are available to help you learn these systems.

Ask questions even if you're totally lost.
There may be times when you feel so lost that you can't even formulate a question. That's okay. Just report this fact to the instructor. Or just ask any question. Often this will lead you to the question you really want to ask.

space for the explanation that you will get later. This space will also be a signal that you missed something. Be honest with yourself when you don't understand.

CONSIDER THE PROS AND CONS OF VOICE RECORDERS

Before you record a lecture, consider the potential pitfalls. Recorders can malfunction. Watching or listening to recorded lectures can take a lot of time—in fact, it can take more time than reviewing written notes. And when you record a lecture, you may be tempted to daydream ("I'll just listen to this later.").

With those warnings in mind, recordings can help you

- Catch up after an absence. If you have to miss a class, ask a classmate to record the lecture for you. Some teachers may even be willing to do this.

- Review your written notes. To create a useful review tool, record yourself as you review your lecture notes. Using your notes as a guide, see whether you can re-create the essence of the lecture. Pretend you're the lecturer.

- Create review materials, such as CDs or MP3s to listen to while you drive.

Make sure that your recording equipment works. During class, set the volume high enough to pick up the speaker. Sitting close and up front can help. Also, back up your recording with written notes. Turn the recorder on and then take notes as if it weren't there. If the recording fails, you'll still have a record of what happened in class.

Note: Before recording, check with your instructors. Some prefer not to be recorded.

CONSIDER THE PROS AND CONS OF LAPTOPS

Laptop computers can be beneficial for note taking, but as with recorders, there are downsides. Laptops can freeze, crash, or run out of battery power. You can get around these disadvantages in several ways.

- Protect your work. Save your data often while taking notes. Regularly back up your computer files.

- Bring paper and pen—just in case. If you have computer problems, you can keep taking notes without missing a beat. Also, you may find it easier to enter diagrams and formulas by hand rather.

- Combine handwritten notes with computer-based notes. This option gives you the best of both worlds. During class, take notes by hand. After class, enter your notes into a word processing or database file. Or use the computer simply to outline or summarize your notes. In either case, save your handwritten notes as a backup.

 You're One Click Away . . .
from more strategies for "showing up" as you take notes.

CRITICAL THINKING
experiment

Listen for key points

Key points are the major ideas in a lecture—the "bottom-line" or "takeaway" messages. Lecturers usually provide verbal clues that they're coming up to a key point. Listen for phrases such as:

The following three factors . . .
The most important thing is . . .
What I want you to remember is . . .
In conclusion . . .

To illustrate and support key points, speakers offer supporting material in the form of examples, facts, statistics, quotations, anecdotes, and other details.

In short, there are two levels of material in a lecture: (1) key points and (2) details that support the key points. Your ability to examine evidence depends on making this distinction.

You can make this distinction in your notes with simple visual cues. For example:

- Highlight key points. As you take notes, graphically emphasize the key points. Underline them, write them in uppercase letters, write them in a different color of ink, or go over them with a highlighter. In your notes, record only the most vivid or important details used to support each key point.

- Use numbered lists to record a sequence of key points. When you want to indicate a series of events or steps that take place in time, number each one in chronological order.

- Format your notes in two columns. In the left-hand column, list the key points. On the right, include the most important details that relate to each point.

To experiment with these suggestions right away, complete the following steps to evaluate your note taking:

1. Select a page or two of class notes that you've taken recently.

2. Circle, underline, or highlight the key points.

3. If you were not able to distinguish the key points from supporting material in your notes, then do some revision. Recopy your notes using the two-column format described above. Show your revised notes to a classmate or to your instructor and ask for feedback.

Finally, reflect on this exercise. Complete the following sentences.

In reviewing my notes, I discovered that . . .

_____

_____

_____

_____

_____

_____

To take more effective notes in the future, I intend to . . .

_____

_____

_____

_____

_____

_____

_____

5

You're One Click Away . . .
from more ways to capture key points and supporting details.

CAPTURE
key words

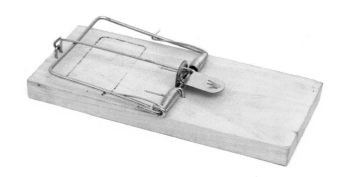

When it comes to notes, more is not necessarily better. Your job is not to write down all of a lecturer's words or even most of them. Taking effective notes calls for split-second decisions about which words are essential to record and which are less important.

An easy way to sort the less important from the essential is to take notes using key words. Key words or phrases contain the essence of communication. They include technical terms, names, numbers, equations, and words of degree: *most, least, faster,* and the like.

Key words are laden with associations. They evoke images and associations with other words and ideas. One key word can initiate the recall of a whole cluster of ideas. A few key words can form a chain: From those words, you can reconstruct an entire lecture.

FOCUS ON NOUNS AND VERBS

In many languages, there are two types of words that carry the essential meaning of most sentences—nouns and verbs. For example, the previous sentence could be reduced to: *nouns + verbs carry meaning. Carry* is a verb; most of the remaining words are nouns.

There are additional ways to subtract words from your notes and still retain the lecturer's meaning:

- **Eliminate adverbs and adjectives.** The words *extremely interesting* can become *interesting* in your notes—or simply an exclamation mark (!)

- **Note the topic followed by a colon and key point.** For instance, *There are seven key principles that can help you take effective notes* becomes *Effective notes: 7 principles.*

- **Use lists.** There are two basic types. A numbered list expresses steps that need to be completed in a certain order. A simple bulleted list includes ideas that are related but do not have to follow a sequential order.

To find more examples of key words, study newspaper headlines. Good headlines include a verb and only enough nouns to communicate the essence of an event or idea.

EXAMPLE: REDUCING SPEECH TO KEY WORDS

To see how key words can be used in note taking, take yourself to an imaginary classroom. You are enrolled in a course on world religion, and today's lecture is an introduction to Buddhism. The instructor begins with these words:

Okay, today we're going to talk about three core precepts of Buddhism. I know that this is a religion that may not be familiar to many of you, and I ask that you keep an open mind as I proceed. Now, with that caveat out of the way, let's move ahead.

First, let's look at the term anicca. By the way, this word is spelled a-n-i-c-c-a. Everybody got that? Great. All right, well, this is a word in an ancient language called Pali, which was widely spoken in India during the Buddha's time—about 600 years before the birth of Jesus. Anicca is a word layered with many meanings and is almost impossible to translate into English. If you read books about Buddhism, you may see it rendered as impermanence, and this is a passable translation.

Impermanence is something that you can observe directly in your everyday experience. Look at any object in your external environment and you'll find that it's constantly changing. Even the most solid and stable things—like a mountain, for example—are dynamic. You could use time-lapse photography to record images of a mountain every day for 10 years, and if you did, you'd see incredible change—rocks shifting, mudslides, new vegetation, and the like.

Following is one way to reduce this section of the lecture to key words:

Buddhism: 3 concepts
#1 = anicca = impermanence.
Anicca = Pali = ancient Indian language (600 yrs b4 Jesus).
Example of anicca: time-lapse photos & changes in mountain.

In this case the original 209 words of the lecture have been reduced to 28. However, this example might be a little sparse for your tastes. Remember that it shows only one possible option for abbreviating your notes. Don't take it as a model to imitate strictly.

A CAVEAT: USE COMPLETE SENTENCES AT CRUCIAL POINTS

Sometimes key words aren't enough. When an instructor repeats a sentence slowly and emphasizes each word, he's sending you a signal. Also, technical definitions are often worded precisely because even a slightly different wording will render the definitions useless or incorrect. Write down key sentences word for word.

ADDITIONAL SUGGESTIONS FOR CAPTURING THE ESSENTIAL INFORMATION

- **Write notes in paragraphs.** When it is difficult to follow the organization of a lecture or to put information into outline form, create a series of informal paragraphs. Use complete sentences for precise definitions, direct quotations, and important points that the instructor emphasizes by repetition or other signals—such as the phrase "This is an important point." For other material, focus on capturing key words.

- **Listen for introductory, concluding, and transition words and phrases.** Examples are "the following three factors," "in conclusion," "the most important consideration," "in addition to," and "on the other hand." These phrases and similar ones signal relationships, definitions, new subjects, conclusions, cause and effect relationships, and examples. They reveal the structure of the lecture. You can use these phrases to organize your notes.

- **Take notes in different colors.** You can use colors as highly visible organizers. For example, you can signal important points with red. Or use one color of ink for notes about the text and another color for lecture notes. Notes that are visually pleasing can be easier to review.

- **Copy material from the board and a PowerPoint presentation.** Record all formulas, diagrams, and problems that the teacher presents on the board or in a PowerPoint presentation. Copy dates, numbers, names, places, and other facts. If it's presented visually in class, put it in your notes. You can even use your own signal or code to flag that material.

- **Plan to get notes for classes you miss.** For most courses, you'll benefit by attending every class session. If you miss a class, catch up as quickly as possible. Early in each term, connect with other students who are willing to share notes. Also contact your instructor. Perhaps there is another section of the same course that you can attend so you won't miss the lecture information. If there is a Web site for your class, check it for assignments and the availability of handouts you missed.

You're One Click Away . . .
from more strategies for reducing ideas to their essence.

Short and sweet— Remember to abbrevi8

Abbreviations can be useful in note taking as well as texting—if you use them consistently. Some abbreviations are standard. If you make up your own abbreviations, write a key explaining them in your notes.

Avoid vague abbreviations. When you use an abbreviation like *comm.* for *committee,* you run the risk of not being able to remember whether you meant *committee, commission, common, commit, community, communicate,* or *communist.*

The following seven principles explain how to use abbreviations in your notes:

Principle: Leave out articles.

Examples: Omit *a, an, the.*

Principle: Leave out vowels.

Examples: Talk becomes *tlk, said* becomes *sd, American* becomes *Amrcn.*

Principle: Use mathematical symbols.

Examples: Plus becomes +, *minus* becomes −, *is more than* becomes >, *is less than* becomes <, *equals or is* becomes =.

Principle: Use arrows to indicate causation and changes in quantity.

Examples: Increase becomes ↑; *decrease* becomes ↓; *causes, leads to,* or *shows that* becomes →.

Principle: Use standard abbreviations and omit the periods.

Examples: Pound becomes *lb, Avenue* becomes *ave.*

Principle: Create words from numbers and letters that you can sound out and combine.

Examples: Before becomes *b4, too* becomes 2.

Principle: Use a comma in place of and.

Example: Freud and Jung were major figures in twentieth-century psychology becomes *20th century psych: Freud, Jung = major figures.*

Note: If you key your notes into word processing files, you can use a "find and replace" command to replace abbreviations with full words.

5

Play with
NOTE-TAKING *formats*

THE CORNELL FORMAT

One option for note taking that has worked for students around the world is the Cornell format. Originally described by Walter Pauk, this approach is now taught across the United States and in other countries as well.[1]

The cornerstone of this system is simple: a wide margin on the left-hand side of the page. Pauk calls this the *cue column,* and using it is the key to the Cornell format's many benefits. To get started with this approach to note taking, take the following steps.

Format your paper. On each page of your notes, draw a vertical line, top to bottom, about two inches from the left edge of the paper. This line creates the cue column—the space to the left of the line. You will use this space later to condense and review your notes.

Pauk also suggests that you leave a two-inch space at the bottom of the page. He calls this the summary area. This space is also designed to be used at a later stage, as you review your notes.

Take notes, leaving the cue column and summary area blank. As you read or listen to a lecture, take notes on the right-hand side of the page. *Do not write in the cue column or summary area.* You'll use these spaces later.

Fill in the cue column. You can reduce your notes to several kinds of entries in the cue column:

- Key questions. Think of the notes you took on the right-hand side of the page as a set of answers. In the cue column, write the corresponding questions. Write one question for each major term or point in your notes.

- Key words. Writing key words will speed the review process later. Also, reading your notes and focusing on extracting key words will further reinforce your understanding of the lecture or reading assignment.

- Headings. Pretend that you are a copy editor at a newspaper, and that the notes you took are a series of articles about different topics. In the cue column, write a headline for each "article." Use actual newspaper headlines—and headings in your textbooks—as models.

Fill in the summary area. See whether you can reduce all the notes on the page to a sentence or two. Add cross-references to topics elsewhere in your notes that are closely related. Explain briefly why the notes on this page matter; if you think the material is likely to appear on a test, note that fact here. Also use the summary area to list any questions that you want to ask in class.

EXAMPLE: NOTES IN CORNELL FORMAT

CUE COLUMN	NOTES
	INTRO TO PHILOSOPHY 1/10/09
What is the origin of the word Philosophy?	Philosophy—from the Greek philosophia— "lover of wisdom"
What do philosophers do?	Philosophers have different views of their main task:
	--reflect on the nature of ultimate reality
	--create a framework to unite all fields of knowledge
	--critically evaluate all claims to knowledge
	Traditional topics in philosophy = 5 areas:
What are 5 traditional topics in philosophy?	1. Determine when a series of assertions is coherent and consistent (logic)
	2. Determine what is ultimately real (ontology)
	3. Determine what constitutes real knowledge (epistemology)
	4. Determine is what is truly valuable (axiology and aesthetics)
	5. Determine what forms of behavior best sustain human society (ethics and politics)
SUMMARY	
Even though philosophers have differing views of their task, there are 5 traditional topics in philosophy.	

OUTLINES

In addition to the Cornell format, another option for note taking is outlining. The traditional Roman-numeral style represents just one option for outlining. By playing with other options, you can discover the power of outlining. Use this tool to reveal relationships between ideas and to categorize large bodies of information.

Outlines consist of *headings*—words, phrases, or sentences arranged in a hierarchy from general to specific:

- In the first or top level of an outline, record the major topics or points that are presented in a lecture or reading assignment.

- In the second level, record the key topics or points that are used to support and explain the first-level headings.

- In the third level, record facts, examples, and other details that relate to each of your second-level headings.

EXAMPLE: NOTES IN OUTLINE FORMAT

Following is an outline of part of this article, based on the above suggestions:

CORNELL FORMAT

Format paper in two vertical columns and summary area at bottom.

Take notes; leave cue column and summary area blank.

Fill in cue column with key questions, key words, or headings.

Fill in summary area.

Notice that first-level headings in this outline are printed in all uppercase (capital) letters. Second-level headings appear in both uppercase and lowercase letters. You could add a third level of headings to this outline by listing the topic sentences for each paragraph in the chapter. These third-level headings could be indented and listed underneath the second-level headings.

CONCEPT MAPS

Concept mapping—explained by Joseph Novak and D. Bob Gowin in their book *Learning How to Learn*—is a way to express ideas in a visual form.[2] Here are the key elements:

- A main concept written at the top of a page.

- Related concepts arranged in a hierarchy, with more general concepts toward the top of a page and more specific concepts toward the bottom.

- Links—lines with words that briefly explain the relationship between concepts.

When you combine concepts with their linking words, you'll often get complete sentences (or sets of coherent phrases). One benefit of concept maps is that they quickly, vividly, and accurately show the relationships between ideas.

EXAMPLE: NOTES IN CONCEPT MAP FORMAT

Excerpt from notes on a reading assignment about nutrition.

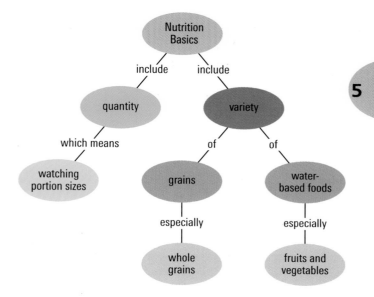

You're One Click Away . . .
from more formats for note taking.

Mine your notes for *added value*

The purpose of taking notes is to consult them later. To some students, that means scanning them once or twice before a test. By that time, however, the notes may raise more questions than they answer.

As an alternative, add value to your notes by updating, condensing, reorganizing, reviewing, and refining them.

The key is to see your notes as living documents—words and images that gain clarity as your understanding of a subject deepens. Create notes that you will understand for weeks, months, or years to come.

REVISE YOUR NOTES

Take your first pass through your notes as soon after each class as possible. Use this time to accomplish the following:

- Fix passages that are illegible.
- Check to see that your notes are labeled with the date and the name of the class.
- Make sure that the pages are numbered.
- Expand on passages that are hard to understand.
- Write out abbreviated words or phrases that might be unclear to you later.
- List questions that you need answered in order to make sense of your notes.

You might find it useful to distinguish between what you wrote in class and what you filled in later. With handwritten notes, edit using a different colored pen or pencil. If you key your notes into a computer, you can use different colored fonts for your edits.

TRANSLATE YOUR NOTES INTO A DIFFERENT FORMAT

If you took notes in the Cornell format, for example, then create separate concept maps to summarize the material. Or, if you used outline format during class, then rewrite key sections of your notes in Cornell format. Use all these formats at different points in your notes for a course, or invent new formats of your own.

Another option is take notes only on the right-hand page of your notebook. Later, use the left-hand page to elaborate on your notes. This page is for anything you want. For example, add charts, diagrams, and drawings. Write review questions, possible test questions, summaries, and outlines,

The benefit of playing with all these formats is that they engage your mind in different ways. Taking notes in Cornell format can help you get a handle on details—key terms and facts. Outlines force you to pay attention to the way that material is structured. And maps are visual devices that help you see connections between many topics at once. Each format yields a different cross-section of the subject matter. And each format deepens your understanding.

REVIEW YOUR NOTES

In terms of reinforcing long-term memory, the *process* you use to review your notes can be just as crucial as the *content* of those notes. Think of notes that have not been reviewed as leaky faucets, constantly dripping, losing precious information until you shut them off with a quick review.

The sooner you review your notes, the better, especially if the class was difficult. In fact, you can start reviewing during class. When your instructor pauses to set up the overhead projector or erase the board, scan your notes. Dot the *i*'s, cross the *t*'s, and write out unclear abbreviations.

Another way to use this technique is to get to your next class as quickly as you can. Then use the four or five minutes before a lecture to review the notes you just took in the previous class.

If you do not get to your notes immediately after class, you can still benefit by reviewing them later in the day. A review right before you go to sleep can also be valuable. And you can do it in just a few minutes—often 10 minutes or less.

Once a week, review all your notes again. The review sessions don't need to take a lot of time. Even a 20-minute weekly review period is valuable. Some students find that a weekend review, say, on Sunday afternoon, helps them stay in continuous touch with the material. Scheduling regular review sessions on your calendar helps develop the habit.

As you review, step back for the larger picture. In addition to reciting or repeating the material to yourself, ask questions about it:

- How does this relate to information I already know, in this field or another?
- Will I be tested on this material?
- What will I do with this material?

- How can I relate it to something that deeply interests me?
- Am I unclear on any points? If so, what exactly is the question I want to ask?

Another important level of review is the kind of studying you do during the week before a major test. This is an intensive phase of learning that can involve many types of activity: creating course summaries, writing mock tests, and taking part in study groups.

REHEARSE YOUR NOTES

When you want to remember a fact or idea, you instinctively rehearse it. Rehearsal can be as simple as repeating the seven digits of a phone number a few times before you dial it—or as complex as an actor who practices lines to learn a one-hour monologue.

The point is this: Information that you rehearse moves into your long-term memory. And information that you do not rehearse can fade completely from your memory in anywhere from a few seconds to a few hours. In more common parlance: If you don't use it, you lose it.

For more effective rehearsal, try the following.

Use a variety of strategies. Recite the points in your notes that you want to remember. Explain these points to someone else. Lead a study group about the topic. Also look for ways to summarize and condense the material. See whether you can take the language from your notes and make it more precise. If you succeed, edit your notes accordingly.

Involve your senses. Make rehearsal a rich, enjoyable experience. Read your notes out loud and use a variety of voices. Sing your notes, making up your own rhymes or songs. Record yourself as you recite your notes, and play music you like in the background.

Use elaborative rehearsal instead of rote memory. Rehearsal is a sophisticated learning strategy that goes well beyond rote repetition. As you review your notes, use rehearsal to move facts and ideas off the page and into your mind. See whether you can elaborate on your notes by using more of your own words and by supplying your own examples.

Build a feedback cycle into your rehearsal. Create a list of key questions that cover the important sections of your notes. Then quiz yourself, or ask a friend to quiz you. To get maximum value from this exercise, evaluate the accuracy of your answers. If you're consistently missing key questions, then consider using a new strategy for reading or note taking.

Allow adequate time. Following the above suggestions means that rehearsal will take more time than mindlessly scanning your notes. It's worth it. Also remember that you can be selective. You don't have to rehearse everything in your notes. Save your most elaborate rehearsal for the most important material.

 You're One Click Away . . .
from more ways to revise, review, and rehearse your notes.

5 ways to improve your handwriting

Many people are resigned to writing illegibly for the rest of their lives. They feel that they have no control over their handwriting. Yet everyone's handwriting does change.

Though handwriting often changes in ways that we fail to notice, you can make a *conscious* effort to change it. The main prerequisite for improving your handwriting is simply the desire to do so. In addition, you can explore the following possibilities.

1. Use creative visualizations. Find
a quiet spot to sit. Relax your whole body, close your eyes, and see yourself writing clearly. Feel the pen as it moves over the page and visualize neat, legible letters as you write them.

2. Revise sloppy writing immediately. Use an erasable pen or pencil.
When you write something sloppily, fix it immediately. At first, you might find yourself rewriting almost everything. This technique can help you learn to write legibly.

3. Dot all i's and cross all t's. The
time you spend dotting and crossing will eliminate time spent scratching your head.

4. Notice problem letters. Go through
your notes and circle letters that you have difficulty deciphering. Practice writing these letters.

5. Be willing to slow down. Weigh
the costs and benefits of writing more slowly as a way to improve your handwriting. If you cannot read what you write, speed is of little use. Also, take fewer notes; write down only what's essential. Learning to take notes efficiently could allow you to improve your handwriting. It will also allow you to spend less time writing and more time learning.

Predict
test questions

Predicting test questions can do more than help you get better grades. It can also keep you focused on the purpose of the course and help you design your learning strategies. Following are legal and constructive ways to outsmart your teacher and reduce surprises at test time.

CREATE A SIGNAL TO FLAG POSSIBLE TEST ITEMS IN YOUR NOTES

Use asterisks (**), exclamation marks (!!), or a *T!* in a circle. Place these signals in the margin next to ideas that seem like possible test items.

LOOK FOR VERBAL CUES FROM YOUR TEACHER

Few teachers will try to disguise the main content of their courses. In fact, most offer repeated clues about what they want you to remember. Many of those clues are verbal. In addition to focusing on *what* lecturers say, pay attention to how they say it.

Repetition. Your teachers may state important points several times or return to those points in subsequent classes. They may also read certain passages word for word from their notes or from a book. Be sure to record all these points fully in your notes.

Common terms. Also note your teachers' "pet phrases"—repeated terms that relate directly to course content. You could benefit from using these terms in essay exams—along with explanations in your own words to show that you truly understand the concepts.

Questions. Pay attention to questions that the instructor poses to the class. These are potential test questions. Write them down, along with some answers.

Emphasis on certain types of content. Some teachers emphasize details—facts, names, dates, technical terms, and the like. Other teachers focus on broad themes and major events. Be alert to such differences. They are clues to the kind of tests you'll have.

Placement of content. Listen closely to material presented at the beginning and end of a lecture. Skilled speakers will often preview or review their key content at these points.

Comments on assigned readings.
When material from reading assignments is also covered extensively in class, it is likely to be on the test. The opposite can also be true: When your teacher emphasizes material that does *not* appear in any assigned reading, that material is likely to be important.

LOOK FOR NONVERBAL CUES FROM YOUR TEACHER

Sometimes a lecturer's body language will give potent clues to key content. He might use certain gestures when making critical points—pausing, looking down at notes, staring at the ceiling, or searching for words. If the lecturer has to think hard about how to make a point, that's probably an important point. Also note the following.

Watch the board or overhead projector. If an instructor takes time to write something down, consider this to be another signal that the material is important. In short: If it's on the board, on a projector, or in a handout, put it in your notes. Use your own signal or code to flag this material.

Watch the instructor's eyes. If an instructor glances at his notes and then makes a point, it is probably a signal that the information is especially important. Anything he reads from his notes is a potential test question.

WRITE PRACTICE TEST QUESTIONS

Save all quizzes, papers, lab sheets, and graded material of any kind. Quiz questions have a way of appearing, in slightly altered form, on final exams. If copies of previous exams are available from your instructor, use them to predict test questions. For science courses and other courses involving problem solving, practice working problems using different variables.

Also brainstorm test questions with other students. This is a great activity for study groups.

REMEMBER THE OBVIOUS

Listen for these words: "This material will be on the test."

You're One Click Away . . .
from more ways to predict test questions.

Taking notes
while *reading*

Taking notes while reading requires the same skills that apply to class notes: picking up key points, capturing key words, and predicting test questions. Use these skills to take notes for review and for research.

REVIEW NOTES

These will look like the notes you take in class. Take review notes when you want more detailed notes than writing in the margin of your text allows. You might want to single out a particularly difficult section of a text and make separate notes. You can't underline or make notes in library books, so these sources will require separate notes too.

Use a variety of formats. Concept maps are useful for review, especially for summaries of overlapping lecture and textbook materials. You can also outline or take notes in paragraph form. Another option is the Cornell method. Use the left-hand column for key words and questions, just as you do in your class notes.

When you read mathematic, scientific, or other technical materials, copy important formulas or equations. Recreate important diagrams and draw your own visual representations of concepts. Also write down data that might appear on an exam.

RESEARCH NOTES

Take research notes when preparing to write a paper or deliver a speech.

One traditional tool for research notes is the mighty 3 × 5 card. Create two kinds of cards: source cards and information cards.

Source cards. These cards identify where you found the information contained in your paper or speech. For example, a source card for a book will show the author, title, date and place of publication, and publisher. Ask your instructor what information to include for each type of source.

When you write source cards, give each source a code—the initials of the author, a number, or a combination of numbers and letters.

A key advantage of using source cards is that you create your bibliography as you do the research. When you are done, simply alphabetize the cards by author and—voilà!—instant bibliography.

Information cards. Write the actual research notes on information cards. At the top of each information card, write the code for the source of the information. For printed sources, also include the relevant page numbers. When recording your own ideas, simply note the source as "me."

Write only one piece of information on each information card— a single quotation, fact, or idea. You can then sort the cards in various ways to construct an outline of your paper or speech.

Avoid plagiarism. When people take words or images from a source and present them as their own, they are committing *plagiarism*. Even when plagiarism is accidental, the consequences can be harsh. If you take a direct quotation from one of your sources, put that material within quotation marks and record the source. Also record the source of any material that you paraphrase or summarize. In addition, always submit your own work. (These are basic guidelines; ask your instructor for more.)

Consider a computer. Another option is to take research notes using a computer. This offers the same flexibility as 3 × 5 cards when it comes to sorting and organizing ideas. However, be especially careful to prevent plagiarism. If you copy text or images from a Web site, separate these notes from your own ideas. Use a different font for copied material or enclose it in quotation marks.

THINK ABOUT NOTES

Whenever you take notes, use your own words as much as possible. When you do this, you are thinking about what you are reading.

Close the book after reading an assignment and quickly jot down a summary of the material. This writing can be loose, without any structure or format. The important thing is to do it right away, while the material is still fresh in your mind. Restating concepts in this way helps you remember them and identify any gaps in your understanding.

✓ Commit to ACTION

Transform your note taking

Think back on the last few lectures you have attended. How would you rate your note-taking skills? As you complete this exercise, think of areas that need improvement.

Discovery Statement

First, recall a recent incident in which you had difficulty taking notes. Perhaps you were listening to an instructor who talked fast. Maybe you got confused and stopped taking notes altogether. Or perhaps you went to review your notes after class, only to find that they made no sense at all.

Describe this incident in more detail, noting how it was challenging for you. I discovered that . . .

_____

_____

_____

_____

_____

Intention Statement

Now review this chapter to find at least five strategies that you can use right away to help you take better notes. Sum up each of those strategies in a few words and note the page numbers where these strategies are explained.

Strategy	Page number
_____	_____
_____	_____
_____	_____
_____	_____
_____	_____

Action Statement

Now gear up for action. Describe a specific situation in which you will apply at least one of the strategies you listed previously. If possible, choose a situation that will occur within the next 24 hours.

_____

_____

_____

_____

_____

_____

_____

After experimenting with these strategies, evaluate how well they worked for you. If you thought of a way to modify any of the strategies so that they can work more effectively, describe those modifications here:

_____

_____

_____

_____

_____

_____

POWER process

Love your problems

Even as you experiment with new strategies for note taking, you might run into some problems keeping up with some instructors and understanding what they say. This is not unusual.

We all have problems and barriers that block our progress or prevent us from moving into new areas. Often, the way we respond to our problems places limitations on what we can be, do, and have.

Problems often work like barriers. When we bump up against one of our problems, we usually turn away and start walking along a different path. And all of a sudden—bump!—we've struck another barrier. And we turn away again.

As we continue to bump into problems and turn away from them, our lives stay inside the same old boundaries. Inside these boundaries, we are unlikely to have new adventures. We are unlikely to keep learning.

There is an alternative. If we respond to problems by loving them instead of resisting them, we can expand the boundaries in which we live our lives.

The word *love* might sound like an overstatement. In this Power Process, the word means to unconditionally accept the fact that your problems exist. The more we deny or resist a problem, the stronger it seems to become. When we accept the fact that we have a problem, we can find effective ways to deal with it.

Suppose one of your barriers is being afraid of speaking in front of a group. You could get up in front of the group and pretend that you're not afraid. Or you could tell yourself, "I'm not going to be scared" and then try to keep your knees from knocking. Generally, these strategies don't work.

A more effective approach is to love your fear. Go to the front of the room, look out into the audience, and say to yourself, "I am scared. I notice that my knees are shaking and my mouth feels dry, and I'm having a rush of thoughts about what might happen if I say the wrong thing. Yup, I'm scared, and I'm not going to fight it. I'm going to give this speech anyway."

The beauty of this Power Process is that you continue to take action—giving your speech, for example—no matter what you feel. You walk right up to the barrier and then *through* it. You might even find that if you totally accept and experience a barrier, such as fear, it shrinks or disappears. And even if that does not happen right away, you still open up to new experiences and gain new chances to learn.

Loving a problem does not need to stop us from solving it. In fact, fully accepting and admitting a problem usually helps us take effective action—which can free us of the problem once and for all.

You're One Click Away . . .
from more ways to love your problems.

6 Maximizing Your Memory and Mastering Tests

Grades:
The truth

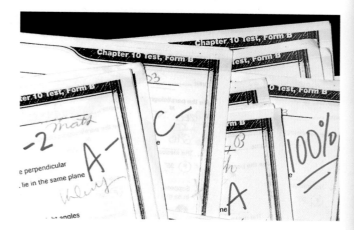

On the surface, tests don't look dangerous. Yet sometimes we treat them as if they are land mines. Suppose a stranger walks up to you on the street and says, "Amiri Baraka first published under another name. What was it?"* Would you tense up or break out in a cold sweat?

Probably not, even if you've never heard of Amiri Baraka. But if you find this question on a test and you don't know the answer, your hands might get clammy. That's because there are lots of misconceptions about grades. Here are some truths about grades:

Grades are not a measure of your intelligence or creativity.

Grades are not an indication of your ability to contribute to society.

Grades are not a measure of your skills or your worth as a human being.

Grades often result from test scores, and a score is only a measure response to items on a test.

Some people think that a test score measures what you accomplished in a course. This is false. If you are blank out, the grade cannot measure what you've learned. The reverse is also true: If you are good at taking tests, the grade won't accurately reflect what you know. If you get a low grade on a test, you are simply a person who got a low grade on a test. Scoring low on important tests—entrance tests for college or med school, bar exams, CPA exams—usually means only a delay.

There's another common confusion about grades—that the way to get good grades is to study. That sounds logical, but what does that word *study* really mean? Skimming your textbooks and notes?

Approach each test as a performance. From this point of view, preparing for a test means *rehearsing*. Study in the way that an actor prepares for a play—by simulating the conditions you'll encounter in the exam room. Do the kinds of tasks that you'll

---

*Amiri Baraka has written more than 40 books, including essays, poems, and plays. He first published under the name LeRoi Jones.

Discover what
YOU WANT
from this chapter

The Discovery Wheel on page 2 includes a section titled *Memory and Tests*. Take some time to go beyond your initial responses to that section. Spend five minutes skimming this chapter. Then complete the following sentences:

On the day of a test, my level of confidence is generally . . .

_____

_____

_____

_____

Some ideas from this chapter that could help me reach a new level of mastery with tests are . . .

_____

_____

_____

_____

_____

When you see **You're One Click Away . . .**, *remember to go to this book's College Success CourseMate for additional content. And for a summary of this chapter, see the Master Student Review Cards at the end of this book.*

6

actually perform during a test: answering questions, solving problems, composing essays, and the like. Rehearse with regular reviews of course content. Also create special review materials, explore the power of study groups, and discover ways to reduce fears of tests. This chapter includes dozens of suggestions on these topics. Use them to transform your experience of tests.

You're One Click Away . . .
from more information about integrity in test taking.

Be ready for your *next test*

When getting ready for tests, remember a key word—*review*. First create effective materials for review. Then use them often.

WRITE REVIEW CHECKLISTS

To begin your test preparation, make a list of what to review in each subject. Include items such as these:

- Reading assignments by chapters or page numbers
- Dates of lectures and major topics covered in each lecture
- Skills you must master
- Key course content—definitions, theories, formulas, sample problems, and laboratory findings

A review checklist is not a review sheet; it is a to-do list. These checklists contain the briefest possible description of each type of material that you intend to review. When you conduct your final review sessions, cross items off each checklist as you study them.

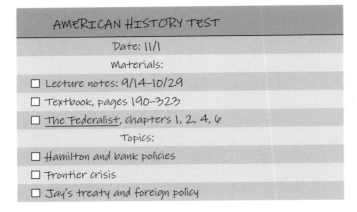

AMERICAN HISTORY TEST
Date: 11/1
Materials:
☐ Lecture notes: 9/14–10/29
☐ Textbook, pages 190–323
☐ The Federalist, chapters 1, 2, 4, 6
Topics:
☐ Hamilton and bank policies
☐ Frontier crisis
☐ Jay's treaty and foreign policy

CREATE SUMMARY NOTES

Summary notes are materials that you create specifically to review for tests. They are separate from notes that you take throughout the term on lectures and readings. Summary notes tie together content from all sources—readings, lectures, handouts, lab sessions, and any other course elements.

You can create summary notes with a computer. Key in all your handwritten notes and edit them into outline form. Or simply create an annotated table of contents for your handwritten notes. Note the date of each lecture, major topics, and main points. Even if you study largely from summary notes, keep the rest of your notes on file. They'll come in handy as backup sources of information.

CREATE FLASH CARDS

Flash cards are like portable test questions. Write them on 3 × 5 cards. On one side of the cards, write key terms or questions. On the other side, write definitions or answers. Buy an inexpensive card file and arrange your flash cards by subject. Carry a pack of flash cards with you whenever you think you might have spare time to review. Also keep a few blank cards with you to make flash cards as you recall new information.

CREATE A MOCK TEST

Make some predictions about what will be on the exam. Review your notes for material that seems important. Recall topics covered in detail during lectures. Write your own exam questions and take this "test" several times before the actual test. Design your mock test to look like the real thing. If possible, write out your answers in the room where the test will actually take place. When you take the real test, you'll be in familiar territory.

GET COPIES OF PREVIOUS TESTS

Old tests can help you plan a review strategy. Copies of previous exams for a class may be available from the instructor, other students, the instructor's department, the library, or the counseling office. In addition, keep a file of tests that have been returned to you.

Caution: If you rely on old tests exclusively, you may gloss over material the instructor has added since the last test. Also, check your school's policy about making past tests available to students.

DO DAILY REVIEWS

Daily reviews include the short pre- and post-class reviews of reading and lecture notes. This is a powerful tool for moving ideas from short-term to long-term memory. Short daily reviews are ideal tasks for small pockets of time, such as waiting for a bus or doing laundry. To make sure you complete these reviews, include them on your daily to-do list.

DO WEEKLY REVIEWS

Review each subject at least once a week. Revisit assigned readings and lecture notes. Do something that forces you to rehearse the material. For example:

- Look over any course summaries you've created and see whether you can re-create them from memory.
- Answer study questions and sample problems from your textbooks.
- Recite the points in your notes that you want to remember.
- Rewrite your notes for greater precision and clarity.

DO MAJOR REVIEWS

Major reviews are usually conducted during the week before finals or other major exams. They integrate concepts and deepen your understanding of material presented throughout the term. *To uncover gaps in knowledge, start major reviews at least three days before the test.*

Major reviews take several hours at a stretch. During long sessions, study the most difficult subjects at the beginning, when you are most alert. Remember that the effectiveness of your review begins to drop after an hour or so unless you give yourself a short rest. Learn your limits by being conscious of the quality of your concentration. When you find it difficult to focus your attention, quit for the day and come back to it tomorrow.

MONITOR YOUR REVIEWS

Each day that you prepare for a test, assess what you have learned and what you still want to learn. See how many items you've covered from your study checklist. Look at the tables of contents in your textbooks and write an *X* next to the sections that you've summarized. This helps you gauge the thoroughness of your reviews and alerts you to areas that still need attention.

KNOW THE LIMITATIONS OF CRAMMING

Cramming won't work if you've neglected all of the reading assignments or skipped most of the lectures. The more courses you have to cram for, the less effective cramming will be. Also cramming is not the same as learning: You won't remember what you cram.

The purpose of cramming is only to make the best of the situation. First, scan your notes, assigned readings, and other course materials to select the most important topics for review. Pick out a *few* of these topics and learn them thoroughly. For example, devote most of your attention to the topic sentences, tables, and charts in a long reading assignment. Then use the time-tested strategy of repetition. Go over your selected material again and again.

You're One Click Away . . .
from more strategies for test preparation.

Seven things to do with your study group

Study groups can lift your mood on days when you just don't feel like working. If you skip a solo study session, no one else will know. If you declare your intention to study with others who are depending on you, then your intention gains strength. Use the following strategies to get the most from your study group meetings.

1. Compare notes. Make sure you all heard the same thing in class and that you all recorded the important information.

2. Work in groups of three at a computer to review a course. Choose one person to operate the keyboard. Others can dictate summaries of lectures and assigned readings.

3. Brainstorm test questions. You can add these to the Test Questions section of your notebook.

4. Take a mock test and share results. Ask each group member to bring four or five sample test questions to a meeting. Create a mock test from these questions, take the test under timed conditions, and share answers.

5. Practice teaching each other. Teaching is a great way to learn something. Turn the material you're studying into a list of topics. Then assign specific topics for each person to teach the group.

6. Create wall-sized concept maps to summarize a textbook or series of lectures. Work on large sheets of butcher paper, or tape together pieces of construction paper.

7. Pair off to do "book reports." One person can summarize an assigned reading. The other person can act like an interviewer on a talk show, posing questions and asking for further clarification.

6

Memory superchargers— *the "six R's"*

To the conscious mind, a memory appears as a discrete mental event—an image, a series of words, the record of a sensation. On a biological level, each of those events involves millions of nerve cells firing chemical messages to each other. Memory is the *probability* that those nerve cells will fire together again in the future. The whole art of improving memory is increasing that probability.

Following are six strategies you can use for this purpose. They all begin with the letter *R*—a convenient hook for your memory.

RELAX

Stress in all its forms—including fear and anxiety—interferes with memory. You can learn about relaxation techniques from books, Web sites, audio and video recordings, and workshops. Some of th orese techniques are sophisticated and take time. However, you can reduce tension at any time simply by noticing your breathing. This will make it deeper and more regular. For a deeper relaxation, deliberately slow down your breathing. Take in more air with each inhalation and release more air with each exhalation.

When you're relaxed, you absorb new information quickly and recall it with greater ease and accuracy. Students who can't recall information under the stress of a final exam can often recite the same facts later when they are relaxed.

Also remember that being relaxed is not the same as being drowsy, zoned out, or asleep. Relaxation is a state of alertness, free of tension, during which your mind can play with new information, roll it around, create associations with it, and apply other memory techniques.

Observe the peaks and valleys in your energy flow during the day, and adjust study times accordingly. Perhaps you experience surges in memory power during the later afternoon evening. You might find that you naturally feel more relaxed and alert during certain hours during the day. Study your most difficult subjects at these times, when your energy peaks.

Many people can concentrate more effectively during daylight hours. The early morning hours can be especially productive, even for those who hate to get up with the sun.

REDUCE

Start by reducing distraction. The simple act of focusing your attention at key moments can do wonders for your memory. Test this idea for yourself: The next time you're introduced to someone, direct 100 percent of your attention to hearing that person's name. Do this consistently and see what happens to your ability to remember names.

Study in a quiet place that is free from distraction. If there's a party at your house, go to the library. If you have a strong attraction to food, don't torture yourself by studying next to your refrigerator. Also remember that two hours of studying in front of the television might equal only 10 minutes of studying where it is quiet.

As an aid to focused attention, avoid marathon study sessions. Plan for shorter, spaced-out sessions. You may find that you can recall more from three 2-hour sessions than one 6-hour session.

Next, reduce the amount of material to master. During your stay in higher education, you will be exposed to thousands of facts and ideas. No one expects you to memorize all of them. To a large degree, the art of memory is the art of selecting what to remember in the first place.

Choose what's essential to remember from reading assignments and lectures. Extract core concepts and key examples. Ask yourself what you'll be tested on, as well as what you want to remember.

When reading, look for chapter previews, summaries, and review questions. Pay attention to anything printed in bold type. Also notice visual elements—tables, charts, graphs, and illustrations. They are all clues pointing to what's important. During lectures, notice what the instructor emphasizes. Anything that's presented visually—on the board, in overheads, or with slides—is probably key.

When you've chosen what you want to remember, then divide the content into manageable chunks. Efficient rehearsal calls for limiting the number of items in your short-term memory at one time. As a rough guide, remember the number seven. When reading a long list of terms, for instance, stop after the first seven or so and see whether you can write definitions for them.

RELATE

The data already in your memory is arranged according to a scheme that makes sense to you. When you introduce new data, relate it to similar data:

- *Create visual associations.* Invent a mental picture of the information you want to remember. You can remember how a personal computer stores files by visualizing the hard disk as a huge filing cabinet. This cabinet is divided into folders that contain documents.

- *Associate course material with something you want.* If you're bogged down in quadratic equations, stand back for a minute. Think about how that math course relates to your goal of becoming an electrical engineer, or to gaining skills that open up new career options for you.

Mnemonics are verbal associations that can increase your ability to recall everything from grocery lists to speeches. There are several varieties, such as these:

- *Acrostics:* For instance, the first letters of the words in the sentence *Every good boy does fine* (E, G, B, D, and F) are the music notes of the lines of the treble-clef staff.

- *Acronyms:* You can make up your own acronyms to recall a series of facts. A common mnemonic acronym is Roy G. Biv, which has helped thousands of students remember the colors of the visible spectrum (**r**ed, **o**range, **y**ellow, **g**reen, **b**lue, **i**ndigo, and **v**iolet). IMPAT helps biology students remember the stages of cell division (**i**nterphase, **p**rophase, **m**etaphase, **a**naphase, and **t**elophase).

- *"Catchy" lists:* Theodore Cheney, author of *Getting the Words Right*, suggests that you remember the "three R's" when editing a paper: *Reduce* the paper to eliminate extraneous paragraphs, *rearrange* the paragraphs that remain into a logical order, and *reword* individual sentences so that they include specific nouns and active verbs.[1]

- *Rhymes:* This simple technique is widely applied. Advertisers often use jingles—songs with rhyming lyrics—to promote products. You can invent original rhymes to burn course material into your long-term memory. Rhymes have been used for centuries to teach basic facts. "I before e, except after c" has helped many a student on spelling tests.

Mnemonics can be useful. They do have two potential drawbacks. First, they rely on rote memorization rather than understanding the material at a deeper level or thinking critically about it. Second, the mnemonic device itself is sometimes complicated to learn and time-consuming to develop. To get the most from mnemonic devices, keep them simple.

RESTRUCTURE

Structure refers to the way that things are organized. When you're faced with a long list of items to remember, look for ways to organize them. Group them into larger categories or arrange them in chronological order.

You can apply this suggestion to long to-do lists. Write each item on a separate 3 × 5 card. Then create a pile of cards for calls to make, errands to run, and household chores. Within each of these categories, you can also arrange the cards in the order you intend to do them.

The same concept applies to the content of your courses. When reading a novel, for example, organize ideas and facts in categories such as plot, characters, and setting:

- To remember the plot, create a timeline. List key events on 3 × 5 cards and arrange the cards to parallel the order of events in the book.

- Group the people in the story into major and minor characters. Again, use 3 × 5 cards to list each character's name along with an identifying feature.

- If geographical setting is important, create a map of the major locations described in the story.

You can also play with different ways to restructure material by using *graphic organizers*. These are preformatted charts that prompt you to visualize relationships among facts and ideas.

One example is a *topic-point-details* chart. At the top of this chart, write the main topic of a lecture or reading assignment. In the left column, list the main points you want to remember. And in the right column, list key details related to each point. Following is the beginning of a chart based on this article:

20 MEMORY TECHNIQUES	
Point	Details
1. Be selective	Choose what not to remember. Look for clues to important material.
2. Make it meaningful	Organize by time, location, category, continuum, oralphabet.
3. Create associations	Link new facts with facts you already know.
4. Learn actively	Sit straight. Stand while studying. Recite while walking.
5. Relax	Release tension. Remain alert.

You could use a similar chart to prompt critical thinking about an issue. Express that issue as a question, and write it at the top. In the left column, note the opinion about the issue. In the right column, list notable facts, expert opinions, reasons, and examples that support each opinion. The example below is about tax cuts as a strategy for stimulating the economy:

STIMULATE THE ECONOMY WITH TAX CUTS?	
Opinion	Support
Yes	Savings from tax cuts allow businesses to invest money in new equipment. Tax cuts encourage businesses to expand and hire new employees.
No	Years of tax cuts under the Bush administration failed to prevent the mortgage credit crisis. Tax cuts create budget deficits.
Maybe	Tax cuts might work in some economic conditions. Budget deficits might be only temporary.

6

Sometimes you'll want to remember the main actions in a story or historical event. Create a time line by drawing a straight line. Place points in order on that line to represent key events. Place earlier events toward the left end of the line and later events toward the right. Following is the start of a time line of events relating the U.S. war with Iraq:

3/19/03 U.S. invades Iraq	3/30/03 Rumsfeld announces location of WMD	4/9/03 Soldiers topple statue of Saddam	5/1/03 Bush declares mission accomplished	5/29/03 Bush: We found WMD

When you want to compare or contrast two things, play with a Venn diagram. Represent each thing as a circle. Draw the circles so that they overlap. In the overlapping area, list characteristics that the two things share. In the outer parts of each circle, list the unique characteristics of each thing. The following diagram compares the two types of journal entries included in this book—Discovery Statements and Intention Statements:

Discovery Statements   Intention Statements

- Describe specific thoughts
- Describe specific feelings
- Describe current and past behaviors

- Are a type of journal entry
- Are based on telling the truth
- Can be written at any time on any topic
- Can lead to action

- Describe future behaviors
- Can include timelines
- Can include rewards

The graphic organizers described here are just a few of the many kinds available. To find more examples, do an Internet search using the key words *graphic organizer*. Have fun, and invent graphic organizers of your own.

RECITE

Recitation is simply speaking about ideas and facts that you want to remember. An informal version of this technique is to inject summaries of your course work into ordinary conversation. When relatives or friends ask what you're studying, seize the moment as an opportunity to recite. Explain what a course is about and mention some of the key topics covered. Describe the three most important ideas or startling facts that you've learned so far.

Informal recitation gains its power from the fact that you need to be brief, distinguishing between major concepts and supporting details. Another option is formal recitation, where you can take more time and go into more depth. Pretend that you've been asked to speak about the topic you're studying. Prepare a brief presentation and deliver it, even if you're the only member of the audience.

Or agree to lead a study group on the topic. One of the best ways to learn something is to teach it.

Some points to remember about recitation include the following.

The "out loud" part is important. Reciting silently, in your head, may be useful—in the library, for example—but it can be less effective than making noise. Your mind can trick itself into thinking it knows something when it doesn't. Your ears are harder to fool.

When you repeat something out loud, you also anchor the concept in two different senses. First, you get the physical sensation in your throat, tongue, and lips when voicing the concept. Second, you hear it. In terms of memory, the combined result is synergistic.

Recitation works best when you use your own words. Say that you want to remember that the "acceleration of a falling body due to gravity at sea level equals 32 feet per second per second." You might say, "Gravity makes an object accelerate 32 feet per second faster for each second that it's in the air at sea level." Putting an idea in your own words forces you to think about it.

Recite in writing. Like speaking, the act of writing is multisensory, combining sight and touch. The mere act of writing down a series of terms and their definitions can help you remember the terms—even if you lose the written list. In addition, writing down what you know quickly reveals gaps in your learning, which you can then go back and fill in. When you're done writing summaries of books or lectures, read what you've written out loud—two forms of recitation.

Recite with visuals. Create diagrams, charts, maps, time-lines, bulleted lists, numbered lists, and other visuals. Even the traditional outline is a visual device that separates major and minor points.

REPEAT

Repetition is a popular memory device because it works. Repetition blazes a trail through the pathways of your brain, making the information easier to recall. Repeat a concept out loud until you know it. Then say it five more times.

Students often stop studying when they think they know material just well enough to pass a test. Another option is to pick a subject apart, examine it, add to it, and go over it until it becomes second nature. Learn the material so well that you could talk about it in your sleep.

olly/Shutterstock.com

This technique—overlearning the material—is especially effective for problem solving in math and science courses. Do the assigned problems, then do more problems. Find another text and work similar problems. Make up your own problems and work those. When you pretest yourself in this way, the potential rewards are speed, accuracy, and greater confidence at exam time.

 **You're One Click Away . . .**
from more memory strategies.

Keep your brain
fit for life

Memories are encoded as physical changes in the brain. And your brain is an organ that needs regular care. Starting now, adopt habits to keep your brain lean and fit for life. Consider these research-based suggestions from the Alzheimer's Association.[2]

1. Challenge your brain with new experiences. Seek out museums, theaters, concerts, and other cultural events. Even after you graduate, consider learning another language or taking up a musical instrument. Talk to people with a wide variety of opinions. New experiences give your brain a workout, much like sit-ups condition your abs.

2. Exercise. Physical activity promotes blood flow to the brain. It also reduces the risk of diabetes and other diseases that can impair brain function.

3. Eat well. A diet rich in dark-skinned fruits and vegetables boosts your supply of antioxidants—natural chemicals that nourish your brain. Examples of these foods are raisins, blueberries, blackberries, strawberries, raspberries, kale, spinach, Brussels sprouts, alfalfa sprouts, and broccoli. Avoid foods that are high in saturated fat and cholesterol, which increase the risk of Alzheimer's disease. Drink alcohol moderately, if at all.

 6

4. Nourish your social life. Having a network of supportive friends can reduce stress levels. In turn, stress management helps to maintain connections between brain cells. Stay socially active by working, volunteering, and joining clubs.

5. Protect your heart. In general, what's good for your heart is good for your brain. Protect both organs by eating well, exercising regularly, managing your weight, staying tobacco-free, and getting plenty of sleep. These habits reduce your risk of heart attack, stroke, and other cardiovascular conditions that interfere with blood flow to the brain.

TEST-TAKING ERRORS—
and ways to avoid them

I f you think of a test as a sprint, remember that there are at least two ways that you can trip: errors due to carelessness and errors that result from getting stuck on a question.

ERRORS DUE TO CARELESSNESS

You can usually catch these errors immediately after your test has been returned to you. And you can avoid many common test-taking errors simply with the power of awareness. Learn about these errors up-front and then look out for them. Here are some examples:

- Mistakes due to skipping or misreading test directions
- Missing several questions in a certain section of the test—a sign that you misunderstood the directions or neglected to study certain topics
- Failing to finish problems that you knew how to answer— such as skipping the second part of a two-part question
- Consistently changing answers that were correct to answers that were incorrect
- Spending so much time on certain questions that you failed to answer others
- Making mistakes when you copy an answer from scratch paper to your answer sheet
- Turning in your test and leaving earlyrather than taking the extra time to proofread your answers

To avoid these types of errors, read and follow directions more carefully. Also, set aside time to proofread your answers.

ERRORS DUE TO GETTING STUCK

You might encounter a question and discover that you don't how to answer it. If this occurs, accept your feelings of discomfort. Take a deep breath. Then use any of the following suggestions:

Read it again, Sam. Eliminate the simplest sources of confusion, such as misreading the question.

Skip the question for now. Simple, but it works. Let your subconscious mind work on the answer while you respond to other questions.

Look for answers in other test questions. A term, name, date, or other fact that escapes you might appear in another question on the test itself. Use other questions to stimulate your memory.

Treat intuitions with care. In quick-answer questions (multiple choice, true/false), go with your first instinct on which answer is correct. If you think your first answer is wrong because you misread the question, do change your answer.

Visualize the answer's "location." Think of the answer to any test question as being recorded someplace in your notes or assigned reading. Close your eyes, take a deep breath, and see whether you can visualize that place—its location in the materials you studied for the test.

Rewrite the question. See whether you can put the question that confuses you into your own words.

Just start writing anything at all. On scratch paper, record any response to the question, noting whatever pops into your head. Instead of just sitting there, stumped, you're doing something—a fact that can reduce anxiety. You may also trigger a mental association that answers the test question.

Write a close answer. If you simply cannot think of an accurate answer to the question, then give it a shot anyway. Answer as best you can, even if you don't think your answer is fully correct. You may get partial credit on some tests.

Eliminate incorrect answers. Cross off the answers that are clearly not correct. The answer you cannot eliminate is probably the best choice.

Before you write, make a quick outline. An outline can help speed up the writing of your detailed essay answer; you're less likely to leave out important facts, and if you don't have time to finish your answer, your outline could win you some points. To use test time efficiently, keep your outline brief. Focus on key words to use in your answer.

You're One Click Away . . .
from more ways to avoid test-taking errors.

experiment

Turn "F" into feedback

When some students get an F as a grade, they interpret that letter as a message: "You are a failure." That interpretation is not accurate. Getting an F means only that you failed a test or an assignment—not that you failed your life.

From now on, experiment with a new way of thinking. Imagine that the letter *F* when used as a grade represents the word *feedback*. An F is an indication that you didn't understand the material well enough. It's an invitation to do something differently before you get your next grade.

The next time that a graded test is returned to you (no matter what the grade), spend at least five minutes reviewing it. Then write your answers to the following questions in the space provided. Use separate paper as needed.

On what material did the teacher base test questions—readings, lectures, discussions, or other class activities?

_____

_____

_____

_____

What types of questions appeared in the test—objective (such as matching items, true/false questions, or multiple choice), short-answer, or essay?

_____

_____

_____

What types of questions did you miss?

_____

_____

_____

_____

Can you learn anything from the instructor's comments that will help you prepare for the next test?

_____

_____

_____

_____

_____

Can you now correctly answer the questions that you missed?

_____

_____

_____

_____

Did you make any of the mistakes mentioned in "Test-taking errors and ways to avoid them" on page 68?

_____

_____

_____

_____

After answering the above questions, write a brief plan for avoiding test-taking errors in the future.

_____

_____

_____

_____

You're One Click Away . . .
from more strategies for turning tests into feedback.

Relax—it's just a test

To perform gracefully under the pressure of exams, put as much effort into mastering your fear of tests as you do into mastering the content of your courses. Think of test-taking skills as the "silent subject" on your schedule, equal in importance to the rest of your courses. If nervousness about tests is a consistent problem for you, that is an ideal point to begin "test taking 101."

OVERPREPARE FOR TESTS

Performing artists know that stage fright can temporarily reduce their level of skill. That's why they often overprepare for a performance. Musicians will rehearse a piece so many times that they can play it without thinking. Actors will go over their parts until they can recite lines in their sleep.

As you prepare for tests, you can apply the same principle. Read, recite, and review the content of each course until you know it cold. Then review again. The idea is to create a margin of mastery that can survive even the most extreme feelings of anxiety.

This technique—overlearning the material—is especially effective for problem solving in math and science courses. Do the assigned problems, then do more problems. Find another text and work similar problems. Make up your own problems and work those. When you pretest yourself in this way, the potential rewards are speed, accuracy, and greater confidence at exam time.

ACCEPT YOUR FEELINGS

Telling someone who's anxious about a test to "just calm down" is like turning up the heat on a pan that's already boiling over: The "solution" simply worsens the problem. Fear and anxiety tend to increase with resistance. The more you try to suppress them, the more intensity the feelings gain.

Roughly speaking, the problem has two levels. First, there's your worry about the test. Second, there's your worry *about* the fact that you're worried.

As an alternative, stop resisting your fear of tests. Simply accept your feelings, whatever they are. See fear as a cluster of thoughts and body sensations. Watch the thoughts as they pass through your mind. Observe the sensations as they wash over you. Let them arise, peak, and pass away. No feeling lasts forever. The moment you accept fear, you take the edge off the feeling and pave the way for its release.

EXAGGERATE YOUR FEAR UNTIL IT DISAPPEARS

Imagine the catastrophic problems that might occur if you fail the test. You might say to yourself, "Well, if I fail this test, I might fail the course, lose my financial aid, and get kicked out of school. Then I won't be able to get a job, so the bank would repossess my car, and I'd start drinking. Pretty soon I'd be a bum on Skid Row, and then. . . ."

Keep going until you see the absurdity of your predictions. Then you can backtrack to discover a reasonable level of concern.

You might be justified in worrying about failing the entire course just because you failed the test. At that point ask yourself, "Can I live with that?" Unless you are taking a skills test in parachute packing and the final question involves jumping out of a plane, the answer will almost always be yes.

ZOOM OUT

When you're in the middle of a test, zoom out. Think the way film directors do when they dolly a camera out and away from an action scene. In your mind, imagine that you're floating away and viewing the situation as a detached outside observer.

From this larger viewpoint, ask yourself whether this situation is worth worrying about. This is not a license to belittle or avoid problems; it is permission to gain some perspective.

Another option is to zoom out in time. Imagine yourself one week, one month, one year, one decade, or one century from today. Assess how much the current situation will matter when that time comes. Then come back to the test with a more detached perspective.

RESIGN YOURSELF TO FAILURE— AND CONTINUE

During a test, you may feel a panic so intense that you see no way out. You might apply all the suggestions listed above and find that none of them work for you in the moment.

If this happens, one option is to simply resign yourself to a low grade on this particular test. Most of the time, you'll be able to live with the consequences. They may not be ideal, but they won't be catastrophic either.

Once you've taken the pressure off yourself, find just one question you think you can answer, anywhere on the test. When you finish that one question, find another. Place 100 percent of your attention on answering the easier questions, one by one. This might be enough to gradually rebuild your confidence and help you complete the test.

USE OTHER STRESS-MANAGEMENT TECHNIQUES

Although the following techniques were not specifically designed for test taking, they can help you achieve a baseline of relaxation in all of your activities. During the week before your next test, set aside a few minutes each day to practice one of the following suggestions.

Breathe. If you notice that you are taking short, shallow breaths, then begin to take longer and deeper breaths. Fill your lungs so that your abdomen rises, then release all the air. Imagine yourself standing on the tip of your nose. Watch the breath pass in and out as if your nose were a huge ventilation shaft for an underground mine.

Describe it. Focus your attention on your anxiety. Tell yourself how large it is, where it is located in your body, what color it is, what shape it is, what texture it is, how much water it might hold if it had volume, and how heavy it is. As you describe anxiety in detail, don't resist it. If you can completely experience a physical sensation, it will often disappear.

Tense and relax. Find a muscle that is tense and make it even more tense. If your shoulders are tense, pull them back, arch your back, and tense your shoulder muscles even more tightly; then relax. The net result is that you can be aware of the relaxation and allow yourself to relax more. You can use the same process with your legs, arms, abdomen, chest, face, and neck.

Use guided imagery. Relax completely and take a quick fantasy trip. Close your eyes, relax your body, and imagine yourself in a beautiful, peaceful, natural setting. Create as much of the scene as you can. Be specific. Use all your senses.

For example, you might imagine yourself at a beach. Hear the surf rolling in and the seagulls calling to each other. Feel the sun on your face and the hot sand between your toes. Smell the sea breeze. Taste the salty mist from the surf. Notice the ships on the horizon and the rolling sand dunes. Use all of your senses to create a vivid imaginary trip.

Focus. Focus your attention on a specific object. Examine the details of a painting, study the branches on a tree, or observe the face of your watch (right down to the tiny scratches in the glass). During an exam, take a few seconds to listen to the hum of the lights in the room. Touch the surface of your desk and notice the texture. Concentrate all your attention on one point. Don't leave room in your mind for fear-related thoughts.

Yell "Stop!" When you notice that your thoughts are racing, that your mind is cluttered with worries and fears, that your thoughts are spinning out of control . . ., mentally yell "Stop!" If you're in a situation that allows it, yell it out loud. Stay in the present moment. Release all thoughts beyond the test.

Exercise aerobically. This is one technique that won't work in the classroom or while you're taking a test. Yet it is an excellent way to reduce body tension. Do some kind of exercise that will get your heart beating at a higher rate and keep it beating at that rate for 15 or 20 minutes. Aerobic exercises include rapid walking, jogging, swimming, bicycling, playing basketball. Do these or another safe activity with the same effects.

Adopt a posture of confidence. Even if you can't control your feelings, you can control your posture. Avoid slouching. Sit up straight, as if you're ready to sprint out of your seat. Look like someone who knows the answers. Notice any changes in your physical and mental alertness.

GET HELP FOR PROLONGED ANXIETY

When stress-management techniques don't work—and when anxiety persists well beyond test times—get help. If you become withdrawn, have frequent thoughts about death or suicide, or feel hopeless or sad for more than a few days, then talk to someone immediately. Seek out a trusted friend. Also see your academic advisor or a counselor at your student health center.

 **You're One Click Away . . .**
from more stress-management strategies.

Math
ESSENTIALS

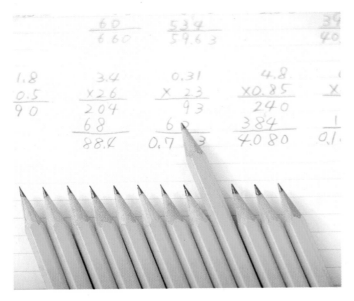

Consider a three-part program for math success. Begin with strategies for overcoming math anxiety. Next, boost your study skills. Finally, let your knowledge shine during tests.

OVERCOME MATH ANXIETY

Many schools offer courses in overcoming math anxiety. Ask your advisor about resources on your campus. Also experiment with the following suggestions.

Connect math to life. Think of the benefits of mastering math courses. You'll have more options for choosing a major and career—which can increase your earning power. Math skills can also put you at ease in everyday situations—calculating the tip for a waiter, balancing your checkbook, working with a spreadsheet on a computer. If you follow baseball statistics, cook, do construction work, or snap pictures with a camera, you'll use math. And speaking the language of math can help you feel at home in a world driven by technology.

Tell the truth. Math is cumulative. Concepts build upon each other in a certain order. If you struggled with algebra, you may have trouble with trigonometry or calculus.

To ensure that you have an adequate base of knowledge, tell the truth about your current level of knowledge and skill. Before you register for a math course, locate assigned texts for the prerequisite courses. If that material seems new or difficult for you, see the instructor. Ask for suggestions on ways to prepare for the course.

Remember that it's okay to continue your study of math from your current level of ability, whatever that level might be.

Change your conversation about math. When students fear math, they often say negative things to themselves about their abilities in these subjects. Many times this self-talk includes statements such as *I'll never be fast enough at solving math problems.* Or *I'm good with words, so I can't be good with numbers.*

Get such statements out in the open and apply some emergency critical thinking. You'll find two self-defeating assumptions lurking there: *Everybody else is better at math and science than I am.* And *Since I don't understand a math concept right now, I'll never understand it.* Both of these are illogical.

Replace negative beliefs with logical, realistic statements that affirm your ability to succeed in math: *Any confusion I feel now will be resolved. I can learn math without comparing myself to others.* And *I will ask whatever questions are needed to aid my understanding.*

Notice your pictures about math. Sometimes what keeps people from succeeding at math is their mental picture of mathematicians. They see a man dressed in a baggy plaid shirt and brown wingtip shoes. He's got a calculator on his belt and six pencils jammed in his shirt pocket.

These pictures are far from the truth. Succeeding in math won't turn you into a nerd. Actually, you'll be able to enjoy school more, and your friends will still like you.

Mental pictures about math can be funny, and they can have serious effects. If math is seen as a field for white males, then women and people of color get excluded. Promoting math success for all students helps to overcome racism and sexism.

Choose your response to stress. Math anxiety is seldom just "in your head." It can also register as sweaty palms, shallow breathing, tightness in the chest, or a mild headache. Instead of trying to ignore these sensations, just notice them without judgment. Over time, simple awareness decreases their power.

In addition, use stress management techniques. "Relax—it's just a test" on page 70 offers a bundle of them.

No matter what you do, remember to breathe. You can relax in any moment just by making your breath slower and deeper. Practice doing this while you study math. It will come in handy at test time.

BOOST STUDY SKILLS FOR MATH

Choose teachers with care. Whenever possible, find a math teacher whose approach to math matches your learning style. Try several teachers until you find one whom you enjoy.

Another option is to ask around. Maybe your academic advisor can recommend math teachers. Also ask classmates to name their favorite math teachers—and to explain the reasons for their choices. Perhaps more than one teacher is offering the math course you'll need.

Take math courses back to back. Approach math in the same way that you learn a foreign language. If you take a year off between Spanish I and Spanish II, you won't gain much fluency. To master a language, you follow each course with a related one. It works the same way with math, which is a language in itself.

Form a study group. During the first week of each math course, organize a study group. Ask each member to bring five problems to group meetings, along with the solutions. Also exchange contact information so that you can stay in touch via e-mail, phone, and instant messaging.

Avoid short courses. Courses that you take during summer school or another shortened term are condensed. You might find yourself doing far more reading and homework each week than you do in longer courses. If you enjoy math, the extra intensity can provide a stimulus to learn. But if math is not your favorite subject, then give yourself extra time. Enroll in courses with more calendar days.

Participate in class. Success in math depends on your active involvement. Attend class regularly. Complete homework assignments *when they're due*—not just before the test. If you're confused, get help right away from an instructor, tutor, or study group. Instructor's office hours, free on-campus tutoring, and classmates are just a few of the resources available to you.

Also support class participation with time for homework. Make daily contact with math.

Ask questions fearlessly. It's a cliché, and it's true: In math, there are no dumb questions. Ask whatever questions will aid your understanding. Keep a running list of them and bring the list to class.

Make your text top priority. Math courses are often text-driven. Class activities closely follow the book. This makes it important to complete your reading assignments. Master one concept before going on to the next, and stay current with your reading. Be willing to read slowly and reread sections as needed.

Read actively. To get the most out of your math texts, read with paper and pencil in hand. Work out examples. Copy diagrams, formulas, and equations. Use chapter summaries and introductory outlines to organize your learning.

From time to time, stop, close your book, and mentally reconstruct the steps in solving a problem. Before you memorize a formula, understand the basic concepts behind it.

Practice solving problems. To get ready for math tests, work *lots* of problems. Find out if practice problems or previous tests are on file in the library, in the math department, or with your math teacher.

Isolate the types of problems that you find the most difficult. Practice them more often. Be sure to get help with these *before* exhaustion or frustration sets in.

To prepare for tests, practice working problems fast. Time yourself. This is a great activity for math study groups.

USE TESTS TO SHOW WHAT YOU KNOW

Practice test taking. Part of preparing for any math test is rehearsal. Instead of passively reading through your text or scanning class notes, do a practice test:

- Print out a set of practice problems and set a timer for the same length of time as your testing period.
- Whenever possible, work these problems in the same room where you will take the actual test.
- Use only the kinds of supporting materials—such as scratch paper or lists of formulas—that will be allowed during the test.
- As you work problems, use deep breathing or another technique to enter a more relaxed state.

Ask appropriate questions. If you don't understand a test item, ask for clarification. The worst that can happen is that an instructor or proctor will politely decline to answer your question.

Write legibly. Put yourself in the instructor's place and imagine the prospect of grading stacks of illegible answer sheets. Make your answers easy to read. If you show your work, underline key sections and circle your answer.

Do your best. There are no secrets involved in getting ready for math tests. Use some stress-management techniques, do your homework, get answers to your questions, and work sample problems. If you've done those things, you're ready for the test and deserve to do well. If you haven't done all those things, then just do the best you can.

Remember that your personal best can vary from test to test, and even day to day. Even if you don't answer all test questions correctly, you can demonstrate what you do know right now.[3]

 You're One Click Away . . .
from more strategies for succeeding in math courses.

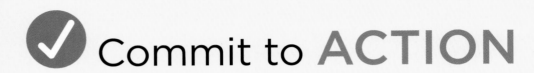

Commit to ACTION

Transform your experience of tests

No matter how you've felt about tests in the past, you can wipe your mental slate clean. Use the following suggestions to transform the ways that you experience tests of all types, from the shortest pop quiz to the longest exam.

Discovery Statement

Mentally re-create a time when you had difficulty taking a test. Do anything that helps you re-experience this event. You could draw a picture of yourself in this situation, list some of the questions you had difficulty answering, or tell how you felt after finding out your score on the test. Briefly describe that experience in the space below.

I discovered that I . . .

_____

_____

_____

_____

_____

_____

_____

_____

Intention Statement

Next, describe how you want your experience of test taking to change. For example, you might write: "I intend to walk into every test I take feeling well rested and thoroughly prepared."

I intend to . . .

_____

_____

_____

_____

_____

_____

Review this chapter, looking for five strategies that can help you turn your intention into reality. List those strategies below and note the page numbers where you read about them.

Strategy	Page number
_____	_____
_____	_____
_____	_____
_____	_____
_____	_____

Action Statement

Finally, prepare for a smooth transition from intention to action. Choose *one* strategy from the above list and describe exactly when and where you will use it.

I will . . .

_____

_____

_____

_____

_____

_____

_____

_____

_____

_____

_____

_____

_____

_____

_____

POWER
process

Detach

This Power Process helps you release the powerful, natural student within you. It is especially useful whenever negative emotions are getting in your way.

When we are attached to something, we think we cannot live without it, just as a drug addict feels he cannot live without drugs. We believe that our well-being depends on maintaining our attachments. We can be attached to just about anything: beliefs, emotions, people, roles, objects. The list is endless.

One person, for example, might be so attached to his car that he takes an accident as a personal attack. Pity the poor unfortunate who backs into this person's car. He might as well back into the owner himself.

Another person might be attached to her job. Her identity and sense of well-being depend on it. She could become depressed if she gets fired.

When we are attached and things don't go our way, we can feel angry, sad, or afraid. Suppose you are attached to getting an A on your physics test. You feel as though your success in life depends on getting that A. As the clock ticks away, you work harder on the test, getting more stuck. That voice in your head gets louder: "I must get an A. I *must* get an A. I MUST GET AN A!"

Now is a time to detach.

Start by getting a broader perspective. Imagine how much this test will matter one week, one year, or one decade from now.

Also pay attention to your thoughts and physical sensations. If you feel stuck, just notice that. If your palms are sweaty and your stomach is one big knot, just admit it. See whether you can just *observe* what's going on, letting go of all your judgments. This is a tranquil spot of pure self-awareness.

In addition, calm your mind and body with relaxation techniques. One simple and effective method is just to close your eyes and observe your breathing. As you do, make a conscious effort to breathe more deeply and slowly. This will help you detach.

Caution: Giving up an *attachment* to being an A student does not mean giving up *being* an A student. Giving up an attachment to a job doesn't mean giving up the job. When you detach, you get to keep your values and goals. However, you know that you will be okay even if you fail to achieve a goal. You are more than your goals. You are more than your thoughts and feelings. These things come and go. Meanwhile, the part of you that can *just observe* is always there and always safe, no matter what happens.

Behind your attachments is a master student. Release that mastery.

Detach.

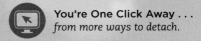

You're One Click Away . . .
from more ways to detach.

Thinking Clearly and Communicating Your Ideas

Critical thinking:
A survival skill

Society depends on persuasion. Advertisers want us to buy their products. Politicians want us to "buy" their stands on the issues. Teachers want us to agree that their classes are vital to success. Parents want us to accept their values. Authors want us to read their words. Broadcasters want us to consume their programs. The business of persuasion impacts all of us.

It's easy to lose our wits in the crosscurrent of competing ideas—unless we develop skills in thinking. When we think effectively, we make choices with open eyes.

Novelist Ernest Hemingway once said that all of us could benefit from having a "built-in, automatic crap detector."[1] That inelegant comment points to a basic truth: As skilled thinkers, we are constantly on the lookout for thinking that's inaccurate, sloppy, or misleading.

At various times in human history, nonsense has been taken for the truth. For example, people believed that:

- Use of blood-sucking leeches is the recommended treatment for most disease.
- Racial intermarriage will lead to genetically inferior children.
- Racial integration of the armed forces will destroy morale.
- Women are incapable of voting intelligently.
- Computers will usher in the age of the paperless office.

The great thinkers of history arose to challenge such ideas. These courageous men and women pointed out that—metaphorically speaking—the emperor had no clothes.

Thinking is a path to freedom from half-truths and deception. You have the right to question everything that you see, hear, and read. Acquiring this ability is a major goal of a liberal education.

In addition, thinking helps us thrive with diversity. Thinking uncovers bias and prejudice. Questioning our assumptions is a first step to communicating with people of other races, ethnic backgrounds, and cultures.

The suggestions for thinking given in this chapter fall into two broad categories. The first is creative thinking, which opens many possible ideas about any topic and many possible solutions to any problem. The second is critical thinking, which narrows down your initial ideas and solutions to those that are most reasonable and workable. In addition, this chapter addresses those skills that allow you to effectively communicate your thoughts, opinions, and ideas to others in written and verbal form.

No one is born a creative or critical thinker. These are learned skills. Use the suggestions in this chapter to claim the thinking powers that are your birthright. The skilled thinker is one aspect of the master student who lives inside you.

Discover what
YOU WANT
from this chapter

The Discovery Wheel on page 2 includes a section titled *Thinking and Writing*. Take some time to go beyond your initial responses to that section. Spend five minutes skimming this chapter. Then complete the following sentences:

When faced with an important problem or a major decision, my first response is usually to . . .

_____

_____

_____

_____

_____

Based on my preview of this chapter, I could think more clearly about problems and decisions by . . .

_____

_____

_____

_____

_____

When you see 🖱 *You're One Click Away . . ., remember to go to this book's College Success CourseMate for additional content. And for a summary of this chapter, see the Master Student Review Cards at the end of this book.*

7

Ways to Create *ideas*

Anyone can think creatively. Use the following techniques to generate ideas about anything—whether you're studying math problems, remodeling a house, or writing a best seller.

CONDUCT A BRAINSTORM

Brainstorming is a technique for creating plans, finding solutions, and discovering new ideas. When you are stuck on a problem, brainstorming can break the logjam. For example, if you run out of money before payday every month, you can brainstorm ways to make your money last longer. You can brainstorm ways to pay for your education. You can brainstorm ways to find a job.

The overall purpose of brainstorming is to generate as many solutions as possible. Sometimes the craziest, most outlandish ideas, while unworkable in themselves, can lead to new ways to solve problems. Use the following steps to try out the brainstorming process:

- **Focus on a single problem or issue.** State your focus as a question. Open-ended questions that start with the words *what, how, who, where,* and *when* often make effective focusing questions.

- **Relax.** Creativity is enhanced by a state of relaxed alertness. If you are tense or anxious, use relaxation techniques. For example, close your eyes and notice your breathing. Then allow yourself to take deeper, longer breaths.

- **Set a quota or goal for the number of solutions you want to generate.** Goals give your subconscious mind something to aim for.

- **Set a time limit.** Use a clock to time it to the minute. Digital sports watches with built-in stopwatches work well. Experiment with various lengths of time. Both short and long brainstorms can be powerful.

- **Allow all answers.** Brainstorming is based on attitudes of permissiveness and patience. Accept every idea. If it pops into your head, put it down on paper. Quantity, not quality, is the goal. Avoid making judgments and evaluations during the brainstorming session. If you get stuck, think of an outlandish idea, and write it down. One crazy idea can unleash a flood of other, more workable solutions.

- **Brainstorm with others.** Group brainstorming is a powerful technique. Group brainstorms take on lives of their own. Assign one member of the group to write down solutions. Feed off the ideas of others, and remember to avoid evaluating or judging anyone's ideas during the brainstorm.

After your brainstorming session, evaluate the results. Toss out any truly nutty ideas, but not before you give them a chance.

FOCUS AND LET GO

Focusing and letting go are alternating parts of the same process. First, focus on a problem or question for a short period of time to the resources of your conscious mind. Then take a break and completely let go of finding a solution or answer. This gives your subconscious mind time to work. When you alternate focusing and relaxing, the conscious and subconscious parts of your brain work in harmony.

Remember that periods of inspiration might last only seconds. Be gentle with yourself when you notice that your concentration has lapsed. That might be a time to let go. This means not forcing yourself to be creative. Practice focusing for short periods at first, and then give yourself a break. In fact, take a nap when you are tired. Thomas Edison took frequent naps. Then the lightbulb clicked on.

CULTIVATE CREATIVE SERENDIPITY

The word *serendipity* was coined by the English author Horace Walpole from the title of an ancient Persian fairy tale, "The Three Princes of Serendip." The princes had a knack for making lucky discoveries. Serendipity is that knack, and it involves more than luck. It is the ability to see something valuable that you weren't looking for.

History is full of people who make serendipitous discoveries. Country doctor Edward Jenner noticed "by accident" that milk-maids seldom got smallpox. The result was his discovery that mild cases of cowpox immunized them. Penicillin was also discovered by accident. Scottish scientist Alexander Fleming was growing bacteria in a laboratory petri dish. A spore of *Penicillium notatum,* a kind of mold, blew in the window and landed in the dish, killing the bacteria. Fleming isolated the active ingredient, which saved thousands of lives.

You can train yourself in the art of serendipity. Keep your eyes open. You might find a solution to an accounting problem in a Saturday morning cartoon. You might discover a topic for your term paper at the corner convenience store. Multiply your contacts with the world. Resolve to meet new people. Join a study or discussion group. Read. Go to plays, concerts, art shows, lectures, and movies. Watch television programs you normally wouldn't watch.

KEEP IDEA FILES

We all have ideas. People who treat their ideas with care are often labeled "creative." They recognize ideas *and* keep track of them.

One way to keep track of ideas is to write them down on 3 x 5 cards. Also keep a journal. Record observations about the world around you, conversations with friends, important or offbeat ideas—anything.

To fuel your creativity, read voraciously, including newspapers and magazines. Keep letter-size file folders of important correspondence, magazine and news articles, and other material. You can also create idea files on a computer using word-processing, outlining, or database software.

COLLECT AND PLAY WITH DATA

Look from all sides at the data you collect. Switch your attention from one aspect to another. Examine each fact, and avoid getting stuck on one particular part of a problem. Turn a problem upside down by picking a solution first and then working backward. Ask other people to look at the data. Solicit opinions.

Look for the obvious solutions or the obvious "truths" about the problem—then toss them out. Ask yourself, "Well, I know X is true, but if X were *not* true, what would happen?" Or ask the reverse: "If that *were* true, what would follow next?"

Put unrelated facts next to each other and invent a relationship between them, even if it seems absurd at first. Make imaginary pictures with the data. Condense it. Categorize it. Put it in chronological order. Put it in alphabetical order. Put it in random order. Order it from most to least complex. Reverse all of those orders. Look for opposites.

It has been said that there are no new ideas—only new ways to combine old ideas. Creativity is the ability to discover those combinations.

CREATE WHILE YOU SLEEP

A part of our mind works as we sleep. You've experienced this fact directly if you've ever fallen asleep with a problem on your mind and awakened the next morning with a solution. For some of us, the solution appears in a dream or just before we fall asleep or wake up.

You can experiment with this process. Ask yourself a question as you fall asleep. Keep pencil and paper or a recorder near your bed. The moment you wake up, begin writing or speaking, and see whether an answer to your question emerges.

Many of us have awakened from a dream with a great idea, only to fall asleep again and lose it forever. To capture your ideas, keep a notebook by your bed at all times. Put the notebook where you can find it easily.

REFINE IDEAS AND FOLLOW THROUGH

Many of us ignore the part of the creative process that involves refining ideas and following through. How many great money-making schemes have we had that we never pursued? How many good ideas have we had for short stories that we never wrote? How many times have we said to ourselves, "You know, what they ought to do is attach two handles to one of those things, paint it orange, and sell it to police departments. They'd make a fortune." And we never realize that we are "they." Genius resides in the follow-through—the application of perspiration to inspiration.

TRUST THE PROCESS

Learn to trust the creative process—even when no answers are in sight. We are often reluctant to look at problems if no immediate solution is at hand. Trust that a solution will show up. Frustration and a feeling of being stuck are often signals that a solution is imminent.

 You're One Click Away . . .
from more strategies for creative thinking.

Ways to REFINE IDEAS

Critical thinking is a path to intellectual adventure. Although there are dozens of possible approaches, the process boils down to *asking and answering questions*. In particular, the following questions can be powerful guides to critical thinking. You will also find a variety of tools for answering those questions. For more handy implements, see *Becoming a Critical Thinker* by Vincent Ryan Ruggiero.

1. WHY AM I CONSIDERING THIS ISSUE?

Critical thinking and personal passion go together. Begin critical thinking with a question that matters to you. Seek a rationale for your learning. Understand why it is important for you to think about a specific topic. You might want to arrive at a new conclusion, make a prediction, choose a major, choose a mate, or solve a pressing problem. By finding a personal connection with an issue, your interest in acquiring and retaining new information increases.

2. WHAT ARE VARIOUS POINTS OF VIEW ON THIS ISSUE?

Imagine Karl Marx, Cesar Chavez, and Warren Buffet assembled in one room to choose the most desirable economic system. Picture Mahatma Gandhi, Nelson Mandela, and General George Patton lecturing at a United Nations conference on conflict resolution. Visualize Al Gore, Bill Gates, and Ban Ki-moon in a discussion about distributing the world's resources equitably. When seeking out alternative points of view, let such scenarios unfold in your mind.

Dozens of viewpoints exist on every important issue—reducing crime, ending world hunger, preventing war, educating our children, and countless other concerns. In fact, few problems have any single, permanent solution. Each generation produces its own answers to critical questions, based on current conditions. Our search for answers is a conversation that spans centuries. On each question, many voices are waiting to be heard.

You can take advantage of this diversity by seeking out alternative views with an open mind. When talking to another person, be willing to walk away with a new point of view—even if it's the one you brought to the table, supported with new evidence.

Examining different points of view is an exercise in analysis, which you can do with the suggestions that follow.

Define terms. Imagine two people arguing about whether an employer should limit health care benefits to members of a family. To one person, the word *family* means a mother, father, and children; to the other person, the word *family* applies to any individuals who live together in a long-term, supportive relationship. Chances are, the debate will go nowhere until these two people realize that they're defining the same word in different ways.

Conflicts of opinion can often be resolved—or at least clarified—when we define our key terms up front. This is especially true with abstract, emotion-laden terms such as *freedom, peace, progress,* or *justice.* Blood has been shed over the meaning of those words. Define them with care.

Look for assertions. Speakers and writers present their key terms in a larger context called an *assertion*. An assertion is a complete sentence that answers a key question. For example, consider this sentence from the article "The essentials of mastery" in Chapter 1: "Mastery means attaining a level of skill that goes beyond technique." This sentence is an assertion that answers an important question: How do we recognize mastery?

Look for at least three viewpoints. When asking questions, let go of the temptation to settle for just a single answer. Once you have come up with an answer, say to yourself, "Yes, that is one answer. Now what's another?" Using this approach can sustain an inquiry, fuel creativity, and lead to conceptual breakthroughs.

Be prepared: The world is complicated, and critical thinking is a complex business. Some of your answers might contradict others. Resist the temptation to have all of your ideas in a neat, orderly bundle.

Practice tolerance. Taking a position on important issues is natural. When we stop having an opinion on things, we've probably stopped breathing. Problems occur when we become so attached to our current viewpoints that we refuse to consider alternatives.

Many ideas that are widely accepted in Western cultures—for example, civil liberties for people of color and the right of women to vote—were once considered dangerous. Viewpoints that seem outlandish today might become widely accepted a century, a decade, or even a year from now. Remembering this idea can help us practice tolerance for differing beliefs. In doing so, make room for new ideas that might alter our lives.

3. HOW WELL IS EACH POINT OF VIEW SUPPORTED?

Uncritical thinkers shield themselves from new information and ideas. As an alternative, you can follow the example of scientists, who constantly search for evidence that contradicts their theories.

To begin, look for logic and evidence. The aim of using logic is to make statements that are clear, consistent, and coherent. As you examine a speaker's or writer's assertions, you might find errors in logic—assertions that contradict each other or assumptions that are unfounded.

Also look at the evidence used to support points of view. Evidence comes in several forms, including facts, expert testimony, and examples. To think critically about evidence, ask questions such as the following:

- Are all or most of the relevant facts presented?

- Are the facts consistent with one another?

- Are facts presented accurately—or in a misleading way?

- Are enough examples included to make a solid case for the viewpoint?

- Do the examples truly support the viewpoint?

- Are the examples typical? That is, could the author or speaker support the assertion with other examples that are similar?

- Is the expert credible—truly knowledgeable about the topic?

As you look for answers, remember to understand before criticizing. Polished debaters are good at summing up their opponents' viewpoints—often better than the people who hold those viewpoints. Likewise, critical thinkers take the time to understand a statement of opinion before agreeing or disagreeing with it.

In the process, you might discover several "hot spots"—topics that provoke strong opinions and feelings. Some examples are abortion, homosexuality, gun control, and the death penalty.

Make a clear intention to accept your feelings about such topics and to continue using critical thinking techniques. One way to cool down is to remember that we can change or even give up our current opinions without giving up ourselves. That's a key message behind the Power Processes: "Ideas are tools" and "Detach."

Also be willing to be uncertain. Some of the most profound thinkers have practiced the art of thinking by using a magic sentence: "I'm not sure yet." In our sound-bite culture, you can set an example by slowing down and taking time to consider many points of view before choosing one. When a society adopts half-truths in a blind rush for certainty, critical thinkers are willing to embrace uncertainty.

4 WHAT IF I COULD COMBINE VARIOUS POINTS OF VIEW OR CREATE A NEW ONE?

The search for truth is like painting a barn door by tossing an open can of paint at it. Few people who throw at the door will miss it entirely. Yet no one can cover the whole door in a single toss.

People who express a viewpoint are seeking the truth. And no reasonable person claims to cover the whole barn door—to understand the whole truth about anything. Instead, each viewpoint can be seen as one approach among many possible alternatives. If you don't think that any one opinion is complete, then see whether you can combine different perspectives on the issue.

Remember to put those perspectives in writing. Thoughts can move at blinding speeds. Writing slows down the thought process. Gaps in logic that slip by us in thought or speech are often exposed when we commit the same ideas to paper. Writing down our thoughts allows us to compare, contrast, and combine points of view more clearly—and become critical thinkers.

7

 You're One Click Away . . .
from more strategies for critical thinking.

Discover the joy of bafflement

The poet Wendell Berry wrote about confusion as an opportunity to learn: "When we no longer know what to do, we have come to our real work, and when we no longer know which way to go, we have begun our real journey. The mind that is not baffled is not employed. The impeded stream is the one that sings."[2] We're all going to experience periods of confusion. You can start preparing for them now—and even learn to welcome confusion as a path to thinking.

This three-step exercise is about becoming confused on purpose—and seeing what possibilities open up as a result. In the process you will generate and collect new ideas—one of the core thinking skills.

1. In the space below, write something that you're sure is true about yourself (for instance: "I'm sure that I will never take a philosophy course").

_____

_____

_____

_____

_____

_____

2. Next, take the same statement and put a question mark after it (for example: "I would never take a philosophy course?"). You might need to rephrase the question for grammatical sense.

_____

_____

_____

_____

_____

_____

3. Are you feeling confused? If so, great. Go a little deeper. Brainstorm some questions related to the one you just wrote. ("In what ways would taking a philosophy course serve my success in school?" "Could taking a philosophy course help me with designing software?") Write your questions in the space below.

_____

_____

_____

_____

_____

_____

_____

4. Finally, circle one of the questions you wrote in step 3. For 10 minutes, brainstorm answers to this question. Write down all your ideas. Don't worry about whether they're logical or practical. Just see whether you can get into a zone of pure creative thinking. Start writing in the space below and continue on separate paper.

_____

_____

_____

_____

_____

_____

_____

Don't fool yourself:
Common mistakes in logic

Over the last few thousand years, philosophers have listed some classic land mines in the field of logic. These common mistakes in thinking are called *fallacies*. The study of fallacies could fill a yearlong course. Following are some examples to get you started. Knowing about them can help you avoid getting fooled.

JUMPING TO CONCLUSIONS

Jumping to conclusions is the only exercise that some lazy thinkers get. This fallacy involves drawing conclusions without sufficient evidence.

Consider the bank officer who hears about a student's failing to pay back an education loan. After that, the officer turns down all loan applications from students. This person has formed a rigid opinion on the basis of hearsay. Jumping to conclusions—also called *hasty generalization*—is at work here.

Following are more examples of this fallacy:

- *When I went to Mexico for spring break, I felt sick the whole time. Mexican food makes people sick.*
- *Google's mission is to "organize the world's information." Their employees must be on a real power trip.*
- *During a recession, more people go to the movies. People just want to sit in the dark and forget about their money problems.*

Each item in the above list includes two statements, and the second statement does not necessarily follow from the first. More evidence is needed to make any possible connection.

ATTACKING THE PERSON

This fallacy flourishes at election time. Consider the example of a candidate who claims that her opponent failed to attend church regularly during the campaign. Candidates who indulge in personal attacks about private matters are attempting an intellectual sleight of hand. They want to divert our attention from the truly relevant issues.

APPEALING TO AUTHORITY

A professional athlete endorses a brand of breakfast cereal. A famous musician features a soft drink company's product in a music video. The promotional brochure for an advertising agency lists all of the large companies that have used its services.

In each case, the people involved are trying to win your confidence—and your dollars—by citing authorities. The underlying assumption is usually this: *Famous people and organizations buy our product. Therefore, you should buy it too.* Or: *You should accept this idea merely because someone who's well-known says it's true.*

Appealing to authority is usually a substitute for producing real evidence. It invites sloppy thinking. When our only evidence for a viewpoint is an appeal to authority, it's time to think more thoroughly.

POINTING TO A FALSE CAUSE

The fact that one event follows another does not necessarily mean that the two events have a cause-and-effect relationship. All we can actually say is that the events might be correlated. For example, as children's vocabularies improve, they can get more cavities. This does not mean that cavities are the result of an improved vocabulary. Instead, the increase in cavities is due to other factors, such as physical maturation and changes in diet or personal care.

THINKING IN ALL-OR-NOTHING TERMS

Consider these statements: *Doctors are greedy. You can't trust politicians. Students these days are in school just to get high-paying jobs; they lack idealism. Homeless people don't want to work.*

These opinions imply the word *all*. They gloss over individual differences, claiming that all members of a group are exactly alike. They also ignore key facts—for instance, that some doctors volunteer their time at free medical clinics and that many homeless people are children who are too young to work. All-or-nothing thinking is one of the most common errors in logic.

BEGGING THE QUESTION

Speakers and writers beg the question when their colorful language glosses over an idea that is unclear or unproven. Consider this statement: *Support the American tradition of individual liberty and oppose mandatory seat belt laws!* Anyone who makes such a statement "begs" (fails to answer) a key question: Are laws that require drivers to use seat belts actually a violation of individual liberty?

 You're One Click Away . . .
from more ways to avoid getting fooled.

Strategies for **effective writing**

Effective writing is essential to your success as a thinker and a student. Papers, presentations, essay tests, e-mail, social networking sites—and even the occasional text message— call for your ability to communicate ideas with force and clarity.

LIST AND SCHEDULE WRITING TASKS

You can divide the ultimate goal—such as a finished paper—into smaller steps to do right away. Estimate how long it will take to complete each step. Start with the date your paper is due and work backward to the present. Say that the due date is December 1, and you have about three weeks to write the paper. To give yourself a cushion, schedule November 28 as your targeted completion date. Plan what you want to get done by November 21, and then list what you want to get done by November 14.

SELECT A TOPIC AND WORKING TITLE

It's easy to put off writing if you have a hard time choosing a topic. However, it is almost impossible to make a wrong choice of topic at this stage. You can choose a different topic later if you find the one you've chosen isn't working out.

Using your instructor's guidelines for a paper or presentation, write down a list of topics that interest you. Write as many of these ideas as you can think of in two minutes. Then choose one topic. If you can't decide, use scissors to cut your list into single items, put them in a box, and pull one out. To avoid getting stuck on this step, set a precise time line: "I will choose a topic by 4 p.m. on Wednesday."

The most common pitfall is selecting a topic that's too broad. "Harriet Tubman" is not a useful topic for your American history paper. Instead, consider "Harriet Tubman's activities as a Union spy during the Civil War." Your topic statement can function as a working title.

WRITE A THESIS STATEMENT

Clarify what you want to say about your topic by summarizing it in one sentence. This sentence is called a thesis statement. Unlike a topic, it is expressed in a complete sentence, including a verb. "Harriet Tubman's activities with the Underground Railroad led to a relationship with the Union army during the Civil War" is a thesis statement.

CONSIDER YOUR PURPOSE

Think about how you'd like your reader or listener to respond after considering your ideas. Do you want your audience to think differently, feel differently, or take a certain action? How you answer these questions greatly affects your writing strategy. If you want someone to *think* differently, make your writing clear and logical. Support your assertions with evidence. If you want someone to *feel* differently, consider crafting a story. Write about a character your audience can empathize with, and describe the actions that this character takes to solve a problem. And if your purpose is to move the reader into *action*, explain exactly what steps to take and offer solid benefits for doing so.

DO INITIAL RESEARCH

At the initial stage, the objective of your research is not to uncover specific facts about your topic. That comes later. First, you want to gain an overview of the subject. Discover the structure of your topic—its major divisions and branches.

OUTLINE

An outline is a kind of map. When you follow a map, you avoid getting lost. Likewise, an outline keeps you from wandering off the topic. To start an outline, gather a stack of 3 x 5 cards. Based on your initial research, brainstorm topics and key points you want to include in your paper. Write one phrase or sentence per card. Then experiment with the cards. Group them into separate stacks, each stack representing one major category. After that, arrange the stacks in order. Finally, arrange the cards within each stack in a logical order. Rearrange them until you discover an organization that you like. If you write with a computer, consider using the outlining feature of your word-processing software.

DO IN-DEPTH RESEARCH

You can find information about research skills in Chapters 4 and 5. Remember that one common technique is to take notes on 3 × 5 cards. Use these cards to record your own ideas and ideas from various sources, such as books, periodicals, and Web sites. Write down one idea or fact per card. This allows you to easily sort cards into different categories based on your outline.

A related option is to key your research notes into a computer file. Again, record one idea or fact in each paragraph of your notes. Record information about the source of each idea or fact (such as author, title, publisher, and publication date) at the end of each paragraph. Label your own ideas separately.

AVOID PLAGIARISM LIKE THE PLAGUE

Using another person's words, images, or other original creations without giving proper credit is called plagiarism. Plagiarism amounts to taking someone else's work and presenting it as your own—the equivalent of cheating on a test. The consequences of plagiarism can range from a failing grade to expulsion from school.

To avoid plagiarism, ask an instructor where to find your school's written policy on this issue. Read this document carefully (no kidding). Ask questions about anything you don't understand.

When writing, be sure to cite a source for each passage, sequence of ideas, or image created by another person. While ideas cannot be copyrighted, the way that any idea is *expressed* in words and images can be.

In addition:

- If you use a direct quote from another writer or speaker, put that person's words in quotation marks. List the source of the quotation as well.
- Paraphrase and summarize with care. Paraphrasing means restating someone else's message in your own words, usually making it shorter and simpler. This does not mean copying a passage word for word and then just rearranging or deleting a few phrases. List a source for paraphrased or summarized material, just as you do for direct quotes.
- When you use the same sequence of ideas as one of your sources—even if you have not quoted, paraphrased, or summarized—cite that source.
- List a source for any idea that is closely identified with a particular person.
- Submit only your own work—not materials that have been written or revised by another person.

WRITE A FIRST DRAFT

Gather your notes and arrange them to follow your outline. Then write about the ideas in your notes. Write in paragraphs, with one main idea per paragraph. If you have organized your notes logically, related facts and ideas will appear close to one another.

At this stage, don't stop to revise your writing. Your goal at this point is simply to finish a complete draft of your paper. Then let your first draft sit for a day or two before you go on to the next step.

One useful technique for writing a first draft is free writing. There's only one rule in free writing: Write without stopping. Set a time limit—say, 10 minutes—and keep your pencil in motion or your fingers dancing across the keyboard the whole time. Give yourself permission to keep writing. Ignore the urge to stop and rewrite, even if you think what you've written isn't very good. There's no need to worry about spelling, punctuation, or grammar. It's okay if you stray from the initial subject. Just keep writing, and let the ideas flow. Experiment with free writing as soon as your instructor assigns a paper.

REVISE, REVISE, REVISE

Schedule plenty of time to slow down and take a microscope to your work. One effective way to revise your paper is to read it out loud. Another technique is to have a friend look over your paper. Though this is never a substitute for your own review, a friend can often see things you miss.

To revise efficiently, first look for pages, paragraphs, sentences, and words that you can cut. Next, rearrange what's left of your draft so that it flows logically. Finally, polish by looking for the following:

- A clear thesis statement
- Sentences that introduce your topic, guide the reader through the major sections of your paper, and summarize your conclusions
- Details—such as quotations, examples, and statistics—that support your conclusions
- Lean sentences that are free of needless words
- Plenty of action verbs and concrete, specific nouns

PROOFREAD

Correct any grammar and punctuation areas. Format your paper or presentation according to your instructor's guidelines and print out a clean copy. Then savor the feeling of finishing your paper. See every writing assignment as a chance to demonstrate mastery.

 You're One Click Away . . .
from more ways to make your writing shine.

7

Writing
and delivering
PRESENTATIONS

Some people tune out during a speech. Just think of all the times you have listened to instructors, lecturers, and politicians. Remember all the wonderful daydreams you had during their speeches?

Your audiences are like you. The way you plan and present your speech can determine the number of audience members who will stay with you until the end. Polishing your speaking and presentation skills can also help you think on your feet and communicate clearly. You can use these skills in any course and in any career you choose.

ANALYZE YOUR AUDIENCE

Developing a presentation is similar to writing a paper. Begin by choosing your topic, purpose, and thesis statement as described in "Strategies for effective writing" on page 84.

Also remember that audiences generally have one question in mind: *So what?* Or, *Why does this matter to me?* They want to know that your presentation relates to their desires. To convince people that you have something worthwhile to say, write down the main point of your presentation. Then see whether you can complete this sentence: *I'm telling you this because. . . .*

WATCH THE TIME

Consider the length of your presentation. Time yourself as you practice speaking. Aim for a lean presentation—just enough to make your point and avoid making your audience restless. Leave your listeners wanting more. When you speak, be brief and then be seated.

COMMUNICATE YOUR MESSAGE IN THREE PARTS

Presentations are usually organized into three main sections: the introduction, the main body, and the conclusion.

Rambling speeches with no clear point or organization put audiences to sleep. Solve this problem with your introduction. State your main point in a way that gets attention. Then give your audience a hint of what's coming next. For example: "More people have died from hunger in the past five years than have been killed in all of the wars, revolutions, and murders in the past 150 years. Yet there is enough food to go around. I'm honored to be here with you today and share a solution to this problem."

In the main body of your presentation, develop your ideas in the same way that you develop a written paper. Cover each point in order. Support each point with facts, quotations, and interesting stories. Also be prepared to offer a source for each of these.

During this part of your presentation, transitions are especially important. Use meaningful pauses and phrases to let people know where you're at and where you're going: "On the other hand, until the public realizes what is happening to children in these countries. . . ." Or, "The second reason hunger persists is. . . ."

For the conclusion, summarize your key points and draw your conclusion in a way that no one will forget. You started with a bang; now finish with drama.

The introduction and conclusion of a speech are the most important sections. Your introduction grabs your audience's attention; your conclusion drives home the main point while making it clear that you've reached the end. Avoid endings such as "This is the end of my speech," and, "Umm, I guess that's it." A simple standby is this: "In conclusion, I want to reiterate three points. . . ."

When you are finished, stop talking.

CREATE SPEAKING NOTES

Some professional speakers recommend writing out your speech in full and then putting key words or main points on a few 3 x 5 cards. Number the cards so that if you drop them, you can quickly put them in order again. As you finish the information on each card, move it to the back of the pile. Write information clearly and in letters large enough to be seen from a distance.

Other speakers prefer to use standard outlined notes instead of cards. Another option is concept mapping. Even an hour-long speech can be mapped on one sheet of paper.

Whatever method you choose, use suggestions from Chapter 3: "Memory" to remember your speech.

CREATE SUPPORTING VISUALS

Presentations often include visuals such as overhead transparencies, flip charts, or slides created with presentation software. These materials can reinforce your main points. Remember that effective visuals complement rather than replace your speaking. If you use too many visuals—or visuals that are too complex—your audience might focus on them and forget about you.

OVERCOME FEAR OF SPEAKING

You may not be able to eliminate fear of public speaking entirely, but you can take three steps to reduce and manage it.

First, prepare thoroughly. Research your topic thoroughly. Knowing your topic inside and out can create a baseline of confidence. To make a strong start, memorize the first four sentences that you plan to deliver, and practice them many times. Delivering them flawlessly when you're in front of an audience can build your confidence for the rest of your speech.

Second, accept your physical sensations. You've probably experienced physical sensations that are commonly associated with stage fright: dry mouth, a pounding heart, sweaty hands, muscle jitters, shortness of breath, and a shaky voice. One immediate way to deal with such sensations is to simply notice them. Tell yourself, "Yes, my hands are clammy. Yes, my stomach is upset. Also, my face feels numb." Trying to deny or ignore such facts can increase your fear. When you fully accept sensations, however, they start to lose power.

Third, focus on content, not delivery. Michael Motley, a professor at the University of California–Davis, distinguishes between two orientations to speaking. People with a *performance orientation* believe that the speaker must captivate the audience by using formal techniques that differ from normal conversation. In contrast, speakers with a *communication orientation* see public speaking simply as an extension of one-to-one conversation. The goal is not to perform but to communicate your ideas to an audience in the same ways that you would explain them to a friend.[3]

Adopting a communication orientation can reduce your fear of public speaking. Instead of thinking about yourself, focus on your message. Your audiences are more interested in *what* you have to say than *how* you say it. Forget about giving a "speech."

Just give people valuable ideas and information that they can use.

PRACTICE YOUR PRESENTATION

The key to successful public speaking is practice. When you practice, do so in a loud voice, which helps your audience to hear you. Your voice sounds different when you talk loudly, and this fact can be unnerving. Get used to it early on.

Practice in the room in which you will deliver your speech. If possible, hear what your voice sounds like over a sound system. If you can't practice your speech in the actual room, at least visit the site ahead of time. Also make sure that the materials you will need for your speech, including any audiovisual equipment, will be available when you want them.

When you practice, consider making an audio or video recording. Many schools have recording equipment available for student use. Listen to or view the finished recording to evaluate your presentation.

As you speak, listen for repeated words and phrases. Examples include *you know*, *kind of*, and *really*, plus any little *uh's*, *umm's*, and *ah*'s. To get rid of them, tell yourself that you intend to notice every time they pop up in your daily speech. When you hear them, remind yourself that you don't use those words anymore.

Keep practicing. Avoid speaking word for word, as if you were reading a script. When you know your material well, you can deliver it in a natural way. Practice your presentation until you could deliver it in your sleep. Then run through it a few more times.

SPEAK UP IN CLASS

You can apply many of the above suggestions to any kind of speaking that you do in class. Get prepared for class discussions by keeping up with your reading and other assignments. In your notes, write out questions to ask in class and other ideas you want to share. Then, when it's your turn to speak, talk loudly enough to be heard, and stick to your point.

In addition, accept any fear that you feel about speaking up in class. You can feel nervous and still join the discussion. Focus on your ideas rather than what other people are thinking about you. Just keep speaking—and celebrating your growing mastery.

 You're One Click Away . . .
from more strategies for effective speaking.

✓ Commit to ACTION

Take the next step in finding your speaking voice

What do you want to improve about your presentation skills? Thinking about past speeches you have made can help you with future presentations you make in the classroom and in the workplace. Being honest about your current skills will open you up to new strategies that will help you succeed.

Think beyond this textbook, as well. Look to successful speakers in your community or in the public eye. In light of their strengths, consider the speaking skills that you'd like to gain.

Discovery Statement

Think back to the last time you were called upon to speak before a group. In the space below, write down what you remember about that situation.

For example, describe the physical sensations you experienced before and during your presentation, the overall effectiveness of your presentation, and any feedback you received from the audience.

I discovered that . . .

_____

_____

_____

_____

_____

_____

_____

_____

Intention Statement

Based on what you wrote above, what would you like to do differently the next time you speak? Describe the most important thing that you could do to become a more effective speaker.

I intend to . . .

_____

_____

_____

_____

Action Statement

Now, review this chapter for five suggestions that could help you make your intention a reality. Summarize each suggestion here along with the related page number.

Strategy	Page number
_____	_____
_____	_____
_____	_____
_____	_____
_____	_____

Finally, choose *one* strategy from the list above that you will definitely use for your next presentation.

I will . . .

_____

_____

_____

_____

_____

_____

_____

_____

_____

_____

_____

_____

_____

_____

_____

_____

Find a bigger problem

Problems seem to follow the same law of physics that gases do: They expand to fill whatever space is available.

Say that the only thing left on your to-do list for today is to write a thank-you letter after a job interview. You could spend the rest of the day thinking about what you're going to say, writing the letter, printing it out, finding an envelope, finding a stamp, going to the post office—and then thinking about all of the things you forgot to say.

Now suppose that you get a phone call with an urgent message: A close friend has been admitted to the hospital and wants you to come right away. It's amazing how quickly and easily that letter can get finished when there's a bigger problem on your plate.

This example makes a point: One way to handle little problems is to find bigger ones. This helps us solve smaller problems in less time and with less energy.

Bigger problems are not in short supply. In fact, there are plenty of big ones: world hunger, child abuse, environmental pollution, terrorism, human-rights violations, drug abuse, street crime, energy shortages, poverty, and wars throughout the world. These problems await your attention and involvement. Use your voice to offer a solution in any arena and make it happen.

From this perspective, the goal becomes not to eliminate problems, but to find problems that are worthy of us. Worthy problems are those that inspire critical and creative thinking.

7

Problems lead us to draw on our talents, define our purpose, and increase our skills. Solving these problems offers the greatest benefits for others and ourselves. Viewed in this way, bigger problems give more meaning to our lives.

Finding a bigger problem does not have to be depressing. In fact, it can be energizing—a reason for getting up in the morning. A huge project can channel your passion and purpose.

When we take on a bigger problem, we play full out. We do justice to our potentials. We love what we do and do what we love. We're awake, alert, and engaged. Playing full out means living our lives as if our lives depended on it.

Take responsibility for problems that are bigger than you are sure you can handle. Then notice how your other problems dwindle in importance—or even vanish.

 You're One Click Away . . .
from more ways to find a bigger problem.

8

Creating Positive Relationships

Notice your "people pictures"—*and let them go*

One of the brain's primary jobs is to manufacture images. Novelists often have mental pictures of the characters that they're about to bring to life. Parents have pictures about what they want their children to become.

These "people pictures" have a profound influence on us. We use such pictures to make predictions about people. And we expect people to act in ways that match those predictions.

This attitude is amazing, considering that we often operate with little, if any, conscious knowledge of our pictures. In fact, our pictures can get in our way.

Take the case of a student who plans to attend a school she hasn't visited. She creates many people pictures. The professors, she imagines, will be as humorous as Jon Stewart and as entertaining as Oprah Winfrey. And her roommate will share her love for hip-hop.

The school turns out to be four gray buildings downtown, next to the bus station. The first class she attends is taught by an overweight, balding professor. He wears a purple and orange bird of paradise tie and has a bad case of the sniffles. In addition, the student's roommate is a country music fan. This hypothetical student gets depressed. She begins to think about dropping out of school.

The problem with people pictures is that they can prevent us from seeing who people really are. In this story, the student's people pictures prevented her from noticing that the professor with the weird tie is an expert in his field *and* a superior teacher. Her pictures also prevented her from seeing that her roommate will gladly listen to all kinds of music.

The next time you discover you are angry, disappointed, or frustrated with someone, look to see which of your people pictures aren't being fulfilled. Having pictures is unavoidable. Letting these pictures control our relationships *is* avoidable. This single attitude change will help you benefit from all the suggestions in this chapter.

Discover what YOU WANT from this chapter

The Discovery Wheel on page 2 includes a section titled *Relationships*. Take some time to go beyond your initial responses to that section. Spend five minutes skimming this chapter. Then complete the following sentences:

To be more effective at managing conflict with people, I could . . .

_____

_____

_____

_____

_____

_____

_____

_____

Some ideas from this chapter that can make a big difference in my relationships are . . .

_____

_____

_____

_____

_____

_____

_____

_____

_____

_____

8

When you see 🔘 **You're One Click Away . . .***, remember to go to this book's Web site at [insert URL] for additional content. And for a summary of this chapter, see the Master Student Review Cards at the end of this book.*

Thriving in a DIVERSE WORLD

Higher education could bring you into the most diverse environment of your life. Your fellow students could come from many different ethnic groups, cultures, and countries. Few institutions in our society can match the level of diversity found in higher education.

To get the most from your education, use this environment to your advantage. Through your encounters with many types of people, you can gain new perspectives and new friends. You can also acquire skills for living in multicultural neighborhoods and working in a global economy.

Cultivate friends from other cultures. Do this through volunteering, serving on committees, or any other activities in which people from other cultures are involved. Through these experiences, your understanding of diversity and "cultural competence" will unfold in a natural, spontaneous way. Also experiment with the following strategies.

SWITCH CULTURAL LENSES

Diversity skills begin with learning about yourself and understanding the lenses through which you see the world. One way to do this is to intentionally switch lenses—to consciously perceive familiar events in a new way.

For example, think of a situation in your life that involved an emotionally charged conflict among several people. Now mentally put yourself inside the skin of another person in that conflict. Ask yourself, "How would I see this situation if I were that person? Or if I were a person of the opposite gender? Or if I were a member of a different racial or ethnic group? Or if I were older or younger?"

Do this consistently and you'll discover that we live in a world of multiple realities. There are many different ways to interpret any event—and just as many ways to respond, given our individual differences.

REFLECT ON EXPERIENCES OF PRIVILEGE AND PREJUDICE

Someone might tell you that he's more likely to be promoted at work because he's white and male—*and* that he's been called "white trash" because he lives in a trailer park.

See whether you can recall incidents such as these from your own life. Think of times when you were favored due to your gender, race, or age. Also think of times when you were excluded or ridiculed based on one of those same characteristics. In doing this, you'll discover ways to identify with a wider range of people.

To complete this process, turn your self-discoveries into possibilities for new behaviors. For example, if you're a younger student, you may tend to join study groups with people who are about your age. If so, then plan to invite an older student to your group's next meeting. When choosing whether to join a campus organization, take into account the diversity of its membership. And before you make a statement about anyone who differs significantly from you, ask yourself, "Is what I'm about to say accurate, or is it based on a belief that I've held for years and never examined?"

LOOK FOR COMMON GROUND

Students in higher education often find that they worry about many of the same things—including tuition bills, the quality of dormitory food, and the shortage of on-campus parking spaces. More important, our fundamental goals as human beings—such as health, physical safety, and economic security—are desires that cross culture lines.

The key is to honor the differences among people while remembering what we have in common. Diversity is not just about our differences—it's about our similarities. On a biological level, less than 1 percent of the human genome accounts for visible characteristics such as skin color. In terms of our genetic blueprint, we are more than 99 percent the same.[1]

LOOK FOR INDIVIDUALS, NOT GROUP REPRESENTATIVES

Sometimes the way we speak glosses over differences among individuals and reinforces stereotypes. For example, a student worried about her grade in math expresses concern over "all those Asian students who are skewing the class curve." Or a white music major assumes that her African American classmate knows a lot about jazz or hip-hop music. We can avoid such errors by seeing people as individuals—not spokespersons for an entire group.

BE WILLING TO ACCEPT FEEDBACK

Members of another culture might let you know that some of your words or actions had a meaning other than what you intended. Perhaps a comment that seems harmless to you is offensive to them. And they may tell you directly about it.

Avoid responding to such feedback with comments such as "Don't get me wrong," "You're taking this way too seriously," or "You're too sensitive."

Instead, listen without resistance. Open yourself to what others have to say. Remember to distinguish between the *intention* of your behavior from its actual *impact* on other people. Then take the feedback you receive and ask how you can use it to communicate more effectively in the future.

If you are new at responding to diversity, then expect to make some mistakes along the way. As long as you approach people in a spirit of tolerance, your words and actions can always be changed.

SPEAK UP AGAINST DISCRIMINATION

You might find yourself in the presence of someone who tells a racist joke, makes a homophobic comment, or utters an ethnic slur. When this happens, you have a right to state what you observe, share what you think, and communicate how you feel.

Depending on the circumstance, you might say:

- "That's a stereotype, and we don't have to accept it."

- "Other people are going to take offense at that. Let's tell jokes that don't put people down."

- "I realize that you don't mean to offend anybody, but I feel hurt and angry by what you just said."

- "As members of the majority culture around here, we can easily forget how comments like that affect other people."

Also keep in mind that someone from a specific ethnic or cultural background can also be the source of negative comments about that culture. Speak up against discriminatory comments from any source.

This kind of speaking may be the most difficult communicating you ever do. And if you *don't* do it, you give the impression that you agree with biased speech.

In response to your candid comments, many people will apologize and express their willingness to change. Even if they don't, you can still know that you practiced integrity by aligning your words with your values.

LOOK FOR DIFFERENCES BETWEEN INDIVIDUALIST AND COLLECTIVIST CULTURES

As you switch lenses, remember some basic differences between cultures. For example, individualist cultures flourish in the United States, Canada, and Western Europe. If your family has deep roots in one of these areas, you were probably raised to value personal fulfillment and personal success. You received recognition or rewards when you stood out from your peers—for example, by earning the highest grades in your class, scoring the most points during a basketball season, or making another individual achievement.

In contrast, collectivist cultures value cooperation over competition. Group progress is more important than individual success. Credit for an achievement is widely shared. If you were raised in such a culture, you probably place a high value on your family and were taught to respect your elders. Collectivist cultures dominate Asia, Africa, and Latin America.

In short, individualist cultures emphasize "I," while collectivist cultures emphasize "we." Forgetting about the differences between them can strain a friendship or wreck an international business deal.

If you were raised in an individualist culture:

- Remember that someone from a collectivist culture may place a high value on "saving face." This involves more than simply avoiding embarrassment. This person may not want to be singled out from other members of a group even for a positive achievement. If you have a direct request for this person or want to share something that could be taken as a personal criticism, save it for a private conversation.

- Respect titles and last names. Although Americans often like to use first names immediately after meeting someone, in some cultures this practice is acceptable only among family members. Especially in work settings, use last names and job titles during your first meetings. Allow time for informal relationships to develop.

- Put messages in context. For members of collectivist cultures, words convey only part of an intended message. Notice gestures and other nonverbal communication as well.

If you were raised in a collectivist culture, you can creatively "reverse" the above list. For instance, remember that direct questions from an American student or coworker are usually meant not to offend but only to clarify an idea. Don't be surprised if you are called by a nickname, if no one asks about your family, or if you are rewarded for a personal achievement. And in social situations, remember that indirect cues might not get another person's attention. Practice asking clearly and directly for what you want.

 You're One Click Away . . .
from more ways to thrive in a diverse world.

Create relationships with *integrity*

R elationships are built on integrity. When we break a promise to be faithful to a spouse, help a friend move to a new apartment, or pay a bill on time, relationships are strained. When we keep our word, relationships work.

WAYS TO MAKE AND KEEP AGREEMENTS

Integrity means making agreements that we fully intend to keep. However, the only way to ensure that we keep *all* of our agreements is either to make none—or to play it safe and only make agreements that pose no risk.

Examining our agreements can improve our effectiveness. Perhaps we took on too much—or too little. Perhaps we did not use all the resources that were available to us—or we used too many. Perhaps we did not fully understand what we were promising. When we learn from our mistakes and our successes, we can build more relationships with integrity.

By making ambitious agreements, we can also stretch ourselves to new possibilities. If we stretch too far and end up breaking an agreement, we can quickly admit our mistake, deal with the consequences, and negotiate a new agreement.

MOVE UP THE LADDER OF POWERFUL SPEAKING

The words used to talk about our agreements fall into several different levels. Think of each level as one rung on a ladder—the ladder of powerful speaking. As we move up this ladder, our speaking leads to more effective action.

Obligation. The lowest rung on the ladder is *obligation*. Words used at this level include *I should, he ought to, someone better, they need to, I must,* and *I had to*. Speaking this way implies that we have few choices—that we are not in control of our lives. When we live at the level of obligation, we feel passive and helpless to change anything.

Note: When we move to the next rung, we leave behind obligation and advance to self-responsibility. All of the remaining rungs reinforce this characteristic.

Possibility. The next rung up is *possibility*. At this level, we examine new options. We play with new ideas, potential solutions, and alternate courses of action. As we do, we become aware of choices that can dramatically affect the quality of our lives. We are not the victims of circumstance. Phrases that signal this level include *I might, I could, I'll consider, I hope to,* and *maybe*.

Preference. From possibility we can move up to *preference*. Here we start to actively *make* choices. The words *I prefer* signal that we're moving toward one set of possibilities over another, perhaps setting the stage for eventual action.

Passion. Above preference is a rung called *passion*. Again, certain words signal this level: *I want to, I'm really excited to do that, I can't wait*. Possibility and passion are both exciting places to be. Even at these levels, though, we're still far from action. Many of us want to achieve lots of things and have no specific plan for doing so.

Planning. We move closer to action with the next rung—*planning*. When people use phrases such as *I intend to, my goal is to, I plan to,* and *I'll try like mad to,* they're at the level of planning. The Intention Statements you write in this book are examples of planning.

Promising. The highest rung on the ladder is *promising*. This is where the power of your word really comes into play. At this level, it's common to use phrases such as these: *I will, I promise to, I am committed, you can count on it*. This is where we bridge from possibility and planning to action. Promising brings many rewards, including relationships built with integrity.

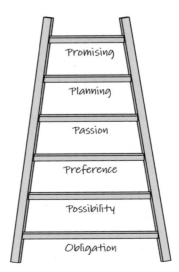

You're One Click Away . . .
from more ways to make and keep powerful agreements.

Commit to ACTION

Practice the art of saying *no*

All your study plans can go down the drain when a friend says, "Time to *parrr-ty!*" Sometimes, succeeding in school means replying with a graceful *no*. Saying no helps you to prevent an overloaded schedule that compromises your health, your relationships, and your grade point average.

Discovery Statement

We find it hard to say no when we make certain assumptions—when we assume that others will think we're rude or that we'll lose friends if we turn down a request.

But think about it: You are in charge of your time only when you have the option to say *no*. Without this option, you are at the mercy of anyone who interrupts you. These will not be relationships based on equality. People who care about you will respect your wishes.

Recall a situation when you wanted to say no to someone but did not. Were you making assumptions about how the other person would react? If so, describe what you were thinking.

I discovered that I . . .

_____

_____

_____

_____

_____

_____

_____

_____

_____

_____

_____

Intention Statement

Next, consider some strategies for giving someone a *no* that's both polite and firm. For instance, you can wait for the request. People who worry about saying no often give in to a request before it's actually been made. Wait until you hear a question: "Would you go to a party with me?"

You can also remind yourself that one no leads to another yes. Saying no to a movie allows you to say yes to getting a paper outlined or a textbook chapter read. Then you can give an unqualified yes to the next social activity.

Describe any strategies that you plan to use the next time you find it difficult to say no.

I intend to . . .

_____

_____

_____

_____

_____

Action Statement

You might find it easier to act on your intention when you don't have to grasp for words. Choose some key phrases in advance. For example: "That doesn't work for me today." "Thanks for asking; my schedule for today is full." Or, "I'll go along next time when my day is clear."

To effectively deliver my next *no*, I will say . . .

_____

_____

_____

_____

_____

_____

8

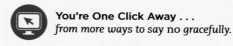 **You're One Click Away . . .**
from more ways to say no gracefully.

12 tools for *deep listening*

People love a good listener. The most popular salespeople, managers, coworkers, teachers, parents, and friends are the best listeners.

To listen well, begin from a clear intention. *Choose* to listen well. Then you can use the following 12 techniques to take your listening to deeper levels.

1. BE QUIET

Silence is more than staying quiet while someone is speaking. Allowing several seconds to pass before you begin to talk gives the speaker time to catch her breath and gather her thoughts. If the message being sent is complete, this short break gives you time to form your response and helps you avoid the biggest barrier to listening—listening with your answer running. If you make up a response before the person is finished, you might miss the end of the message, which is often the main point.

2. DISPLAY OPENNESS

You can display openness through your facial expression and body position. Uncross your arms and legs. Sit up straight. Face the other person and remove any physical barriers between you, such as a pile of books.

3. SEND ACKNOWLEDGMENTS

Let the speaker know periodically that you are still there. Words and nonverbal gestures of acknowledgment convey to the speaker that you are interested and that you are receiving her message. Examples are "Uh huh," "Okay," "Yes," and head nods. These acknowledgments do not imply your agreement. They just indicate that you are listening.

4. RELEASE DISTRACTIONS

Even when your intention is to listen, you might find your mind wandering. Thoughts about what *you* want to say or something you want to do later might claim your attention.

There's a simple solution: Notice your wandering mind without judgment. Then bring your attention back to the act of listening.

There are times when you might not want to listen. You might be fully distracted by your own concerns. Be honest. Don't pretend to listen. You can say, "What you're telling me is important, but I'm not able to listen well right now. Can we set aside another time to talk about this?" Sometimes it's okay not to listen.

5. SUSPEND JUDGMENTS

Listening and agreeing are two different activities. As listeners, our goal is to fully receive another person's message. This does not mean that we're obligated to agree with the message. Once you're confident that you accurately understand a speaker's point of view, you are free to agree or disagree with it. One key to effective listening is understanding *before* evaluating.

6. LISTEN FOR REQUESTS AND INTENTIONS

An effective way to listen to complaints is to look for the request hidden in them. "This class is a waste of my time" can be heard as "Please tell me what I'll gain if I participate actively in class." "The instructor talks too fast" might be asking "What strategies can I use to take notes when the instructor covers material rapidly?"

We can even transform complaints into intentions. Take this complaint: "The parking lot by the dorms is so dark at night that I'm afraid to go to my car." This complaint can lead to "I intend to talk to someone who can see that a light gets installed in the parking lot."

Viewing complaints as requests and intentions gives us more choices. We can stop responding with defensiveness ("What does he know anyway?"), resignation ("It's always been this way and always will be"), or indifference ("It's not my job"). We can choose whether to grant the request or help people translate their complaint into an action plan.

7. ALLOW EMOTION

In the presence of full listening, some people will share things that they feel deeply about. They might cry, shake, or sob. If you feel uncomfortable when this happens, see whether you can accept the discomfort for a little while longer. Emotional release can bring relief and trigger unexpected insights.

8. NOTICE VERBAL AND NONVERBAL MESSAGES

You might point out that the speaker's body language seems to be the exact opposite of her words. For example: "I noticed you said you are excited, but to me you look bored."

Keep in mind that the same nonverbal behavior can have various meanings across cultures. Someone who looks bored might simply be listening in a different way.

9. FEED BACK MEANING

Summarize the essence of that person's message: "Let me see whether I understood what you said . . ." or "What I'm hearing you say is. . . ." Often, the other person will say, "No, that's not what I meant. What I said was. . . ."

There will be no doubt when you get it right. The sender will say, "Yeah, that's it," and either continue with another message or stop sending when she knows you understand.

When you feed back meaning, be concise. This is not a time to stop the other person by talking on and on about what you think you heard.

10. BE CAREFUL WITH QUESTIONS AND ADVICE

Questions are directive. They can take conversations in a new direction, which may *not* be where the speaker wants to go. Ask questions only to clarify the speaker's message. Later, when it's your turn to speak, you can introduce any topic that you want.

Also be cautious about advice. Unsolicited advice can be taken as condescending or even insulting. Skilled listeners recognize that people are different, and they do not assume that they know what's best for someone else.

11. ASK FOR MORE

Full listening with unconditional acceptance is a rare gift. Many people have never experienced it. They are used to being greeted with resistance, so they habitually stop short of saying what they truly think and feel. Help them change this habit by routinely asking, "Is there anything more you want to say about that?" This sends the speaker a message that you truly value what she has to say.

12. STAY OPEN TO THE ADVENTURE OF LISTENING

Receiving what another person has to say is an act of courage. Listening fully—truly opening yourself to the way another person sees the world—means taking risks. Your opinions may be challenged. You may be less certain or less comfortable than you were before.

Along with the risks come rewards. Listening in an unguarded way can take your relationships to a new depth and level of honesty. This kind of listening can open up new possibilities for thinking, feeling, and behavior. And when you practice full listening, other people are more likely to listen when it's your turn to speak.

You're One Click Away . . .
from more strategies for deep listening.

7 steps to effective complaints

Sometimes relationship building involves making a complaint. Whining, blaming, pouting, screaming, and yelling insults usually don't get results. Here are some guidelines for complaining effectively:

1. Go to the source.
Start with the person who is most directly involved with the problem.

2. Present the facts without blaming anyone.
Your complaint will carry more weight if you document the facts. Keep track of names and dates. Note which actions were promised and which results actually occurred.

3. Go up the ladder to people with more responsibility.
If you don't get satisfaction at the first level, go to that person's direct supervisor. Requesting a supervisor's name will often get results. Write a letter to the company president.

4. Ask for commitments.
When you find someone who is willing to solve your problem, get him to say exactly what he is going to do and when.

5. Use available support.
There are dozens of groups as well as government agencies willing to get involved in resolving complaints. Contact consumer groups or the Better Business Bureau. Trade associations can sometimes help. Ask city council members, county commissioners, state legislators, and senators and representatives. All of them want your vote, so they are usually eager to help.

6. Take legal action, if necessary.
Small claims court is relatively inexpensive, and you don't have to hire a lawyer. These courts can handle cases involving small amounts of money (usually up to a few thousand dollars). Legal aid offices can sometimes answer questions.

7. Don't give up.
Assume that others are on your team. Many people are out there to help you. State what you intend to do and ask for their partnership.

8

Manage conflict
with "I" messages

When conflict occurs, we often make statements about another person. We say such things as these:

"You are rude."
"You make me mad."
"You must be crazy."
"You don't love me anymore."

These are "You" messages. Usually they result in defensiveness. The responses might be:

"I am not rude."
"I don't care."
"No, *you* are crazy."
"No, *you* don't love *me!*"

"You" messages are hard to listen to. They label, judge, blame, and assume things that might or might not be true. They demand rebuttal.

The next time you're in conflict with someone, consider replacing "You" messages with "I" messages:

"You are rude" might become "I feel upset."
"You make me mad" could be "I feel angry."
"You must be crazy" can be "I don't understand."
"You don't love me anymore" could become "I'm afraid we're drifting apart."

"I" messages don't judge, blame, criticize, or insult. They don't invite the other person to counterattack. "I" messages are also more accurate. They stick to the facts and report our own thoughts and feelings.

Suppose a friend asks you to pick her up at the airport. You drive 20 miles and wait for the plane. No friend. You decide your friend missed her plane, so you wait three hours for the next flight. No friend. Perplexed and worried, you drive home. The next day, you see your friend downtown.

"What happened?" you ask.
"Oh, I caught an earlier flight."
"You are a rude person," you reply.

Instead, look for and talk about the facts—the observable behavior. Everyone will agree

that your friend asked you to pick her up, that she did take an earlier flight, and that you did not receive a call from her. But the idea that she is rude is not a fact—it's a judgment. Perhaps she had an emergency and was unable to call.

When you see your friend, choose an "I" message instead: "I waited and waited at the airport. I was worried about you. I didn't get a call. I feel angry and hurt. I don't want to waste my time. Next time, you can call me when your flight arrives, and I'll be happy to pick you up."

An "I" message can include any or all of the following five elements:

1. Observations.
Describe the facts—the indisputable, observable realities. Talk about what you, or anyone else, can see, hear, smell, taste, or touch. Avoid judgments, interpretations, or opinions. Instead of saying, "You're a slob," say, "Last night's lasagna pan was still on the stove this morning."

2. Feelings.
Describe your own feelings. It is easier to listen to "I feel frustrated" than to "You never help me." Stating how you feel about another's actions can be valuable feedback for that person.

3. Wants.
You are far more likely to get what you want if you *say* what you want. If someone doesn't know what you want, she doesn't have a chance to help you get it. Ask clearly. Avoid demanding or using the word *need*. Most people like to feel helpful, not obligated. Instead of saying, "Do the dishes when it's your turn, or else!" say, "I want to divide the housework fairly."

4. Thoughts.
Communicate your thoughts, and use caution. Beginning your statement with the word "I" doesn't make it an "I" message. "I think you are a slob" is a "You" judgment in disguise. Instead, say, "I'd have more time to study if I didn't have to clean up so often."

5. Intentions.
The last part of an "I" message is a statement about what you intend to do. Have a plan that doesn't depend on the other person. For example, instead of "From now on we're going to split the dishwashing evenly," you could say, "I intend to do my share of the housework and leave the rest."

 You're One Click Away . . .
from more ways to resolve conflict.

✓ Commit to ACTION

Write an "I" message

The purpose of this exercise is to help you experiment with "I" messages. Practice in the space below, but also start practicing this with the next person you communicate with, whether it's a teacher, roommate, friend, parent, or child. Watch how making this small shift in language can make a big change in your relationships.

Discovery Statement

Pick something about a teacher, friend, or family member that irritates you. Then pretend that you are talking to the person who is associated with this irritation. In the space below, write down what you would say to this person as a "You" message.

I discovered that I would say . . .

_____
_____
_____
_____
_____
_____
_____
_____
_____
_____
_____
_____
_____
_____
_____
_____
_____
_____
_____

Intention Statement

Now consider the possibility of sending a different message. How interested are you in actually using "I" messages with the person described above?

There are several possible levels of commitment. For example, you might choose to deliver a few "I" messages to this person and then see how well they work. Or you might commit to using "I" messages on a permanent basis with this person—and with other key people in your life. Describe your current level of commitment to using "I" messages in the space below.

I intend to . . .

_____
_____
_____
_____
_____
_____
_____

Action Statement

Give some thought to exactly what you'll say if you do use this technique. Take the "You" message above and rewrite it as an "I" message. Include at least the first three elements suggested in "Manage conflict with 'I' messages" on page 98.

I will say . . .

_____
_____
_____
_____
_____
_____
_____
_____
_____
_____

 You're One Click Away . . .
from more ways to deliver an effective "I" message.

8

LEADING
high-performance teams

Working in teams helps you to develop several transferable skills. One is sociability—taking an interest in people, valuing what they think, and understanding how they feel. Another is understanding social systems in organizations and operating effectively in them. Teamwork also gives you a chance to practice all the communication skills explored in this chapter.

In the workplace, teams abound. To research their book *When Teams Work Best,* Frank LaFasto and Carl Larson studied 600 teams. These ranged from the Mount Everest climbing team to the teams that produced the Boeing 747 airplane—the world's largest aircraft and a product of 75,000 blueprints. Teams take on all kinds of complex, time-consuming projects.[2]

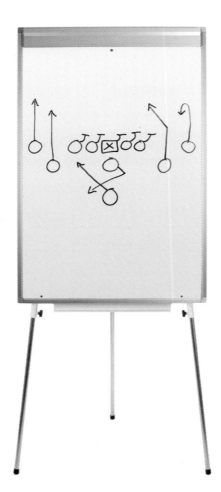

KNOW THE PITFALLS

Research indicates many potential problems with teams, including the following:[3]

- Dependence on a dominant leader
- "Group think" that excludes new ideas
- Fear of taking risks
- "Social loafing"—the tendency of people to take less action when working as part of a group than when working alone
- Taking on too many goals
- Adopting ideas that most group members disagree with because members choose not to share their true thoughts and feelings

APPLY THE CYCLE OF LEARNING TO TEAMS

One way to prevent such problems is to select team members based on the cycle of learning as described in Chapter 2: "Using Your Learning Styles." Remember David Kolb's idea that people learn from experience through four kinds of activity that occur in a repeating cycle. Teams learn in the same way. To create a successful team, choose members who will

- Get fully involved with the team and commit to its purpose (concrete experience).
- Talk about the team's experiences and stay open to new ideas (reflective observation).
- Think critically about which agreements and actions will achieve the team's purpose (abstract conceptualization).
- Make decisions and take action (active experimentation).

Not everyone will have all these skills, so invite members with a variety of learning styles. Look beyond your circle of friends and people who tend to think and act alike. Your team is more likely to succeed with a variety of people who can choose tasks based on their strengths and preferences.

Moving through the cycle of learning is easier when the team is an optimal size. Think carefully about how many people to include. There is no magic number that will guarantee a successful team. Keep it small enough to manage—and large enough to achieve the team's goals.

Your team members might say that they are too busy to bother with the full cycle of learning. As an alternative, simply ask them to reflect on their prior experience. During your first meeting, set aside time to talk about everyone's prior experience with teams. Share your best and worst experiences. Based on that discussion, create your own list of what makes for a successful team. Then make some basic agreements about ways to prevent the problems you've experienced with teams in the past.

EVEN OUT THE WORKLOAD

One potential trap for teams is that one person ends up doing most of the work. This person might feel resentful and complain. If you find yourself in this situation, transform your complaint into a request. Instead of scolding team members for being lazy, request help. Ask team members to take over tasks that you've been doing. Delegate specific jobs.

SHARE ROLES

Teams often begin by choosing a leader with a vision, charisma, and expertise. As your team matures, however, consider letting other members take turns in a leadership role. This is one way to encourage a diversity of viewpoints and help people expand their learning styles.

PREPARE FOR DIFFERENT ATTITUDES ABOUT TEAMS

During much of the previous century, many large businesses and nonprofit organizations were organized as hierarchies with multiple layers—executives, middle-level managers, supervisors, and employees. People who worked for such companies had jobs with clearly defined and limited responsibilities. Collaborations among employees in different departments were rare.

In contrast, teams present a new picture of how to operate in the workplace. And old pictures die hard. Companies may give lip service to the idea of teams and yet fall back into traditional practices. Managers might set up teams but offer little training to help people function in this new working environment.

You can prepare for this situation now. While you are in school, seize opportunities to work collaboratively. Form study groups. Enroll in classes that include group projects. Show up for your next job with teamwork skills. At the same time, remember that some of your coworkers may not share your assumptions about the value of teams. By demonstrating your abilities, you help them to form new pictures.

APPLY THE POWER PROCESSES

People talk a lot about *empowering* teams. One answer is to take your cue from the word *empowered* and see whether you can apply the Power Processes in this book to team work.

For example, use the Power Process "Ideas are tools." Teams tend to fizzle when they create new ideas that meet with immediate skepticism or outright rejection. After proposing changes to a company's existing policies and procedures, team members might face resistance: "This suggestion will never work." "That's just not the way we do things around here." "We can't break with tradition." These responses are examples of groupthink, which happens when a team automatically rules out new options simply because they're . . . well, *new.*

People who want a team to succeed will treat its ideas as tools. Instead of automatically looking for what's wrong with a proposal, look for potential value. Even a proposal that seems outlandish at first might become workable with a few modifications.

Also consider "Be here now." Concentration and focused attention are features of effective students *and* effective teams. When a team tries to tackle too many problems or achieve too many goals, it gets distracted. Members can forget the team's purpose and lose their enthusiasm for the project. Restore the focus by asking: "What is the single most important goal that our team can meet?" and "What is the single most important thing we can do *now* to meet that goal?"

You're One Click Away . . .
from more teamwork strategies.

You are *already* a *leader*

No one can escape leadership. Every time you speak, you lead others in some small or large way. Every time you take action, you lead others through your example. Every time you ask someone to do something, you are leading that person. To lead effectively, consider the following suggestions.

Embrace change. Leaders change the status quo. They create new products, develop new services, start new businesses, found new organizations, and pass new legislation. They recognize good ideas early on and then tirelessly promote them.

Get back on purpose. Leadership is the art of helping others lift their eyes to the horizon—keeping them in touch with the ultimate value and purpose of a project. When you lead a project, speak a lot about the end result and the potential value of what you're doing.

Move people into action. A leader's vision has little power until people get behind it. That vision cannot be forced on anyone. Instead, leaders enlist wide support for new projects through the sheer force of enthusiasm. Their passion for a new project spreads to people at all levels of an organization. In addition:

- **Make requests—lots of them.** An effective leader is a request machine. Making requests, both large and small, is an act of respect. When we ask a lot from others, we demonstrate our respect for them and our confidence in their abilities.

- **Delegate.** Ask a coworker or classmate to take on a job that you'd like to see done. Ask the same of your family or friends. Delegate tasks to the mayor of your town, the governor of your state, and the leaders of your country. Suggest projects that are important to you. Then find people who can lead the effort.

- **Follow up.** What we don't inspect, people don't respect. When other people agree to do a job for you, follow up to see how it is going. This can be done in a way that communicates your respect and interest—not your fear that the project might flounder.

8

Try on a new interpretation

The purpose of this exercise is to see the difference between behaviors and interpretations. Understanding this difference can help you think more accurately about what other people say and do. In turn, this thinking skill can help you prevent and resolve conflict.

A *behavior* is a physical action that we can directly observe. When we describe behaviors, we're stating facts. In contrast, an *interpretation* is a statement of opinion about what a behavior means.

The following chart lists two behaviors and two different ways to interpret each behavior.

Behavior	Interpretation #1	Interpretation #2
Someone enters a classroom 10 minutes after a lecture starts.	"She's too irresponsible to get to a lecture on time."	"She's normally on time; maybe her car broke down at the last minute."
Someone gets up during a conversation and runs out of the room.	"He ran out of the room because he was so angry with me."	"maybe he left the room suddenly because he got a text message about an emergency."

In both cases, Interpretation #1 places blame and invites an argument. Interpretation #2 avoids blame and invites further conversation rather than argument. Interpretation #1 increases conflict, while Interpretation #2 decreases conflict.

With this distinction in mind, think of a recent situation when you were in conflict with someone. In the chart below, brainstorm a list of any behaviors that were involved in this conflict. List each behavior on a separate line. Then think of two ways to interpret each behavior. Finally, place a plus sign (+) next to any interpretation that could increase conflict. Then place a minus sign (−) next to any interpretation that could decrease conflict.

Behavior	Interpretation #1	Interpretation #2

 You're One Click Away . . .
from more examples of the differences between observations and interpretations.

POWER process

Choose your conversations

Relationships flourish or die based on the quality of conversations. Some conversations create bridges of understanding and bring people closer together. Others create division and leave people with feelings of fear, frustration, or sadness.

Conversations have power over what we think, feel, and do. They shape our attitudes, our decisions, our emotions, and our actions. If you want clues about what a person will be like tomorrow, listen to what she's talking about today. We become our conversations.

Given that conversations are so powerful, it's amazing that few people act on this fact. Most of us swim in a constant sea of conversations, almost none of which we carefully and thoughtfully choose.

For example, there are the random conversations we have with friends, relatives, and other people. If we flip on the radio or television, or if we surf the Web, millions of other conversations await us. Thanks to modern technology, many of these conversations take place in high-quality sound, high-resolution images, and living color, 24 hours each day.

Even in the midst of all these voices, we have the power to choose our conversations. Certain conversations create real value for us. They give us fuel for reaching our goals. Others distract us from what we want. We can choose more of the conversations that support and sustain us.

The conversations you have are dramatically influenced by the people you associate with. If you want to change your attitudes about almost anything—prejudice, politics, religion, humor—then seek out new people and start some new conversations. Instead of complaining about problems, start talking about solutions. Instead of rehashing mistakes from the past, start talking about new possibilities for the future. Instead of focusing on what's missing from your life, start talking about the things you appreciate.

Spend time with people who speak about and live consistently with the attitudes you value. In this way you can use conversations to change habits. You can use conversations to create new options in your life. You can use conversations to meet your goals, inspire your team, and create more loving relationships.

Choose your conversations.

 You're One Click Away . . .
from more ways to choose your conversations.

8

9

Choosing Greater Health

Wake up to health

We expect to experience health challenges as we age. Even youth, though, is no guarantee of good health. Over the last three decades, obesity among young adults has tripled. Twenty-nine percent of young men smoke. And 70 percent of deaths among adults age 18 to 29 result from unintentional injuries, accidents, homicide, and suicide.[1]

Your success in school is directly tied to your health. Lack of sleep and exercise have been associated with lower grades. So have alcohol use, tobacco use, gambling, and chronic health conditions.[2] And any health habit that undermines your success in school can also undermine your success in later life.

The word *health* is similar in origin to *whole, hale, hardy,* and even *holy*. Implied in these words are qualities often associated with healthy people: alertness, vitality, vigor. Healthy people meet the demands of daily life with energy to spare. Illness or stress might slow them down, but they bounce back. They know how to relax, create loving relationships, and find satisfaction in work.

Perhaps *health* is one of those rich, multilayered concepts that we can never define completely. That's okay. We can still adopt habits that sustain our well-being. One study found that people lengthened their lives an average of 14 years by adopting just four habits: staying tobacco-free, eating more fruits and vegetables, exercising regularly, and drinking alcohol in moderation if at all.[3]

In the end, your definition of *health* comes from your own experience. To a large extent, your level of health is your creation. Health is a choice you make with each action that you take. You have two basic options. One is to remain unaware of your habits and their consequences. This leaves your health up to chance.

The second option is to apply the cycle of mastery mentioned throughout this book: Become aware of your current health habits (discovery), choose new habits (intention), then translate your intentions into action.

The purpose of this chapter is to promote the second choice. Create health by experimenting with the suggestions that follow.

Discover what YOU WANT from this chapter

The Discovery Wheel on page 2 includes a section titled *Health*. Take some time to go beyond your initial responses to that section. Spend five minutes skimming this chapter. Then complete the following sentences.

Right now, my top health concern is . . .

_____

_____

_____

_____

_____

_____

_____

_____

Some ideas from this chapter that can help me respond to that concern are . . .

_____

_____

_____

_____

_____

_____

_____

_____

_____

_____

When you see 🖱 *You're One Click Away . . ., remember to go to this book's College Success CourseMate for additional content. And for a summary of this chapter, see the Master Student Review Cards at the end of this book.*

9

✓ Commit to ACTION

Take a fearless look at your health

Take a few minutes right now to take a detailed look at your health. If you generally look and feel healthy, then understanding your body better can help you be aware of what you're doing well. If you are not content with your current level of health, you can discover some ways to adjust your personal habits and increase your sense of well-being.

As with the Discovery Wheel exercise in Chapter 1, the usefulness of this exercise is determined by your honesty and courage.

PART ONE

To begin, draw a simple outline of your body on a separate piece of paper. You might have positive and negative feelings about various internal and external parts of your body. Label the parts and include a short description of the attributes you like or dislike—for example, straight teeth, fat thighs, clear lungs, double chin, straight posture.

PART TWO

The body you just drew reflects your past health practices. To discover how well you take care of your body, complete the following sentences. Again, if you're concerned about privacy, then do this writing on a separate sheet of paper.

Eating

1. What I know about the way I eat is . . .

_____
_____
_____

2. What I would most like to change about my diet is . . .

_____
_____
_____

3. My eating habits lead me to be . . .

_____
_____
_____

Exercise

1. The way I usually exercise is . . .

_____
_____

2. The last time I did 20 minutes or more of heart/lung (aerobic) exercise was . . .

_____
_____
_____

3. As a result of my physical conditioning, I feel . . .

_____
_____
_____

4. And I look . . .

_____
_____
_____

5. It would be easier for me to work out regularly if I . . .

_____
_____
_____

6. The most important benefit for me in exercising more is . . .

_____
_____
_____

Drug use

1. My history of cigarette smoking is . . .

_____
_____
_____

2. An objective observer would say that my use of alcohol is . . .

_____
_____
_____

3. In the last 10 days, the number of alcoholic drinks I have had is . . .

_____
_____
_____

4. I would describe my use of coffee, colas, and other caffeinated drinks as . . .

_____
_____
_____

5. I have used the following illegal drugs in the past week:

_____
_____
_____

6. I take the following prescription drugs:

_____
_____
_____

7. When it comes to drugs, what I am sometimes concerned about is . . .

_____
_____
_____

Relationships

1. Someone who knows me fairly well would say that my emotional health is . . .

_____
_____
_____

2. The way I look and feel has affected my relationships by . . .

_____
_____
_____

3. My use of drugs or alcohol has been an issue with . . .

_____
_____
_____

4. The best thing I could do for myself and my relationships would be to . . .

_____
_____

Sleep

1. The average number of hours I sleep each night is . . .

_____
_____

2. On weekends I normally sleep . . .

_____
_____

3. I have trouble sleeping when . . .

_____
_____

4. Last night, the quality of my sleep was . . .

_____
_____

5. Overall, the quality of my sleep is usually . . .

_____
_____
_____

Following up

1. In doing this exercise, I discovered that my top three concerns about my health is . . .

_____
_____
_____

2. I could make a big difference in my health by changing some of my habits. Specifically, I intend to . . .

_____
_____
_____

3. I will act on my intention today by . . .

_____
_____
_____

9

Prevent and treat *eating disorders*

Eating disorders affect many students. These disorders involve serious disturbances in eating behavior. Examples are overeating or extreme reduction of food intake, as well as irrational concern about body shape or weight. Women are much more likely to develop these disorders than are men, though cases are on the rise among males.

Bulimia involves cycles of excessive eating and forced purges. A person with this disorder might gorge on a pizza, doughnuts, and ice cream and then force herself to vomit. Or she might compensate for overeating with excessive use of laxatives, enemas, or diuretics.

Anorexia nervosa is a potentially fatal illness marked by self-starvation. People with anorexia may practice extended fasting or eat only one kind of food for weeks at a time.

Binge eating disorder leads to many of the same symptoms as bulimia, without the purging behaviors.

These disorders are not due to a failure of willpower. They are real illnesses in which harmful patterns of eating take on a life of their own.

Eating disorders can lead to many complications, including life-threatening heart conditions and kidney failure. Many people with eating disorders also struggle with depression, substance abuse, and anxiety. They need immediate treatment to stabilize their health. This is usually followed by continuing medical care, counseling, and medication to promote a full recovery.

If you're worried you might have an eating disorder, visit a doctor, campus health service, or local public health clinic. If you see signs of an eating disorder in someone else, express your concern with "I" messages, as explained in Chapter 8: "Creating Positive Relationships."

For more information, contact the National Eating Disorders Association at 1-800-931-2237 or online at www.nationaleatingdisorders.org.

Choose your *fuel*

Food is your primary fuel for body and mind. And even though you've been eating all your life, the demands of higher education are bound to affect the amount of time that you spend on planning and preparing meals.

There have been hundreds of books written about nutrition. One says don't drink milk. Another says the calcium provided by milk is an essential nutrient we need daily. Although such debate seems confusing, take comfort. There is actually wide agreement about how to fuel yourself for health.

Today, federal nutrition guidelines are summarized visually as a *food pyramid*. The idea is to eat more of the foods shown in the bigger sections of the pyramid and less of those in the smaller sections. To see an example and build your personal food pyramid, go online to www.mypyramid.gov.

The various food pyramids agree on several core guidelines:[4]

- Emphasize fruits, vegetables, whole grains, and fat-free or low-fat milk and milk products.

- Include lean meats, poultry, fish, beans, eggs, and nuts.

- Choose foods that are low in saturated fats, trans fats, cholesterol, salt (sodium), and added sugars.

Michael Pollan, a writer for the *New York Times Magazine*, spent several years sorting out the scientific literature on nutrition.[5] He boiled the key guidelines down to seven words in three statements:

- *Eat food*. In other words, choose whole, fresh foods over processed products with a lot of ingredients.

- *Mostly plants*. Fruits, vegetables, and grains are loaded with chemicals that help to prevent disease. Plant-based foods, on the whole, are also lower in calories than foods from animals (meat and dairy products).

- *Not too much*. If you want to manage your weight, then control how much you eat. Notice portion sizes. Pass on snacks, seconds, and desserts—or indulge just occasionally.

Finally, forget diets. *How* you eat can matter more than *what* you eat. If you want to eat less, then eat slowly. Savor each bite. Stop when you're satisfied instead of when you feel full. Use meal times as a chance to relax, reduce stress, and connect with people.

You're One Click Away . . .
from more healthy ways to fuel your body.

Choose to EXERCISE

Exercise promotes weight control and reduces the symptoms of depression. It also helps to prevent heart attack, diabetes, and several forms of cancer.[6] In addition, exercise refreshes your body and your mind. If you're stuck on a math problem or blocked on writing a paper, take an exercise break. Use the following simple ways to include more physical activity in your life.

Stay active throughout the day. Park a little farther from work or school. Walk some extra blocks. Take the stairs instead of the elevator. For an extra workout, climb two stairs at a time. An hour of daily activity is ideal, but do whatever you can.

Adapt to your campus environment. Look for exercise facilities on campus. Search for classes in aerobics, swimming, volleyball, basketball, golf, tennis, and other sports. Intramural sports are another option.

Do what you enjoy. Stay active over the long term with aerobic activities that you enjoy, such as martial arts, kickboxing, yoga, dancing, or rock climbing. Check your school catalog for classes. Find several activities that you enjoy, and rotate them throughout the year. Your main form of activity during winter might be ballroom dancing, riding an exercise bike, or skiing. In summer, you could switch to outdoor sports. Whenever possible, choose weight-bearing activities such as walking, running, or stair climbing.

Get active early. Work out first thing in the morning. Then it's done for the day. Make it part of your daily routine, just like brushing your teeth.

Exercise with other people. Making exercise a social affair can add a fun factor and raise your level of commitment.

Before beginning any vigorous exercise program, consult a health care professional. This is critical if you are overweight, over age 60, in poor condition, or a heavy smoker, or if you have a history of health problems.

You're One Click Away . . .
from more ways to make exercise a regular part of your life.

7 ways to stay healthy
in (almost) no time

The best intentions to stay healthy can go out the window when you have only 20 minutes to eat between classes or when you don't get home from classes until 10 p.m. The more hurried you become, the more important it becomes to take care of yourself. Following are 7 little things you can do to experience maximum health benefits in minimum time:

1. When you're in a hurry, eat vegetarian. There's no meat to thaw or cook. In the time it takes to cook a pot of pasta, you can cut and steam some fresh vegetables.

2. For a quick, nutritious meal, choose cereal. Buy whole grain cereal and add skim milk.

3. Make healthier choices from vending machines. Instead of soda, choose bottled water. Also choose packages of nuts or whole grain crackers instead of candy.

4. Eat more fruit. It's still the world's most portable, nutritious food. For a meal that takes almost no time to prepare, combine fresh fruit with some nuts and whole grain crackers.

5. Switch to whole grain bread. Choosing whole grain over wheat takes no extra time from your schedule. And the whole grain comes packed with more nutrients than white bread.

6. Park farther away from your destination. You'll build some exercise time into your day without having to join a gym.

7. Whenever possible, walk. Walk between classes or while taking a study break. Instead of meeting a friend for a restaurant meal or a movie, go for a walk instead.

From *Student's Guide to Succeeding at Community College*, First Edition. Copyright 2007 Wadsworth, a part of Cengage Learning, Inc. Reproduced by permission. **www.cengage.com/permissions**

9

Choose freedom from *distress*

A little tension before a test, a presentation, or a date is normal. That feeling can keep you alert and boost your energy. The problem comes when tension is persistent and extreme. That's when average levels of stress turn into *distress*.

The number of students in higher education who cope with high levels of stress and other mental health issues is steadily increasing.[7] According to the American College Health Association, 31 percent of college students report that they have felt so depressed that it was difficult to function. Almost half of students say that they've felt overwhelming anxiety, and 60 percent report that they've felt very lonely.[8] Suicide is the second leading cause of death on college campuses.[9]

You can take simple and immediate steps toward freedom from distress. Start with your overall health. Your thoughts and emotions can get scrambled if you go too long feeling hungry or tired. Use the suggestions in this chapter for eating, exercise, and sleep.

Also remember that the suggestions in "Relax—it's just a test" on page 70 can help you manage *any* form of distress. Start with those strategies, then experiment with the following ideas for more freedom from distress.

MAKE CONTACT WITH THE PRESENT MOMENT

If you feel anxious, see whether you can focus your attention on a specific sight, sound, or other sensation that's happening in the present moment. In a classroom, for example, take a few seconds to listen to the sounds of squeaking chairs, the scratching of pencils, the muted coughs. Focus all of your attention on one point—anything other than the flow of thoughts through your head. This is one way to use the Power Process: "Be here now" as a simple and quick stress-buster.

SCAN YOUR BODY

Awareness of physical sensations can be an immediate and effective response to distress. Discover this for yourself by bringing awareness to each area of your body.

To begin, sit comfortably and close your eyes. Focus your attention on the muscles in your feet, and notice whether they are relaxed. Tell the muscles in your feet that they can relax.

Move up to your ankles, and repeat the procedure. Next, go to your calves and thighs and buttocks, telling each group of muscles to relax.

Do the same for your lower back, diaphragm, chest, upper arms, lower arms, fingers, upper back, shoulders, neck, jaw, face, and scalp.

USE GUIDED IMAGERY

This technique can work especially well after a body scan. For example, you might imagine yourself at a beach. Hear the surf rolling in and the seagulls calling to each other. Feel the sun on your face and the hot sand between your toes. Smell the sea breeze. Taste the salty mist from the surf. Notice the ships on the horizon and the rolling sand dunes. Use all of your senses to create a vivid imaginary trip.

Find a place that works for you, and practice getting there. When you become proficient, you can return to it quickly for trips that might last only a few seconds. With practice, you can use this technique even while you are taking a test.

DON'T BELIEVE EVERYTHING YOU THINK

Stress results not from events in our lives but from the way we *think* about those events. One thought that sets us up for misery is *People should always behave in exactly the way I expect.* Another one is *Events should always turn out exactly as I expect.* A more sane option is to dispute such irrational beliefs and replace them with more rational ones: *I can control my own behavior, but not the behavior of others.* And *Some events are beyond my control.* Changing our beliefs can reduce our stress significantly.

Another way to deal with stressful thoughts is to release them altogether. Meditation is a way to do this. While meditating, you simply notice your thoughts as they arise and pass. Instead of reacting to them, you observe them. Eventually, your stream of thinking slows down. You might enter a state of deep relaxation that also yields life-changing insights.

Many religious organizations offer meditation classes. You can also find meditation instruction through health care providers and community education programs.

PRACTICE DETACHMENT

Beyond questioning your thoughts is detaching from them. To *detach* means to step back from something and see it as separate from ourselves. When we detach from an emotion, we no longer identify with it. We no longer say, "*I* am afraid" or "*I* am sad." We say something like "There's fear again" or "I feel sadness right now." Using language such as this offers us a way to step back from our internal experiences and keep them in perspective.

You might find it especially useful to detach from your thoughts with ideas from Acceptance and Commitment Therapy.[10] Take an anxiety-producing thought—such as *I always screw up on tests*—and do any of the following:

- Repeat the thought over and over again out loud until it becomes just a meaningless series of sounds.
- Repeat the thought while using the voice of a cartoon character such as Mickey Mouse or Homer Simpson.
- Rephrase the thought so that you can sing it to the tune of a nursery rhyme or the song "Happy Birthday."
- Preface the thought with "I'm having the thought that . . ." (*I'm having the thought that I always screw up on tests.*)
- Talk back to your mind by saying, "That's an interesting thought, mind; thanks a lot for sharing." Or simply say, "Thanks, mind."

SOLVE PROBLEMS

Although you can't "fix" a bad feeling in the same way that you can fix a machine, you can choose to change a situation associated with that feeling. There might be a problem that needs a solution. You can use feeling bad as your motivation to take action.

Sometimes an intense feeling of sadness, anger, or fear is related to a specific situation in your life. Describe the problem. Then brainstorm solutions, and choose one to implement. Reducing your course load, cutting back on hours at work, getting more financial aid, delegating a task, or taking some other concrete action might solve the problem and help you feel better.

STAY ACTIVE

A related strategy is to do something—*anything* that's constructive, even if it's not a solution to a specific problem. For example, mop the kitchen floor. Clean out your dresser drawers. Iron your shirts. This sounds silly, but it works.

The basic principle is that you can separate emotions from actions. It is appropriate to feel miserable when you do. It's normal to cry and express your feelings. It is also possible to go to class, study, work, eat, and feel miserable at the same time. Unless you have a diagnosable problem with anxiety or depression, you can continue your normal activities until the misery passes.

SHARE WHAT YOU'RE THINKING AND FEELING

There are times when negative thoughts and emotions persist even when you take appropriate action. Tell a family member or friend about your feelings. This is a powerful way to gain perspective. The simple act of describing a problem can sometimes reveal a solution or give you a fresh perspective.

ASK FOR HELP

Student health centers are not just for treating colds, allergies, and flu symptoms. Counselors expect to help students deal with adjustment to campus, changes in mood, academic problems, and drug use disorders. Your tuition helps to pay for health services. It's smart to use them now.

Students with anxiety disorders, clinical depression, bipolar disorder, and other diagnoses might get referred to a psychiatrist or psychologist who works off campus. The referral process can take time, so seek help right away.

You can find resources to promote mental health even if your campus doesn't offer counseling services. First, find a personal doctor—one person who can coordinate all of your health care. This person can refer you to a mental health professional if it seems appropriate.

Second, remember a basic guideline about *when* to seek help: whenever problems with your thinking, moods, or behaviors consistently interfere with your ability to sleep, eat, go to class, work, or create positive relationships.

These two suggestions can also work after you graduate. Promoting mental health is a skill to use for the rest of your life.

You're One Click Away . . .
from more ways to manage distress.

9

Alcohol and other drugs:
The truth

We are a drug-using society. Of course, some of those uses are therapeutic and legal, including taking drugs as prescribed by a doctor.

The problem comes when we turn to drugs as *the* solution to any problem. Are you uncomfortable? Often the first response is "Take something." We live in times when reaching for instant comfort via chemicals is condoned and encouraged. If you're bored, tense, or anxious, you can drink a can of beer, down a glass of wine, or light up a cigarette. If you want to enhance your memory, you can take a "smart drug," which might include stimulants such as caffeine. And these are only the legal options.

COMPARE THE PAYOFF TO THE COST

There is at least a temporary payoff in using alcohol, tobacco, caffeine, cocaine, heroin, and other drugs. The payoff can be relaxation, self-confidence, comfort, excitement, or the ability to pull an all-nighter. At times, the payoff is avoiding rejection or defying authority.

In addition to the payoffs, there are costs. And sometimes these are much greater than the payoff. This is true for people who care about little else except finding and using drugs—friends, school, work, and family be damned.

Some people will stop using a drug when the consequences get serious enough. Other people don't stop. They continue their self-defeating behaviors, no matter the consequences for themselves, their friends, or their families. At that point, the problem goes beyond abuse. It's a disorder, commonly called addiction.

With addiction, the costs can include overdose, infection, and lowered immunity to disease. These can be fatal. Long-term heavy drinking, for example, damages every organ system in the human body. And about 440,000 Americans die annually from the effects of cigarette smoking.[11]

YOU GET TO CHOOSE

Lectures about the reasons for avoiding alcohol and drug abuse and addiction can be pointless. We don't take care of our bodies because someone says we should. We might take care of ourselves when we see that the costs of using alcohol and other drugs outweigh the benefits.

The truth is that getting high can be fun. In our culture, getting high has become synonymous with having a good time. Acknowledging that alcohol, tobacco, and other drugs can be fun infuriates a lot of people. Remember that this acknowledgment is *not* the same as condoning drug use. The point is this: People are more likely to change their relationship to drugs when they're convinced that using them leads to more pain than pleasure over the long run. You choose. It's your body.

The technical term for addiction is *alcohol use disorder* or *substance use disorder*. This disease has many signs, for example:

- Failing to meet major requirements for work or school
- Feeling strong cravings for drugs
- Continued use of drugs even when it leads to physical danger
- Taking drugs in larger doses over longer periods of time
- Persistent failure in reducing or quitting drug use
- Continued drug use despite other harmful consequences

Remember that behaviors such as gambling can also take on a life of their own and overtake commitments to school, work, and family. Fortunately, help is available for all such disorders. Consider the following suggestions.

USE RESPONSIBLY

Show people that you can have a good time without alcohol or other drugs. If you do choose to drink, consume alcohol with food. Pace yourself. Take time between drinks.

Avoid promotions that encourage excess drinking. "Ladies Drink Free" nights are especially dangerous. Women are affected more quickly by alcohol, making them targets for rape. Also stay out of games that encourage people to guzzle. And avoid people who make fun of you for choosing not to drink.

PAY ATTENTION

Whenever you use alcohol or another drug, do so with awareness. Then pay attention to the consequences. Act with deliberate decision rather than out of habit or under pressure from others.

ADMIT PROBLEMS

People with active addictions are a varied group—rich and poor, young and old, successful and unsuccessful. Often these people do have one thing in common: They are masters of denial. They deny that they are unhappy. They deny that they have hurt anyone. They are convinced that they can quit any time they want. They sometimes become so good at hiding the problem from themselves that they die.

TAKE RESPONSIBILITY FOR RECOVERY

Nobody plans to become addicted. If you have pneumonia, you seek treatment and recover without shame. Approach addiction in the same way. You can take responsibility for your recovery without blame or shame.

GET HELP

Two broad options exist. One is the growing self-help movement. The other is formal treatment. People who seek help often combine the two.

Many self-help groups are modeled after Alcoholics Anonymous (AA)—one of the oldest and most successful programs in this category. Groups based on AA principles exist for many other problems as well.

Some people feel uncomfortable with the AA approach. Other resources exist for them, including private therapy and group therapy. Also investigate organizations such as Women for Sobriety, the Secular Organizations for Sobriety, and Rational Recovery. Use whatever works.

Treatment programs are available in almost every community. They might be residential (you live there for weeks or months at a time) or outpatient (you visit several hours a day). Find out where these treatment centers are located by calling a doctor, a mental health professional, or a local hospital. If you don't have insurance, it is usually possible to arrange some other payment program. Cost is no reason to avoid treatment.

GET HELP FOR A FRIEND OR FAMILY MEMBER

You might know someone whose behavior meets the criteria for a drug use disorder. If so, you have every right to express your concern to that person. Wait until the person is clearheaded. Then mention specific incidents. For example: "Last night you drank five beers when we were at my apartment, and then you wanted to drive home. When I offered to call a cab for you instead, you refused." Also be prepared to offer a source of help, such as the phone number of a local treatment center.

You're One Click Away . . .
from more ways to choose your relationship to alcohol and other drugs.

Protect yourself
from sexually transmitted infections

Some common STIs are chlamydia, gonorrhea, and syphilis. Sexual contact can also spread the human papillomavirus (HPV, the most common cause of cervical cancer) and the human immunodeficiency virus (HIV, the virus that causes AIDS). Know how to protect yourself.

STIs can result from vaginal sex, oral sex, anal sex—or any other way that people contact semen, vaginal secretions, and blood. People with a sexually transmitted infection (STI) might feel no symptoms for years and not even discover that they are infected. Without treatment, some of these infections can lead to infertility, cancer, heart disease, or even death.[12]

Most STIs can be cured if treated early. (Herpes and AIDS are important exceptions.) Prevention is better.

Make careful choices about sex.
Abstain from sex, or have sex exclusively with one person who is free of infection and has no other sex partners. These are the only ways to be absolutely safe from STIs.

Make careful choices about drug use.
People are more likely to have unsafe sex when drunk or high. Also remember that sharing needles or other paraphernalia with drug users can spread STIs.

Talk to your partner.
Before you have sex with someone, talk about the risk of STIs. If you are infected, tell your partner.

Talk to your doctor.
See your family doctor or someone at the student health center about STIs. Some methods of contraception, such as using condoms, can also prevent STIs. Also ask about vaccinations for hepatitis B and HPV infection, symptoms of STIs, and when to get screened for STIs.

You're One Click Away . . .
from more ways to prevent STIs and unwanted pregnancy.

9

Addiction—how do I know?

People who have problems with drugs and alcohol can hide this fact from themselves and from others. And any of us can find it hard to admit that a friend or loved one has a problem.

The purpose of this exercise is to give you an objective way to look at your relationship with drugs or alcohol. There are signals that indicate when drug or alcohol use calls for getting treatment. Answer the following questions quickly and honestly with yes, no, or n/a (not applicable). If you are concerned about someone else, rephrase each question using his/her name.

_____ Are you uncomfortable discussing drug abuse?

_____ Are you worried about your own drug or alcohol use?

_____ Are any of your friends worried about your drug or alcohol use?

_____ Have you ever hidden from a friend, spouse, employer, or coworker the fact that you were drinking?

_____ Do you sometimes use alcohol or drugs to escape lows rather than to produce highs?

_____ Have you ever gotten angry when confronted about your use?

_____ Do you brag about how much you consume?

_____ Do you think about or do drugs when you are alone?

_____ Do you store up alcohol, drugs, cigarettes, or caffeine (in coffee or soft drinks) to be sure you won't run out?

_____ Does having a party almost always include alcohol or drugs?

_____ Do you try to control your drinking so that it won't be a problem? ("I drink only beer.")

_____ Do you often explain to other people why you are drinking? ("It's my birthday." "It's a hot day.")

_____ Have you changed friends to accommodate your drinking or drug use?

_____ Has your behavior changed in the last several months? (Grades down? Lack of motivation?)

_____ Do you drink or use drugs to relieve tension?

_____ Do you have medical problems that could be related to drinking or drugs?

_____ Have you ever decided to quit drugs or alcohol and then changed your mind?

_____ Have you had any fights, accidents, or similar incidents related to drinking or drugs in the last year?

_____ Has your use ever caused a problem at home?

_____ Do you envy people who go overboard with alcohol or drugs?

_____ Have you ever told yourself you can quit at any time?

_____ Have you ever been in trouble with the police after or while you were drinking?

_____ Have you ever missed school or work because you had a hangover?

_____ Have you blacked out during or after drinking?

_____ Do you wish that people would mind their own business when it comes to your use of alcohol or drugs?

_____ Is the cost of alcohol or other drugs taxing your budget or resulting in financial stress?

_____ Do you need increasing amounts of the drug to produce the desired effect?

_____ When you stop taking the drug, do you experience withdrawal?

_____ Do you spend a great deal of time obtaining and using alcohol or other drugs?

_____ Have you used alcohol or another drug when it was physically dangerous to do so (such as when driving a car or working with machines)?

_____ Have you been arrested or had other legal problems resulting from the use of a substance?

Now count the number of times you answered yes. If the total is more than one, then consider talking with a professional. This does not necessarily mean that you are addicted. It does point out that alcohol or other drugs could be adversely affecting your life. Talk to someone with training in recovery from chemical dependency. If you filled out this questionnaire about another person and you answered yes two or more times, then your friend might need help. Seek out a counselor and a support group such as Alcoholics Anonymous.

POWER process

Surrender

Life can be magnificent and satisfying. It can also be devastating.

Sometimes there is too much pain or confusion. Problems can be too big and too numerous. Life can bring us to our knees. A broken relationship with a loved one, a sudden diagnosis of cancer, or total frustration with a child's behavior problem can leave us feeling overwhelmed—powerless.

In these troubling situations, the first thing we can do is to admit that we don't have all the resources to handle the problem. No matter how hard we try and no matter what skills we bring to bear, some problems remain out of our control. When this is the case, we can tell the truth: "It's too big and too mean. I can't handle it."

Desperately struggling to control a problem can easily result in the problem's controlling us. Surrender is letting go of being the master in order to avoid becoming the slave.

Many traditions point to the power of surrendering. Western religions speak of surrendering to God. Hindus say surrender to the Self. Members of Alcoholics Anonymous talk about turning their lives over to a Higher Power. Agnostics might suggest surrendering to the dictates of reason or the principles of science. Others might speak of surrendering to their intuition, their inner guide, or their conscience.

Surrendering simply means asking for help. We don't have to go it alone. Other people have faced traumatic problems and survived. We can benefit from their experience.

Surrender is *not* "giving up." This is not a suggestion to quit and do nothing about your problems. You can apply all of your energy and skill to solving a problem—and still surrender at the same time. You can surrender to a toothache even while calling the dentist.

Surrendering means giving up the belief that we control everything. We can stop acting as general manager of the universe. We can open up the support from other people. And that creates a space for something new in our lives.

9

You're One Click Away . . .
from more ways to surrender to big problems and ask for help.

10

Choosing Your Major and Planning Your Career

Give up the myth of "someday"

It's tempting to postpone changes in our lives until we're really feeling "ready" for them—perhaps next week, next month, next year, or some other day that's more convenient. Other people reinforce this notion by telling you that your life will *really* start the day when you.... (Fill in the blank with phrases such as *graduate from college, get married, have kids, get promoted,* or *retire*.)

Agreeing with these statements can condemn us to a life of perpetual waiting. Using this logic, we could wait our whole life to start living.

There's a mistaken idea about planning that adds to the problem. This is the assumption that life works only when you complete your to-do list. Happiness, fulfillment, and satisfaction will come someday in the future, when you achieve your next goal, then the next one, and the one after that.

That doesn't sound like much fun. However, there is another option: You can give up the myth of "someday." This means taking a new attitude toward the future. In fact, one of the best ways to get what you want in the future is to realize that you do not have a future. The only time you have is right now.

The problem with this idea is that some students might think, "No future, huh? Terrific! Party time!" Giving up the myth of "someday," however, is not the same as living only for today and forgetting about tomorrow. Nor is it a call to abandon goals. Goals are useful tools when we use them to direct our actions right now. Goals allow us to live fully in the present.

The idea is to make commitments for the future that change your action in the present. Set a goal that might take years to accomplish—and then enjoy every step along the way. Start now by using this chapter to choose your major, plan your career, find your place in the global economy, and otherwise create the life of your dreams.

Just start doing it today.

You're One Click Away . . .
from more suggestions for choosing what's next in your life.

Discover what YOU WANT from this chapter

The Discovery Wheel on page 2 includes a section titled *Major and Career*. Take some time to go beyond your initial responses to that section. Spend five minutes skimming this chapter. Then complete the following sentences:

When I complete my education, I want to be able to . . .

_____

_____

_____

_____

_____

_____

_____

_____

_____

_____

Some ideas from this chapter that can help me meet that goal are . . .

_____

_____

_____

_____

_____

_____

_____

_____

_____

10

When you see 🖥 *You're One Click Away . . ., remember to go to this book's College Success CourseMate for additional content. And for a summary of this chapter, see the Master Student Review Cards at the end of this book.*

Discovering the skilled person
YOU ALREADY ARE

When meeting with an academic advisor, some students say, "I've just been taking general education and liberal arts courses. I haven't got any marketable skills." Think again.

TWO KINDS OF SKILLS

Few words are as widely misunderstood as *skill*. Defining it carefully can have an immediate and positive impact on your career planning.

One dictionary defines *skill* as "the ability to do something well, usually gained by training or experience." Some skills—such as the ability to speak a second language, repair fiberoptic cables, or do brain surgery—are acquired through formal schooling, on-the-job training, or both. These abilities are called *technical skills*. People with such skills have mastered a specialized body of knowledge needed to do a specific kind of work.

However, there is another category of skills that we develop through experiences both inside and outside the classroom. We may never receive formal training to develop these abilities. Yet they are key to success in the workplace. These are *transferable skills*. Transferable skills help people thrive in any job—no matter what technical skills they have.

Perhaps you've heard someone described this way: "She's really smart and knows what she's doing, but she's got lousy people skills." People skills—such as listening, managing conflict, and problem solving—are prime examples of transferable skills.

SUCCEEDING IN MANY SITUATIONS

Transferable skills are often invisible to us. The problem begins when we assume that a given skill can be used in only one context, such as a particular course or a particular job. Thinking in this way places an artificial limit on our possibilities.

As an alternative, think about the things you routinely do to succeed in school. Analyze your activities to isolate specific skills and how they might apply in other situations.

Consider, for example, the task of writing a research paper. This calls for skills such as these:

- *Planning* by setting goals for completing your outline, first draft, second draft, and final draft.
- *Managing time* to meet your writing goals.
- *Interviewing* people who know a lot about the topic of your paper.
- *Researching* by using the Internet and campus library to discover key facts and ideas to include in your paper.
- *Writing* to present those facts and ideas in an original way.
- *Editing* your drafts for clarity and correctness.

Now consider the kinds of jobs that draw on these skills. For instance, you could transfer your skill at writing papers to a possible career in journalism, technical writing, or advertising copywriting. You could use your editing skills to work in the field of publishing as a magazine or book editor. Interviewing and research skills could help you enter the field of market research. The abilities to plan, manage time, and meet deadlines will help you succeed in all the jobs mentioned so far.

Here's another example. Say that you work part-time as an administrative assistant at a computer dealer that sells a variety of hardware and software. You take phone calls from potential customers, help current customers solve problems using their computers, and attend meetings where your coworkers plan ways to market new products. You are developing skills at *selling, serving customers,* and *working on teams*.

The basic idea is to take a cue from the word *transferable*. Almost any skill you use to succeed in one situation can *transfer* to success in another situation. The concept of transferable skills opens you up to discovering how skilled you already are. Almost everything you do in school can be applied to your career—if you consistently pursue this line of thought. Getting past the I-don't-have-any-skills syndrome means that you can approach job hunting with more confidence. As you uncover these hidden assets, your list of qualifications will grow as if by magic.

You're One Click Away . . .
from more information about the nature of skills.

50 *transferable* skills

There are literally hundreds of transferable skills. To learn more, check out O*Net OnLine, a Web site from the federal government at http://online.onetcenter.org/skills. You'll find tools for discovering your skills and matching them to specific occupations. More information on careers and job hunting is available through CareerOneStop at www.careeronestop.org.

SELF-DISCOVERY AND SELF-MANAGEMENT SKILLS

1. Assessing your current knowledge and skills
2. Seeking out opportunities to acquire new knowledge and skills
3. Choosing and applying learning strategies
4. Showing flexibility by adopting new attitudes and behaviors

For more information about self-discovery skills, review Chapters 1, 2, and 9.

TIME MANAGEMENT SKILLS

5. Scheduling due dates for projects and goals
6. Choosing technology and applying it to goal-related tasks
7. Choosing materials and facilities needed to meet goals
8. Designing other processes, procedures, or systems to meet goals
10. Working independently to meet projects and goals on schedule
9. Planning projects for teams
10. Managing multiple projects at the same time
11. Monitoring progress toward goals

For more information about these skills, review Chapter 3.

READING SKILLS

12. Reading for key ideas and major themes
13. Reading for detail
14. Reading to synthesize information from several sources
15. Reading to find strategies for solving problems or meeting goals

For more information about reading skills, review Chapter 4.

NOTE-TAKING SKILLS

16. Taking notes on material presented verbally, in print, or online
17. Creating graphs and other visuals to summarize and clarify
18. Organizing information in digital and paper forms
19. Researching information online or in the library
20. Gathering data through research or primary sources

For more information about note-taking skills, review Chapter 5.

TEST-TAKING AND RELATED SKILLS

21. Using test results and other assessments to improve performance
22. Working cooperatively in study groups and project teams
23. Managing stress
24. Applying scientific findings and methods to solve problems
25. Using mathematics to do basic computations and solve problems

For more information about this group of skills, review Chapters 6 and 8.

THINKING SKILLS

26. Thinking to create new ideas, products, or services
27. Thinking to evaluate and improve ideas, products, or services
28. Evaluating material presented verbally, in print, or online
29. Choosing appropriate strategies for making decisions
30. Choosing ethical behaviors
31. Diagnosing the sources of problems
32. Stating problems accurately and generating solutions
33. Weighing benefits and costs of potential solutions
34. Choosing and implementing solutions

For more information about thinking skills, review Chapter 7.

COMMUNICATION SKILLS

35. Assigning and delegating tasks
36. Coaching, consulting, and counseling
37. Editing publications
38. Giving people feedback about the quality of their performance
39. Interpreting and responding to nonverbal messages
40. Interviewing people
41. Leading meetings and project teams
42. Listening fully (without judgment or distraction)
43. Preventing and resolving conflicts
44. Responding to complaints
45. Speaking to diverse audiences
46. Writing and editing

For more information about communication skills, review Chapter 8.

MONEY SKILLS

47. Monitoring income and expenses
48. Raising funds
49. Decreasing expenses
50. Estimating costs and preparing budgets

For more information about money skills, review Chapter 3.

 You're One Click Away . . .
from more examples of transferable skills.

✓ Commit to ACTION

Inventory your skills

This exercise is about discovering your skills. Before you begin, gather 100 blank 3 × 5 cards. Allow about one hour to complete the following steps.

Step 1

Recall your activities during the past week or month. To refresh your memory, review your responses to Commit to Action: "Discover where your time goes" on page 24. (You might even benefit from doing that exercise again.) Write down as many activities as you can, listing each one on a separate 3 × 5 card. Include work-related activities, school activities, and hobbies.

In addition to daily activities, recall and write down any rewards you've received or recognition of your achievements. Examples include scholarship awards, athletic awards, and recognitions for volunteer work.

Spend 20 minutes on this step, listing all of the activities, rewards, and recognitions you can recall.

Step 2

Next, look over your activity cards. Then take another 20 minutes to list any specialized knowledge or procedures needed to complete those activities or gain those awards and recognitions. These are your *technical skills*. For example, tutoring a French class requires a working knowledge of that language. (See "Discovering the skilled person you already are" on page 118 for more on technical skills.) You might be able to list several technical skills for any one activity, recognition, or reward.

Write each technical skill on a separate card, and label it "technical skill."

Step 3

Go over your activity cards one more time. Now look for examples of *transferable skills*—those that could be applied to a variety of jobs. For instance, giving a speech or working as a salesperson in a computer store requires the ability to persuade people. You can use this ability in just about any career you choose. Write each of your transferable skills on a separate card labeled "transferable skill."

Congratulations—you now have a detailed picture of your current skills. Take a few minutes to reflect on the experience of creating that picture. Complete the following sentences:

While listing my skills, I was surprised to discover that . . .

_____

_____

_____

_____

_____

_____

New skills that I intend to develop include . . .

_____

_____

_____

_____

_____

_____

To develop those skills, I will take specific steps, including . . .

_____

_____

_____

_____

Keep your lists of technical and transferable skills on hand when planning your career, choosing your major, writing your résumé, and preparing for job interviews. As you gain new skills, be sure to add them to your lists.

 **You're One Click Away . . .**
from more ways to identify your skills.

Four ways to choose your major

One decision that concerns many students in higher education is the choice of an academic major. Here is an opportunity to apply your skills at critical thinking, decision making, and problem solving. Use the following four suggestions as a guide.

1. DISCOVER OPTIONS

Follow the fun. Perhaps you look forward to attending one of your classes and even like completing the assignments. This is a clue to your choice of major. See whether you can find lasting patterns in the subjects and extracurricular activities that you've enjoyed over the years. Look for a major that allows you to continue and expand on these experiences.

Also brainstorm answers to the following questions, putting your ideas in writing.

- What do you enjoy doing most with your unscheduled time?
- Imagine that you're at a party and having a fascinating conversation. What is this conversation about?
- What Websites do you frequently visit or have bookmarked in a Web browser?
- What kind of problems do you enjoy solving—those that involve people? Products? Ideas?
- What interests are revealed by your choices of reading material, television shows, and other entertainment?
- What would an ideal day look like for you? Describe where you'd live, who would be with you, and what you'd do throughout the day. Do any of these visions suggest a possible major?

Questions like these are not frivolous. They can uncover a "fun factor" that energizes you to finish the work of completing a major.

Consider ability. In choosing a major, ability counts as much as interest. Einstein enjoyed playing the violin, but his love of music didn't override his choice of a physics career. In addition to considering what you enjoy, think about times and places when you excelled. List the courses that you "aced," the work assignments that you mastered, and the hobbies that led to rewards or recognition. Let your choice of a major reflect a discovery of your passions *and* potentials.

Use formal techniques for self-discovery. Consider questionnaires that are designed to correlate your interests with specific majors. Examples include the Strong Interest Inventory and the Self-Directed Search. Your academic advisor or someone at your school's career-planning office can give you more details.

Remember that questionnaires can help you gain self-knowledge. However, what you *do* with that knowledge is entirely up to you. No one else can choose your major for you.

Link to long-term goals. Your choice of a major might fall into place once you determine what you want in life. Before you choose a major, back up to a bigger picture. List your core values, such as contributing to society, achieving financial security and professional recognition, enjoying good health, or making time for fun. Also write down specific goals that you want to accomplish in 5 years, 10 years, or even 50 years from today.

Many students find the prospect of getting what they want in life justifies all of the time, money, and day-to-day effort invested in going to school. Having a major gives you a powerful incentive for attending classes, taking part in discussions, reading textbooks, writing papers, and completing other assignments. When you see a clear connection between finishing school and creating the life of your dreams, the daily tasks of higher education become charged with meaning.

Ask other people. Key people in your life might have valuable suggestions about your choice of major. Ask for their ideas and listen with an open mind.

At the same time, release yourself from any pressure to choose a major or career that fails to interest you. If you make a choice based solely on the expectations of other people, you could end up with a major or even a career you don't enjoy.

Gather information. Check your school's catalog or Web site for a list of available majors. Here is a gold mine of information. Take a quick glance and highlight all the majors that interest you. Then talk to students who have declared them.

Also read descriptions of courses required for these majors. Chat with instructors who teach courses in these areas and ask for

10

copies of their class syllabi. Go the bookstore and browse required texts.

Based on all this information, write a list of prospective majors. Discuss them with an academic advisor and someone at your school's career-planning center.

Invent a major. When choosing a major, you do not need to limit yourself to those listed in your school catalog. Many schools now have flexible programs that allow for independent study. Through such programs you might be able to combine two existing majors or invent an entirely new one of your own.

Consider a complementary minor. You can add flexibility to your academic program by choosing a minor to complement or contrast with your major. The student who wants to be a politician could opt for a minor in English; all of those courses in composition can help in writing speeches. Or the student with a major in psychology might choose a minor in business administration, with the idea of managing a counseling service someday. An effective choice of a minor can expand your skills and career options.

Think critically about the link between your major and your career. Your career goals might largely dictate your choice of a major. On the other hand, you might be able to pursue a rewarding career by choosing among *several* different majors. Remember that many people work happily in jobs with little relationship to their major.

2. MAKE A TRIAL CHOICE

At many schools, declaring a major offers some benefits. For example, you might get priority when registering for certain classes and qualify for special scholarships or grants.

Don't delay such benefits. Even if you feel undecided today, you probably have many ideas about what your major will be. Choose one soon.

Do a simple experiment. Pretend that you have to choose a major today. Based on the options that you've already discovered, write down the first three ideas that come to mind. Review the list for a few minutes and then just choose one.

Hold onto your list. It reflects your current intuition or "gut feelings," and it may come in handy during the next step. This step might confirm your trial choice of major—or return you to one of the other majors that you had originally listed.

3. EVALUATE YOUR TRIAL CHOICE

When you've made a trial choice of major, take on the role of a scientist. Treat your choice as a hypothesis and then design a series of experiments to evaluate and test it. For example, you can try the following suggestions:

- Schedule office meetings with instructors who teach courses in the major. Ask about required course work and career options in the field.
- Discuss your trial choice with an academic advisor or career counselor.
- Enroll in a course related to your possible major. Remember that introductory courses might not give you a realistic picture of the workloads involved in advanced courses. Also, you might not be able to register for certain courses until you've actually declared a related major.
- Find a volunteer experience, internship, part-time job, or service-learning project related to the major.
- Interview students who have declared the same major. Ask them in detail about their experiences and suggestions for success.
- Interview someone who works in a field related to the major.
- Think about whether you can complete your major given the amount of time and money that you plan to invest in higher education.
- Consider whether declaring this major would require a transfer to another program or even another school.

If these factors confirm your choice of major, celebrate that fact. If they result in choosing a new major, celebrate that outcome as well.

Also remember that higher education represents a safe place to test your choice of major. As you sort through your options, help is always available from administrators, instructors, advisors, and peers.

4. CHOOSE AGAIN

Keep your trial choice of a major in perspective. There is no single "correct" choice. Your unique collection of skills is likely to provide the basis for majoring in several fields.

Odds are that you'll change your major at least once—and that you'll change careers several times during your life. One benefit of higher education is mobility. You can gain skills and knowledge that help you move into a new major or career field at any time.

Viewing a major as a one-time choice that determines your entire future can raise your stress levels. Instead, look at choosing a major as the start of a continuing path that involves discovery, intention, and passionate action, a decision that evolves during the rest of your life.

 You're One Click Away . . .
from more ways to choose your major.

Commit to ACTION

Declare your major today

Pretend that you are required to choose a major today. Of course, your choice is not permanent. You can change it in the future. The purpose of this exercise is simply to begin a process that will lead to declaring an official major.

1. To begin, review your responses to Commit to Action: "Inventory your skills" on page 120.

2. Next, look at your school's catalog (print or online) for a list of majors. Print out this list or make a copy of it.

Based on knowledge of your skills and your ideas about your future career, cross out all of the majors that do not interest you. You will probably eliminate well over half the list.

From the remaining majors on the list, circle those that you're willing to consider.

Now, scan the majors that you circled and look for those that interest you the most. See whether you can narrow your choices down to five. List those majors here.

_____

_____

_____

_____

_____

_____

_____

_____

_____

_____

_____

_____

_____

Write an asterisk next to the major that interests you most right now. *This is your trial choice of major.*

Don't stop there. Now, move into action. Review the article "Four ways to choose your major" on page 121. Then list the suggestions from that article that you will definitely use. List those suggestions below, including at least one action that you will take within the next 24 hours.

I will . . .

_____

_____

_____

_____

_____

_____

_____

_____

_____

_____

_____

_____

_____

10

Create your *career*

There's an old saying: "If you enjoy what you do, you'll never work another day in your life." A satisfying and lucrative career is often the goal of education. If you clearly define your career goals and your strategy for reaching them, then you can plan your education effectively.

Career planning involves continuous exploration. There are dozens of effective paths to take. Begin now with the following ideas.

YOU ALREADY KNOW A LOT ABOUT YOUR CAREER PLAN

When people go to school to gain skills, they often start discovering things that they don't know. Career planning is different. You can begin by realizing how much you know right now.

In fact, you've already made many decisions about your career. This is true for young people who say, "I don't have any idea what

I want to be when I grow up." It's also true for midlife career changers.

Consider the student who can't decide whether she wants to be a cost accountant or a tax accountant and then jumps to the conclusion that she is totally lost when it comes to career planning. Or take the student who doesn't know whether he wants to be a veterinary assistant or a nurse.

These people forget that they already know a lot about their career choices.

The person who is debating tax accounting versus cost accounting already knows that she doesn't want to be a doctor, playwright, or taxicab driver. She also knows that she likes working with numbers and balancing books.

The person who is choosing between veterinary assistance and nursing has already ruled out becoming a lawyer, computer programmer, or teacher. He just doesn't know yet whether he has the right bedside manner for horses or for people.

Such people have already narrowed their list of career choices to a number of jobs in the same field—jobs that draw on the same core skills. In general, they already know what they want to be when they grow up.

Demonstrate this for yourself. Find a long list of occupations. (One source is *The Dictionary of Occupational Titles,* a government publication available at many libraries and online.) Using a stack of 3×5 cards, write down randomly selected job titles, one title per card. Then sort through the cards and divide them into two piles. Label one pile "Careers I've Definitely Ruled Out for Now." Label the other pile "Careers I'm Willing to Consider."

You might go through a stack of 100 such cards and end up with 95 in the "definitely ruled out" pile and five in the "willing to consider" pile. This demonstrates that you already have many ideas about the career you want.

YOUR CAREER IS A CHOICE, NOT A DISCOVERY

Many people approach career planning as if they were panning for gold. They keep sifting through dirt, clearing away dust, and throwing out rocks. They are hoping to strike it rich and discover the perfect career.

Other people believe that they'll wake up one morning, see the heavens part, and suddenly know what they're supposed to do. Many of them are still waiting for that magical day to dawn.

We can approach career planning in a different way. Instead of seeing a career as something we discover, we can see it as something we choose. We don't find the right career. We create it.

There's a big difference between these two approaches. Thinking that there's only one "correct" choice for your career can lead to a lot of anxiety: "Did I discover the right one?" "What if I made a mistake?"

Viewing your career as your creation helps you relax. Instead of anguishing over finding the right career, you can stay open to possibilities. You can choose one career today, knowing that you can choose again later.

Suppose that you've narrowed your list of possible careers to five, and you're still unsure. Then just choose one. Any one. Many people will have five careers in a lifetime anyway. You might be able to pursue all five of your careers, and you can do any one of them first. The important thing is to choose.

One caution is in order. Choosing your career is not something to do in an information vacuum. Rather, choose after you've done a lot of research. That includes research into yourself—your skills and interests—and a thorough knowledge of what careers are available.

YOU'VE GOT A WORLD OF CHOICES

Our society offers a limitless array of careers. You no longer have to confine yourself to a handful of traditional categories, such as business, education, government, or manufacturing. People are constantly creating new products and services to meet new demands. The number of job titles is expanding so rapidly that we can barely keep track of them.

For instance, there are people who work as *ritual consultants*, helping people to plan weddings, anniversaries, graduations, and other ceremonies. *Auto brokers* visit dealers, shop around, and buy a car for you. *Professional organizers* walk into your home or office and advise you on managing workflow and organizing your space. *Pet psychologists* help you raise a happy and healthy animal. *Life coaches* assist you in setting and achieving goals.

In addition to choosing the *content* of your career, you have many options for the *context* in which you work. You can work full-time. You can work part-time. You can commute to a cubicle in a major corporation. Or you can work at home and take the one-minute commute from your bedroom to your desk. You can join a thriving business—or create one of your own.

PLAN BY NAMING NAMES

One key to making your career plan real and to ensuring that you can act on it is naming. Go back over your plan to see whether you can include specific names whenever they're called for.

Name your job.
Take the skills you enjoy using and find out which jobs use them. What are those jobs called? List them. Note that one job might have different names.

Name your company.
Name the agency or organization you want to work for. If you want to be self-employed or start your own business, then name the product or service you'd sell.

Name your contacts.
Take the list of organizations you just compiled. Which people in these organizations are responsible for hiring? List those people and contact them directly. If you choose self-employment, list the names of possible customers or clients.

Name more contacts.
Expand your list of contacts by brainstorming with your family and friends. Come up with a list of names—anyone who can help you with career planning and job hunting. Write each of these names on a 3 × 5 card or Rolodex card. Or use a contact manager on a computer.

Name your location.
Ask whether your career choices are consistent with your preferences about where to live and work. For example, someone who wants to make a living as a studio musician might consider living in a large city such as New York or Toronto. This contrasts with the freelance graphic artist who conducts his business mainly by phone and e-mail. He might be able to live anywhere and still pursue his career.

Name your career goal for others to hear.
Develop a "pitch"—a short statement of your career goal that you can easily share with your contacts. For example: "After I graduate, I plan to work in the travel business. I'm looking for an internship in an international travel agency for next summer. Do you know of any agencies that take interns?" Consider everyone you meet a potential member of your job network, and be prepared to talk about what you do.

Note: Career planning services at your school can help with all of the above tasks. Make an appointment to see someone at that office right away.

TEST YOUR CHOICE—AND BE WILLING TO CHANGE

On the basis of all the thinking you've done, make a trial career choice. Then look for experiences that can help you evaluate that choice. Here are some examples of actions you can take:

- Contact people who are actually doing the job you're researching and ask them a lot of questions about what it's like (an *information interview*).
- Choose an internship or volunteer position in a field that interests you.
- Get a part-time or summer job in your career field.
- If you enjoy such experiences, then you've probably made a wise career choice. The people you met might be sources of recommendations, referrals, and employment in the future. If you did *not* enjoy your experiences, then celebrate what you learned about yourself. Now you're free to refine your initial career choice or go in a new direction.

Remember that career plans are made to be changed and refined as you gain new information about yourself and the world. If your present career no longer feels right, you can choose again—no matter what stage of life you're in. The process is the same, whether you're choosing your first career or your fifth.

10

You're One Click Away . . .
from more career planning strategies.

Commit to ACTION

Plan your career now

Write your career plan. Now. That's right—*now.* Get started with the process of career planning, even if you're not sure where to begin.

Your response to this exercise could be just a rough draft of your plan, which you can revise and rewrite many times. The point is to start a conversation about your career choice—and to get your ideas in writing.

The format of your plan is up to you. You could include many details, such as the next job title you'd like to have, the courses required for your major, and other training that you want to complete. You could list the names of companies to research and people that could hire you. You could also include target dates to complete each of these tasks.

Another option is to represent your plan visually. Consider using charts, timelines, maps, or drawings. You can generate these by hand or with computer software.

To prime your thinking, complete the following sentences. Use the space below and continue on additional paper as needed.

The skills I most enjoy using include . . .

_____

_____

_____

_____

_____

Careers that require these skills include . . .

_____

_____

_____

_____

_____

Of those careers, the one that interests me most right now is . . .

_____

_____

_____

_____

_____

_____

_____

The educational and work experiences that would help me prepare for this career include . . .

_____

_____

_____

_____

_____

_____

The immediate steps I will take to pursue this career are . . .

_____

_____

_____

_____

_____

_____

Finding your place in the new *world of work*

One generation ago, only factory workers worried about automation—being laid off and replaced by machines. Today, employees in a variety of fields might fear losing their jobs to computer-driven robots or to workers across the globe who will do the same job for a fraction of the wages.

You are entering a global economy. Your toughest competitors for a new job might be people from India or China with technical skills and a blazing fast Internet connection.

Employers can now hire from a global workforce. Project teams in the future will include people from several nations who connect via e-mail, cell phones, teleconferencing, and digital devices that have yet to be invented.

You can thrive in this global economy. It will take foresight and a willingness to learn, along with the following strategies.

Complete your education.

According to *Tough Choices or Tough Times: The Report of the New Commission on the Skills of the American Workforce,* the United States will remain an economic powerhouse only if its citizens are educated to do creative work—research, development, design, marketing, sales, and management. Careers in these areas are the least likely to be outsourced.[1]

The authors of *Tough Choices* also note that people with computer skills and strong backgrounds in mathematics and science will have key tools to succeed in the new global economy. They will also need to work with abstract ideas, think creatively, learn quickly, write well, develop new products, and work on culturally diverse project teams. Higher education can help you develop these skills.

Create a long-term career plan.

When planning your career, look beyond your next job. Think in terms of a career *path*. Discover opportunities for advancement and innovation over the long term.

If you're a computer programmer, for example, think about what you could do beyond writing code—perhaps by becoming a systems analyst or software engineer.

If you're a musician, find out how you could use the Internet to promote your band, book gigs, and distribute recordings.

If you're a stockbroker, plan to offer more than advice about buying and selling. Help your clients plan their retirement and fund their children's college education as well.

No matter what your plan, consider gaining sales and marketing skills. Every organization depends on people who can bring in new customers and clients. If you can attract new sources of revenue, you'll be harder to replace.

Develop two key sets of skills.

In *The New Division of Labor: How Computers Are Creating the Next Job Market,* Frank Levy and Richard J. Murnane describe two sets of skills that will not be taken over by robots or computers.[2]

First is *expert thinking.* This is the ability to work with problems that cannot be solved simply by applying rules. The doctor who successfully treats a person with a rare set of symptoms offers an example of expert thinking. So does the mechanic who repairs an engine defect that the computer diagnostics missed.

Second is *complex communication*—the ability to find information, explain it to other people, and persuade them how to use it. An example is the engineer who convinces his colleagues that his design for a disk drive filter will outstrip the competition and reduce production costs. Complex communication is essential to education, sales, marketing, and management.

Even in a high-tech world, there will always be a need for the human touch. Learn to lead meetings, guide project teams, mentor people, spot new talent, and create long-term business relationships. Use creative thinking to develop new products and services, reduce expenses, save energy, and attract new customers and clients. Also use critical thinking skills to turn your ideas into reality. You'll offer employers something that they cannot get from a software package, robot, or any other source.

 You're One Click Away . . .
from more strategies for succeeding in a global economy.

10

Examine beliefs about careers and jobs

Belief #1: *The best way to plan a career is to enter a field that's in demand.*

This statement sounds reasonable. However, you might find it practical to choose a career that's not in demand right now. Even in careers that are highly competitive, job openings often exist for qualified people who are passionate about the field. Also, jobs that are "hot" right now might be "cool" by the time you complete your education. In a constantly changing job market, your own interests and values could guide you as reliably as current trends.

Belief #2: *The best way to find a job is through "want ads" and online job listings.*

There's a problem with these job-hunting strategies: *Many job openings are not advertised.* According to Richard Bolles, author of *What Color Is Your Parachute? A Practical Manual for Job-Hunters and Career-Changers,* employers turn to help wanted listings, résumés, and employment agencies only as a last resort. When jobs open up, they prefer instead to hire people they know— or people who walk through the door and prove that they're excellent candidates for available jobs.[3]

Now, based on the above examples, do some critical thinking of your own. Evaluate each of the following beliefs, stating whether you agree with it. Also provide some reasons for your agreement or disagreement.

Belief #3: *Writing a career plan now is a waste of time. I'll just have to change it later.*

_____

_____

_____

_____

_____

Belief #4: *Writing a résumé is a waste of time until you're actually ready to hunt for a job.*

_____

_____

_____

_____

_____

_____

_____

_____

_____

_____

_____

_____

_____

_____

_____

_____

_____

You're One Click Away . . .
from strategies for successful job hunting, including résumé writing and job interviewing.

The Discovery Wheel, *reloaded*

The purpose of this book is to give you the opportunity to change your behaviors. This exercise gives you a chance to see what behaviors you have changed on your journey toward becoming a master student. Answer each question quickly and honestly. Record your results on the Discovery Wheel that follows, and then compare it with the one you completed in Chapter 1.

As you complete this self-evaluation, keep in mind that *your scores might be lower here than on your earlier Discovery Wheel.* That's okay. Lower scores might result from increased self-awareness, honesty, and other valuable assets.

As you did with the earlier Discovery Wheel, read the following statements and give yourself points for each one. Use the point system described below. Then add up your point total for each category and shade the Discovery Wheel on page 130 to the appropriate level.

5 points
This statement is always or almost always true of me.

4 points
This statement is often true of me.

3 points
This statement is true of me about half the time.

2 points
This statement is seldom true of me.

1 points
This statement is never or almost never true of me.

1. _____ I can clearly state my overall purpose in life.
2. _____ I can explain how school relates to what I plan to do after I graduate.
3. _____ I capture key insights in writing and clarify exactly how I intend to act on them.
4. _____ I am skilled at making transitions.
5. _____ I seek out and use resources to support my success.

_____ Total score (1) *Purpose*

1. _____ I enjoy learning.
2. _____ I make a habit of assessing my personal strengths and areas for improvement.
3. _____ I monitor my understanding of a topic and change learning strategies if I get confused.

4. _____ I use my knowledge of various learning styles to support my success in school.
5. _____ I am open to different points of view on almost any topic.

_____ Total score (2) *Learning Styles*

1. _____ I can clearly describe what I want to experience in major areas of my life, including career, relationships, financial well-being, and health.
2. _____ I set goals and periodically review them.
3. _____ I plan each day and often accomplish what I plan.
4. _____ I will have enough money to complete my education.
5. _____ I monitor my income, keep track of my expenses, and live within my means.

_____ Total score (3) *Time and Money*

1. _____ I ask myself questions about the material that I am reading.
2. _____ I preview and review reading assignments.
3. _____ I relate what I read to my life.
4. _____ I select strategies to fit the type of material I'm reading.
5. _____ When I don't understand what I'm reading, I note my questions and find answers.

_____ Total score (4) *Reading*

1. _____ When I am in class, I focus my attention.
2. _____ I take notes in class.
3. _____ I can explain various methods for taking notes, and I choose those that work best for me.
4. _____ I distinguish key points from supporting examples.
5. _____ I put important concepts into my own words.

_____ Total score (5) *Notes*

1. _____ The way that I talk about my value as a person is independent of my grades.
2. _____ I often succeed at predicting test questions.
3. _____ I review for tests throughout the term.
4. _____ I manage my time during tests.
5. _____ I use techniques to remember key facts and ideas.

_____ Total score (6) *Memory and Tests*

1. _____ I use brainstorming to generate solutions to problems.
2. _____ I can detect common errors in logic and gaps in evidence.
3. _____ When researching, I find relevant facts and properly credit their sources.
4. _____ I edit my writing for clarity, accuracy, and coherence.
5. _____ I prepare and deliver effective presentations.

_____ Total score (7) *Thinking and Communicating*

10

1. _____ Other people tell me that I am a good listener.
2. _____ I communicate my upsets without blaming others.
3. _____ I build rewarding relationships with people from other backgrounds.
4. _____ I effectively resolve conflict.
5. _____ I participate effectively in teams and take on leadership roles.

_____ Total score (8) *Relationships*

1. _____ I have enough energy to study, attend classes, and enjoy other areas of my life.
2. _____The way I eat supports my long-term health.
3. _____ I exercise regularly.
4. _____ I can cope effectively with stress.
5. _____ I am in control of any alcohol or other drugs I put into my body.

_____ Total score (9) *Health*

1. _____ I have a detailed list of my skills.
2. _____ I have a written career plan and update it regularly.
3. _____ I use the career-planning services offered by my school.
4. _____ I participate in internships, extracurricular activities, information interviews, and on-the-job experiences to test and refine my career plan.
5. _____ I have declared a major related to my interests, skills, and core values.

_____ Total score (10) *Major and Career*

Using the total score from each category, shade in each section of the blank Discovery Wheel. If you want, use different colors. For example, you could use green for areas you want to work on.

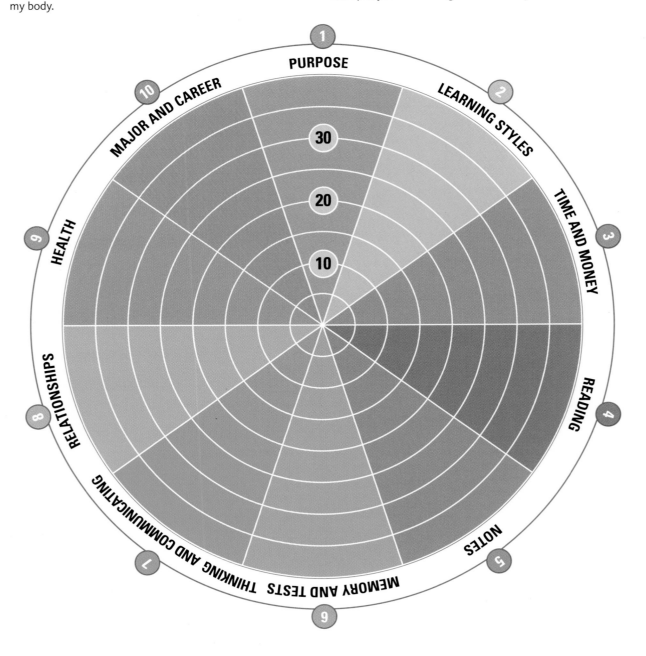

REFLECT ON YOUR DISCOVERY WHEEL

Take this opportunity to review both of the Discovery Wheels you completed in this book. Write your scores from each section of the Discovery Wheel from Chapter 1 in the chart below. Then add your scores for each section of the Discovery Wheel that you just completed.

	Chapter 1	Chapter 10
Purpose		
Learning Styles		
Time and Money		
Reading		
Notes		
Memory and Tests		
Thinking and Communicating		
Relationships		
Health		
Major and Career		

Finally, summarize your insights from doing the Discovery Wheels. Then declare how you will use these insights to promote your continued success.

Comparing the Discovery Wheel in this chapter with the Discovery Wheel in Chapter 1, I discovered that I . . .

_____

_____

_____

_____

_____

_____

_____

_____

_____

_____

In the next six months, I intend to review the following articles from this book for additional suggestions I could use:

_____

_____

_____

_____

_____

_____

_____

_____

_____

_____

_____

_____

_____

_____

_____

_____

_____

_____

_____

_____

10

You're One Click Away . . .
from an online version of this exercise.

Commit to ACTION

Create your future with a lifeline

On a large sheet of paper, draw a horizontal line. This line will represent your entire lifetime.

Now add key events in your life to this line in chronological order. Focus on key events that have already occurred in your life. Examples are your birth date, your first day at school, the date of your graduation from high school, and the date that you enrolled in higher education. Plot each of these events on a separate point on your lifeline. Label each point with a date.

Now extend your lifeline into the future. Write down key events and outcomes that you *want* to occur in the future. Think about the events you'd like to experience 1 year, 3 years, 5 years, and 10 or more years from now. Examples might include graduation from school, career milestones, major trips you'd like to take, and retirement. Again, plot these events as points on your lifeline, and add a projected date for each one.

As you create this map of your possible future, work quickly in the spirit of a brainstorm. Choose events that align with your core values. Also remember that this plan for your life can be revised at any time.

Afterward, take a few minutes to reflect on your lifeline. Complete the following sentences:

Discovery

In creating my lifeline, I discovered that the key things I want to create in my future include . . .

_____

_____

_____

_____

_____

_____

_____

_____

_____

Intention

The next key event on my lifeline that I definitely intend to create is . . .

_____

_____

_____

_____

_____

_____

_____

_____

_____

_____

_____

Action

The actions that I will take to create this event include . . .

_____

_____

_____

_____

_____

_____

_____

_____

_____

_____

_____

Note: You can write Discovery, Intention, and Action Statements for any event or outcome listed on your lifeline.

You're One Click Away . . .
from doing this exercise online.

I create it all

This power process is about the difference between two distinct positions in life: being a victim and being responsible.

Consider a student who flunks a test. "Another F!" the student says. "That teacher couldn't teach her way out of a wet paper bag. How could I read with a houseful of kids making noise all the time? And then later some friends came over and wanted to hang out, and then we ordered a pizza, and then. . . ."

The problem with this viewpoint is that it's all about making excuses. The student is robbing himself of the power to get any grade other than an F. He's giving all of his power to a bad teacher, noisy children, and friends. This is being a victim.

Instead, the student could react like this: "Another F! Well, hmmm . . . . How did I choose this F? What did I do to create it? Well, I didn't review my notes after class. That might have done it." Or "I studied in the same room with my children while they watched TV. Then I partied with my friends the night before the test. Well, that probably helped me fulfill some of the requirements for getting an F." This is being responsible.

See whether you can apply this example to some of the circumstances in your life. Accidents happen. There are events that you cannot predict or control. Sometimes you might feel like a victim. But if you're willing to look, you'll find that other events followed from choices that you made. You were responsible.

Responsibility is "response-ability"—the ability to choose a response. When faced with any circumstance—even one that you do not control—you can choose what you say next and what you do next. This does not mean that you have divine powers. It simply means that you have a choice.

Throughout history, people have used this Power Process, even if they didn't call it by the same name. Viktor Frankl, a psychiatrist and a survivor of Nazi concentration camps, was one. He created courage and dignity out of horror and humiliation. Reflecting on his experiences at Auschwitz, he wrote, "Everything can be taken from a man but one thing: the last of the human freedoms—to choose one's own attitude in any given set of circumstances, to choose one's own way."[4]

Right now, thousands of people are living productive lives and creating positive experiences out of challenging events. These include chronic illnesses, physical disabilities, poverty, abuse, and neglect.

Whenever you feel like a victim, remember "I create it all." It's simply a tool for creative thinking. Use it whenever you can. When you do, you will instantly open up a world of choices. You will create new options for your major, your career, and every other area of your life. You will give yourself power.

You're One Click Away . . .
from more ways to master self-responsibility.

10

Endnotes

CHAPTER 1

1. Matthew Landrus, *Treasures of Leonardo Da Vinci,* New York, HarperCollins, 2006.

CHAPTER 2

1. David A. Kolb, *Experiential Learning: Experience as the Source of Learning and Development,* Englewood Cliffs, NJ: Prentice-Hall, 1984.
2. Howard Gardner, Frames of Mind: The Theory of Multiple Intelligences, New York: Basic Books, 1993.

CHAPTER 3

1. Jane B. Burka and Lenora R. Yuen, *Procrastination: Why You Do It, What to Do About It,* Reading, MA, Addison-Wesley, 1983.

CHAPTER 5

1. Walter Pauk and Ross J. Q. Owens, How to Study in College, 10th ed., Florence, KY, Cengage, 2011.
2. Joseph Novak and D. Bob Gowin, *Learning How to Learn,* New York, Cambridge University Press, 1984.

CHAPTER 6

1. Theodore Cheney, *Getting the Words Right: How to Revise, Edit and Rewrite,* Cincinnati, OH, Writer's Digest, 1983.
2. Alzheimer's Association, "Brain Health," 2009, http://www.alz.org/brainhealth/overview.asp (accessed January 27, 2010).
3. This article incorporates detailed suggestions from reviewer Frank Baker.

CHAPTER 7

1. Robert Manning, "Hemingway in Cuba," *Atlantic Monthly,* August 1965, http://www.theatlantic.com/issues/65aug/6508manning.htm (accessed January 30, 2010).
2. Arthur L. Costa and Bena Kallick, "Habit Is a Cable . . . : Quotations to Extend and Illuminate Habits of Mind," June 6, 2003, http://www.habits-of-mind.net (accessed April 22, 2010).
3. M. T. Motley, *Overcoming Your Fear of Public Speaking: A Proven Method,* New York: Houghton Mifflin, 1998.

CHAPTER 8

1. Maia Szalavitz, "Race and the Genome," Howard University Human Genome Center, March 2, 2001, http://www.genomecenter.howard.edu/article.htm (accessed April 14, 2010).
2. Frank LaFasto, "The Zen of Brilliant Teams," Center for Association Leadership, July 2002, www.asaecenter.org/PublicationsResources/articledetail.cfm?ItemNumber=13295 (accessed March 17, 2010).
3. Anna B. Adams, D. Christopher Kayes and David A. Kolb, "Experiential learning in teams," Experience-Based Learning Systems, 2004, http://www.learningfromexperience.com/images/uploads/experiential-learning-in-teams.pdf (viewed March 18, 2009).

CHAPTER 9

1. Centers for Disease Control and Prevention, "Health Habits of Adults Aged 18-29 Highlighted in Report on Nation's Health," February 18, 2009, www.cdc.gov/media/pressrel/2009/r090218.htm (accessed April 14, 2010).
2. University of Minnesota, "Health and Academic Performance: Minnesota Undergraduate Students," www.bhs.umn.edu/reports/HealthAcademicPerformanceReport_2007.pdf, 2007 (accessed April 10, 2010).
3. Kay-Tee Khaw, Nicholas Wareham, Sheila Bingham, Ailsa Welch, Robert Luben, and Nicholas Day, "Combined Impact of Health Behaviours and Mortality in Men and Women: The EPIC-Norfolk Prospective Population Study," *PLoS Medicine* 5, no. 1, 2008, www.plosmedicine.org/article/info:doi/10.1371/journal.pmed.0050012 (accessed April 10, 2009).
4. U.S. Department of Agriculture, "MyPyramid.gov," mypyramid.gov/guidelines/index.html, 2009 (accessed April 10, 2010).
5. Michael Pollan, "Unhappy Meals," *New York Times,* January 28, 2007, http://www.nytimes.com/2007/01/28/magazine/28nutritionism.t.html (accessed April 10, 2010).
6. Harvard Medical School, *HEALTHbeat: 20 No-Sweat Ways to Get More Exercise,* Boston, Harvard Health Publications, October 14, 2008.
7. Mary Duenwald, "The Dorms May Be Great, but How's the Counseling?" *New York Times,* October 26, 2004, www.nytimes.com/2004/10/26/health/psychology/26cons.html?_r=1 (accessed April 14, 2010).
8. American College Health Association, *American College Health Association–National College Health Assessment II: Reference Group, Executive Summary Fall 2008,* www.acha-ncha.org/docs/ACHA-NCHA_Reference_Group_ExecutiveSummary_Fall2008.pdf, 2009 (accessed April 9, 2010).
9. M. Schaffer, E. L. Jeglic, and B. Stanley, "The Relationship between Suicidal Behavior, Ideation, and Binge Drinking among College Students," *Archives of Suicide Research* 12, no. 2, 2008, pp. 124–132.
10. Steven C. Hayes, *Get Out of Your Mind and Into Your Life: The New Acceptance and Commitment Therapy* (Oakland, CA: New Harbinger, 2004).
11. U.S. Centers for Disease Control and Prevention, "2004 Surgeon General's Report—The Health Consequences of Smoking," http://www.cdc.gov/tobacco/data_statistics/sgr/2004/, 2004 (accessed April 10, 2010).
12. Centers for Disease Control and Prevention, "Trends in Reportable Sexually Transmitted Diseases in the United States, 2007," www.cdc.gov/nchhstp/newsroom/docs/STDTrendsFactSheet.pdf, 2009 (accessed April 9, 2010).

CHAPTER 10

1. National Center on Education and the Economy, *Tough Choices or Tough Times: The Report of the New Commission on the Skills of the American Workforce,* San Francisco, Jossey-Bass, 2007.
2. Frank Levy and Richard J. Murnane, *The New Division of Labor: How Computers Are Creating the Next Job Market,* Princeton, NJ, Princeton University Press, 2004), pp. 47–48.
3. Richard N. Bolles, *What Color Is Your Parachute? A Practical Manual for Job-Hunters and Career-Changers,* Berkeley, CA, updated annually.
4. Viktor Frankl, *Man's Search for Meaning,* New York, Simon & Schuster, 1970, p. 104.

Further Reading

Adler, Mortimer, and Charles Van Doren. *How to Read a Book: The Classic Guide to Intelligent Reading.* New York: Touchstone, 1972.

Allen, David. *Getting Things Done: The Art of Stress-Free Productivity.* New York: Penguin, 2001.

Belsky, Scott. *Making Ideas Happen: Overcoming the Obstacles Between Vision and Reality.* New York: Portfolio, 2010.

Bolles, Richard N. *What Color Is Your Parachute? A Practical Manual for Job-Hunters and Career-Changers.* Berkeley, CA: Ten Speed, updated annually.

Boston Women's Health Book Collective. *Our Bodies, Ourselves: A New Edition for a New Era.* New York: Touchstone, 2005.

Buzan, Tony. How to Mind Map: *Make the Most of Your Mind and Learn to Create, Organize and Plan.* New York: Thorsons/Element, 2003.

Chaffee, John. *Thinking Critically,* Tenth Edition. Florence, KY: Cengage, 2012.

Colvin, George. *Talent is Overrated: What Really Separates World-Class Performers from Everybody Else.* New York: Portfolio, 2008.

Coplin, Bill. *10 Things Employers Want You to Learn in College.* Berkeley, CA: Ten Speed, 2003.

Covey, Stephen R. *The Seven Habits of Highly Effective People: Powerful Lessons in Personal Change.* New York: Simon & Schuster, 1989.

Davis, Deborah. *The Adult Learner's Companion,* Second Edition. Florence, KY: Cengage, 2012.

Downing, Skip. *On Course: Strategies for Creating Success in College and in Life,* Sixth Edition. Florence, KY: Cengage, 2011.

Elgin, Duane. *Voluntary Simplicity.* New York: Morrow, 1993.

Ellis, Dave. *Becoming a Master Student,* Thirteenth Edition. Florence, KY: Cengage, 2011.

Ellis, Dave. *Falling Awake: Creating the Life of Your Dreams.* Rapid City, SD: Breakthrough Enterprises, 2000.

Facione, Peter. *Critical Thinking: What It Is and Why It Counts.* Millbrae, CA: California Academic Press, 1996.

Fletcher, Anne. *Sober for Good.* Boston: Houghton Mifflin, 2001.

From Master Student to Master Employee, Third Edition. Florence, KY: Cengage, 2011.

Gawain, Shakti. *Creative Visualization.* New York: New World Library, 1998.

Glasser, William. *Take Effective Control of Your Life.* New York: HarperCollins, 1984.

Godin, Seth. *Linchpin: Are You Indispensable?* New York: Portfolio, 2010.

Golas, Thaddeus. *The Lazy Man's Guide to Enlightenment.* New York: Bantam, 1993.

Greene, Susan D., and Melanie C. L. Martel. *The Ultimate Job Hunter's Guidebook,* Fifth Edition. Florence, KY: Cengage, 2008.

Hallowell, Edward M. *CrazyBusy: Overstretched, Overbooked, and About to Snap!* New York: Ballantine, 2006.

Keyes, Ken, Jr. *Handbook to Higher Consciousness.* Berkeley, CA: Living Love, 1974.

Kolb, David A. *Experiential Learning: Experience as the Source of Learning and Development.* Englewood Cliffs: Prentice-Hall, 1984.

Levy, Frank, and Richard J. Murname. *The New Division of Labor: How Computers Are Creating the Next Job Market.* Princeton, NJ: Princeton University Press, 2004.

Newport, Cal. *How to Win at College.* New York: Random House, 2005.

Nolting, Paul D. *Math Study Skills Workbook,* Fourth Edition. Florence, KY: Cengage, 2011.

Pirsig, Robert. *Zen and the Art of Motorcycle Maintenance.* New York: Perennial Classics, 2000.

Raimes, Anne and Maria Jerskey. *Universal Keys for Writers,* Second Edition. Florence, KY: Cengage, 2008.

Ram Dass. *Be Here Now.* Santa Fe, NM: Hanuman Foundation, 1971.

Robinson, Adam. *What Smart Students Know: Maximum Grades, Optimum Learning, Minimum Time.* New York: Crown, 1993.

Ruggiero, Vincent Ryan. *Becoming a Critical Thinker,* Sixth Edition. Florence, KY: Cengage, 2009.

Schacter, Daniel L. *Searching for Memory: The Brain, the Mind, and the Past.* New York: HarperCollins, 1997.

Toft, Doug, ed. *Master Student Guide to Academic Success.* Florence, KY: Cengage, 2005.

Trapani, Gina. *Lifehacker: 88 Tech Tricks to Turbocharge Your Day.* Indianapolis, IN: Wiley, 2007.

Ueland, Brenda. *If You Want to Write: A Book About Art, Independence and Spirit.* St. Paul, MN: Graywolf, 1987.

U.S. Department of Education. *Funding Education Beyond High School: The Guide to Federal Student Aid.* Published yearly, http://studentaid.ed.gov/students/publications/student_guide/index.html.

Watkins, Ryan, and Michael Corry. *E-learning Companion: A Student's Guide to Online Success,* Third Edition. Florence, KY: Cengage, 2011.

Wurman, Saul Richard. *Information Anxiety 2.* Indianapolis: QUE, 2001.

Photo and Illustration Credits

Chapter 1: p. viii: (l) Image copyright © William Casey. Used under license from Shutterstock.com; Edmond Van Hoorick/Jupiter Images; Ted Humble-Smith/Getty Images; © Luca Tettoni/Corbis; DAJ/Jupiter Images; Buena Vista Images/Jupiter Images; Katsuo Yamagishi / SPORT / Jupiter Images; Skip Brown/National Geographic/Getty Images; Image copyright © Andrey Burmakin. Used under license from Shutterstock.com; p. viii: (t) © razihusin/Shutterstock.com; p. viii: (c) © sashkin/Shutterstock.com; viii: (bc) yuyangc/Shutterstock.com; p. xiii: (c) Galina Barskaya/Shutterstock.com; p. 1: (tl) © razihusin/Shutterstock.com; p. 5: (tl) Pierre Desrosiers/Getty Images; p. 5: (tcl) Aaron Lindber/Getty Images; p. 5: (tc) Hola Images/Getty Images; p. 5: (tcr) Jamie Grill/Getty Images; p. 5: (br) Jose Luis Pelaez/Getty Images; p. 5: (br) © sashkin/Shutterstock.com; p. 8: (tr) yuyangc/Shutterstock.com; p. 10: (tl) Courtesy of Jennie Long; p. 10: (bl) Courtesy of Jennifer Jarding; p. 10: (tr) Courtesy of Alex Denizard; p. 10: (br) Courtesy of the Washington Speakers Bureau; p. 11: (tl) © Bettmann/CORBIS; p. 11: (tr) Photo by John Lamparski/WireImage; p. 13: (c) Image copyright © Evgeny Vasenev. Used under license from Shutterstock.com

Chapter 2: p. 14: (r) © Robert Kneschke/Shutterstock.com; p. 14: (t) Tanya Constantine/Getty Images; p. 14: (t) Tim Laman/Getty Images; p. 14: (t) Scott T. Baxter/Getty Images; p. 14: (t) Vladimir Godnik/Getty Images; p. 14: (t) Meg Takamura/Getty Images; p. 14: (t) Doug Menuez/Photodisc/Getty Images; p. 14: (t) Gregor Schuster/Getty Images; p. 14: (t) Stockbyte/Getty Images; p. 14: (t) Stockbyte/Getty Images; p. 15: (tl) Tanya Constantine; p. 15: (tl) Tim Laman/Getty Images; p. 15: (tl) Scott T. Baxter/Getty Images; p. 15: (tl) Vladimir Godnik/Getty Images; p. 15: (tl) Getty Images; p. 15: (tl) Doug Menuez/Getty Images; p. 15: (tl) Gregor Schuster/Getty Images; p. 15: (tl) George Doyle/Getty Images; p. 15: (tl) Stockbyte/Getty Images; p. 17: (c) © Noam Armonn/Shutterstock.com

Chapter 3: p. 18: (l) Image copyright © Monkey Business Images. Used under license from Shutterstock.com; p. 18: (c) Fuse/Jupiter Images; p. 18: (tc) PaulPaladin/Shutterstock.com; p. 18: (bc) Temych/Shutterstock.com; p. 18: (t) design56/Shutterstock.com; p. 18: (b) Laurent Renault/Shutterstock.com; p. 19: (tc) design56/Shutterstock.com; p. 22: (tc) PaulPaladin/Shutterstock.com: p. 27: (tl) Fuse/Jupiter Images; p. 28: (tr) Temych/Shutterstock.com; p. 29: (tl) Laurent Renault/Shutterstock.com; p. 31: (c) Image copyright ©. Used under license from Shutterstock.com

Chapter 4: p. 32: (r) Image copyright © Francesco Ridolfi. Used under license from Shutterstock.com; p. 32: (tc) Jim Craigmyle/Corbis; p. 32: (tc) Jim Craigmyle/Corbis; p. 32: (c) Jim Craigmyle/Corbis; p. 32: (bc) © moodboard/Corbis; p. 32: (t) © MartinaK/Shutterstock.com; p. 32: (b) © Elnur/Shutterstock.com; p. 33: (tl) © MartinaK/Shutterstock.com; p. 34: (tl) Jim Craigmyle/Corbis; p. 34: (tcl) Jim Craigmyle/Corbis; p. 36: (cl) Jim Craigmyle/Corbis; p. 38: (tl) © moodboard/Corbis; p. 41: (tc) © Elnur/Shutterstock.com; p. 43: (c) Image copyright © Alex Staroseltsev. Used under license from Shutterstock.com

Chapter 5: p. 44: (r) Image copyright © Monkey Business Images. Used under license from Shutterstock.com; p. 44: (bc) Image Source/Jupiter Images; p. 44: (t) © Denis and Yulia Pogostins/Shutterstock.com; p. 44: (tc) © Katrina Brown/Shutterstock.com; p. 44: (tc) © Greg Hinsdale/Corbis; p. 44: (c) © Norberto Mario Lauria/Shutterstock.com; p. 44: (bc) © filipw/Shutterstock.com; p. 44: (b) © photoroller/Shutterstock.com; p. 44: (bc) © Jouke Van Keulen/Shutterstock.com; p. 45: (tl) © Denis and Yulia Pogostins/Shutterstock.com; p. 46: (tr) © Katrina Brown/Shutterstock.com; p. 47: (tr) © Greg Hinsdale/Corbis; p. 50: (tr) © Norberto Mario Lauria/Shutterstock.com; p. 52: (tl) © filipw/Shutterstock.com; p. 54: (tl) © Jouke Van Keulen/Shutterstock.com; p. 56: (tl) Image Source/Jupiter Images; p. 57: (tl) © photoroller/Shutterstock.com; p. 59: (c) Image copyright © Kapu. Used under license from Shutterstock.com

Chapter 6: p. 60: (l) Image copyright © Monkey Business Images. Used under license from Shutterstock.com; p. 60: (b) © Bloomimage/Corbis; p. 60: (t) © Bill Aron / PhotoEdit; p. 60: (tc) © Dennis Owusu-Ansah/Shutterstock.com; p. 60: (c) © M. Dykstra/Shutterstock.com; p. 60: (c) © zimmytws/Shutterstock.com; p. 60: (bc) © cameilia/Shutterstock.com; p. 61: (tl) © Bill Aron / PhotoEdit; p. 62: (tr) © Dennis Owusu-Ansah/Shutterstock.com; p. 64: (c) © M. Dykstra/Shutterstock.com; p. 67 olly/Shutterstock.com; p. 68: (tl) © zimmytws/Shutterstock.com; p. 70: (c) © cameilia/Shutterstock.com; p. 72: (tl) © Bloomimage/Corbis; p. 75: (c) Image copyright © Gorilla. Used under license from Shutterstock.com

Chapter 7: p. 76: (l) Image copyright © AVAVA. Used under license from Shutterstock.com; p. 76: (tc) Floresco Productions/Getty Images; p. 76: (t) © RTImages/ Shutterstock.com; p. 76: (c) © Zoran Vukmanov Simokov/Shutterstock.com; p. 76: (c) © Zoran Vukmanov Simokov/Shutterstock.com; p. 76: (bc) © Reddogs/Shutterstock.com; p. 76: (b) © James Steidl/Shutterstock.com; p. 77: (tl) © RTImages/ Shutterstock.com; p. 78: (cr) Floresco Productions/Getty Images; p. 78: (tr) maigi/Shutterstock.com; p. 80: (tr) © Zoran Vukmanov Simokov/Shutterstock.com; p. 83: (tr) © Zoran Vukmanov Simokov/Shutterstock.com; p. 84: (tr) © Reddogs/Shutterstock.com; p. 86: (tr) © James Steidl/Shutterstock.com; p. 89: (c) Image copyright © Jan Martin Will. Used under license from Shutterstock.com

Chapter 8: p. 90: (l) Image copyright © Andresr. Used under license from Shutterstock.com; p. 90: (tc) David Madison/Photographer's Choice/Getty Images; p. 90: (t) ©Bayanova Svetlana/Shutterstock.com; p. 90: (c) © Stefanovi/Shutterstock.com; p. 90: (c) © James Steidl/Shutterstock.com; p. 90: (bc) © Dmitrijs Mihejevs/Shutterstock.com; p. 90: (b) ©J. Helgason/Shutterstock.com; p. 91: (tl) © Bayanova Svetlana/Shutterstock.com; p. 92: (tr) David Madison/Photographer's Choice/Getty Images; p. 94: (tl) © Stefanovi/Shutterstock.com; p. 96: (bc) © James Steidl/Shutterstock.com; p. 98: (bc) ©Dmitrijs Mihejevs/Shutterstock.com; p. 100: (bl) © J. Helgason/Shutterstock.com; p. 103: (c) Image copyright © Supri Suharjoto. Used under license from Shutterstock.com

Index

Reviewing notes, 54–55, 62–63
Revising writing, 85
Rhymes, 65
Risk taking, 17

S

Saying no, 22, 95
Self-discovery skills, 119
Serendipity, 79
Sexually transmitted
  infections, 113
Shorthand, 48
Skills
  inventory, 120
  transferable, 118–120
Sleep, thinking process, 79
Smallpox, 79
Social life, 67
Source cards, 57
Speaking, reading, 38
Speed, reading, 41
STIs, 113
Stress management, 70–71, 72–73,
  75, 87, 110–111
Student loans, 29
*Student's Guide to Succeeding at
  Community College,* 109
Study groups, 46, 63, 73
Success, essentials, 6–7
Suicide, 71
Summary notes, 62
Support networks, 12
Surrender, 115
Syphilis, 113

T

Teams, 100–101
Technical skills, 118

Tests
  Action Statement, 74
  Commit to Action, 74
  Critical Thinking Experiment, 69
  detachment, 75
  Discovery Statement, 74
  Discovery Wheel, 3
  errors, 68, 69
  grades, 61, 69
  Intention Statement, 74
  math, 72–73
  memory, improving, 64–67
  Power Process, 75
  predicting questions, 56
  preparing for, 62–63
  skills, transferable, 119
  stress management, 70–71, 72–73
Text, marking, 36–37
The New Division of Labor, 127
Thesis statements, 84
Thinking
  brainstorming, 78, 82
  Critical Thinking Experiment, 82
  Discovery Wheel, 2–3
  expert, 127
  focusing and letting go, 78
  idea files, 79
  logic mistakes, 83
  overview, 77
  refining ideas, 80–81
  serendipity, 79
  skills, transferable, 119
  sleeping, 79
  viewpoints, 80–81
  writing strategies, 84–85
Time management
  changing behavior, 22–23
  Commit to Action, 24–26
  Discovery Wheel, 3
  overview, 19

  procrastination, 22, 27
  skills, 119
To-do list, 22–23
Tolerance, viewpoints, 81
Tough Choices or Tough Times, 127
Transferable skills, 118–120
Transition words, note-taking, 51
Trial choice, major, 122

U

Underlining text, 36–37
Using book, 7

V

Values, 6
Verbal messages, 96–97
Verbs, note-taking, 50
Victimhood, 133
Viewpoints, ideas, 80–81
Visual associations, 64–65
Visuals, presentations, 87
Voice recording lectures, 48

W

Walpole, Horace, 79
*What Color Is Your
  Parachute?,* 128
When Teams Work Best, 100
Work, planning for, 127
Writing
  plagiarism, 85
  presentations, 86–87
  strategies, 84–85

Y

You're One Click Away, defined, 1

144

1 Getting Started and Getting Involved

MAKE THE TRANSITION TO HIGHER EDUCATION

- **Connect** to resources—campus clubs and organizations, and school and community services.
- **Meet** with your academic advisor.
- **Attend** every class and participate actively.
- **Take the initiative** to meet new people.
- **Share your feelings** with friends, family members, and a counselor.

REMEMBER THREE SUCCESS ESSENTIALS

- **Discovery**—telling the truth about your current thoughts, feelings, behaviors, and circumstances.
- **Intention**—committing to make specific changes in behavior.
- **Action**—using consistent behavior changes to produce new results in life.

USE THE DISCOVERY WHEEL

Apply the cycle of discovery, intention, and action to 10 areas of your life:

- **Purpose**—knowing what you want to accomplish in school and over the course of your life.
- **Learning Styles**—knowing how you prefer to perceive and process information and being willing to expand your preferences.
- **Time and Money**—setting goals, taking action to achieve them, balancing expenses and income, and securing enough money to complete your education.
- **Reading**—previewing your assignments, asking questions about the material, and reviewing the answers.

- **Notes**—focusing your attention in class, separating key points from supporting materials, and putting ideas in your own words.
- **Memory and Tests**—separating your grades from your self-concept, reviewing course material, and using test time effectively.
- **Thinking and Communicating**—creating ideas, refining ideas, and effectively presenting them through writing and speaking.
- **Relationships**—listening effectively, sharing your thoughts and feelings in a respectful way, and collaborating on group projects.
- **Health**—eating to manage weight, exercising regularly, and meeting the demands of life with energy to spare.
- **Major and Career**—translating your interests, abilities, and values into an academic plan and role in the workplace.

DISCOVER WHAT YOU WANT

- Discovering what you want makes it more likely that you'll get what you want.
- Discovering what you want greatly enhances your odds of succeeding in higher education.
- Every day, you can do one thing—no matter how simple or small—that takes you closer to getting what you want.
- Look for connections between your passions and your coursework.
- Do the suggested activities in this book, including the Discovery Wheel, Critical Thinking Experiments, and Commit to Action exercises.

Using Your Learning Styles

Risk being a fool

LEARNING STYLES ESSENTIALS

According to psychologist David Kolb, we learn best through four kinds of activity:

- **Concrete experience**—absorbing information through our five senses.

- **Reflective observation**—creating ideas that make sense of events.

- **Abstract conceptualization**—integrating our initial ideas into general models of how the world works.

- **Active experimentation**—using our models to make predictions and plan behaviors.

TAKE YOURSELF THROUGH THE COMPLETE CYCLE OF LEARNING

Ask the following questions to experience each mode of learning:

- **Why?** to make a personal connection with a subject to be learned (Mode 1).

- **What?** to discover the main points, facts, and procedures related to that subject (Mode 2).

- **How?** to test ideas through action (Mode 3).

- **What if?** to apply ideas in new contexts (Mode 4).

EXPLORE SEVERAL VIEWS OF LEARNING STYLES

- The Learning Style Inventory in this book is based on David Kolb's ideas about learning from experience.

- Howard Gardner of Harvard University developed the theory of multiple intelligences, which describes 8 unique ways of learning.

- The VAK system focuses on how we learn from visual, auditory, and kinesthetic experience.

- Approach the topic of learning styles as a way to experiment, have fun, and promote your success in school.

- Remember that deep learning takes place when we embrace a variety of styles and strategies.

MAKE YOUR LEARNING STYLES WORK FOR YOU

- Keep your learning preferences in mind as you choose courses, declare a major, and plan your career.

- Expect classmates and workers to demonstrate many different styles.

- Look for clues to different learning styles.

- Collaborate with people and resolve conflict while staying aware of differences in learning styles.

- Cope with differences in teaching styles by using all four modes of learning.

- Remember that any learning styles inventory is just a snapshot of how you learn today.

- See learning as a continuous a process, as well as a series of outcomes.

- Keep your focus on answering two key questions: "How do I currently learn?" and "How can I become a more successful learner?"

RISK BEING A FOOL

We learn by taking appropriate risks. Remember:

- We are all fallible human beings.

- Learning includes making mistakes.

- This is not a suggestion to be foolhardy or to "fool around."

3 Taking Charge of Your Time and Money

SET GOALS

- Brainstorm a list of what you want to experience in all areas of your life.
- Restate your wants as goals—specific outcomes with clear due dates.
- On your to-do list and calendar, list the actions you'll take to achieve your goals.

TAKE BACK YOUR TIME

We cannot "manage" time, but we can manage our productivity:

- Complete key tasks immediately, whenever that's appropriate.
- Delegate tasks that are better handled by other people.
- Say no to low-priority projects.
- Use a calendar to schedule commitments that are tied to a specific date.
- Write reminders about things to do in the future—and reviewing those reminders regularly.
- Schedule challenging tasks for times when our energy peaks.
- Look beyond today to get an overview of our commitments over the coming months.

DISCOVER WHERE YOUR TIME GOES

- Choose a specific period of time to monitor—one day, a week, or a month.
- During this period, record each of your activities and how long they last.
- At the end of the day, week, or month, total up how much time you spent on each activity.
- Based on the results of your time monitoring, choose to spend more or less time on certain activities.

END PROCRASTINATION

- Check for attitudes—such as perfectionism and fear of taking risks—that promote procrastination.
- Accept feelings of discomfort about a task and then move into action.
- Break large goals down into tasks that you can complete in 10 minutes or less.
- Remember that you can start a task even when you don't feel "motivated."

END MONEY WORRIES

- Monitor how much money you earn and spend each month.
- Live within your means by increasing income and decreasing expenses.
- Use credit cards with caution.
- Borrow as little money as possible and select loans carefully.

BE HERE NOW

You can be more effective at any task when you give it your full attention:

- Simply become aware distractions of instead of trying to resist them.
- Enter the present moment by tuning into sights, sounds, and other sensations.
- Keep returning your attention to the task at hand.
- Notice any self-judgments about how often you get distracted—and release those thoughts as well.
- See this Power Process as a path to practical benefits—saving time, getting more out of classes, becoming a better listener, reading with more comprehension, enjoying meals, and even having more fun at parties.

Achieving Your Purpose for Reading

APPROACH READING ASSIGNMENTS WITH A THREE-PART STRATEGY

To extract key ideas and information:

- **Question** the text by previewing it, outlining it, and listing what you want to discover.

- **Read** with focused attention, make multiple passes through the text, and find answers to your questions.

- **Review** by reflecting on those answers, reciting them, and returning to them at regular intervals in the future.

TAKE YOUR READING SKILLS TO A HIGHER LEVEL

- When reading a difficult text, mark the places where you get confused and look for a pattern in your marks.

- Isolate key words—usually nouns and verbs—and define them.

- Read difficult passages out loud several times.

- Skip to the end of an article or chapter and look for a summary of the key points.

- Stop at least once during each chapter or section to summarize what you understand—and list questions about what you do not understand.

- Pose your questions to an instructor, tutor, or classmate.

- Take a break from reading and come back to the text with a fresh perspective.

- Focus on the sections of the text that directly answer your questions; skim or skip the rest.

- Adjust your reading pace, based on the difficulty of the text.

THINK CRITICALLY ABOUT WHAT YOU READ

- Remember that two cornerstones of critical thinking are the abilities to test logic and look for evidence.

- Make a list of the main points in what you read, along with the facts, examples, and expert testimony used to support each point.

- Review what you read to see if key terms are defined clearly.

- Be alert for statements that contradict each other.

- Look for assumptions—statements that are taken as true and offered without evidence.

IDEAS ARE TOOLS

- Notice your immediate response to new ideas.

- Instead of rejecting new ideas, look for their potential value.

- if an idea doesn't work for you today, then be willing to consider it again tomorrow

Participating in Class and Taking Notes

5

NOTE-TAKING ESSENTIALS

- Set the stage for note taking by completing your reading assignments on schedule.

- Arrive early to class, sit in front, and use the spare time to review previous notes.

- Label notebooks with your name, your phone number, the class name, and the date of the notes.

- Leave blank space in your notes so that you can add related information later.

- Write on only one side of each piece of paper.

- Use a three-ring binder to store notes.

- As you take notes in class, use the Power Process: "Be here now" to release distractions.

- Accurately record ideas even when you disagree with them.

- Focus on a speaker's content rather than appearance or presentation style.

- Record your own comments and questions in a separate section of your notes.

- Reduce a speaker's ideas to key words—essential nouns and verbs that are rich in associations.

- Write crucial points in complete sentences that use the instructor's exact words.

- Look for verbal and nonverbal clues from your instructor about which material is most important.

- Write review and research notes based on your reading, taking care to credit your sources and avoid plagiarism.

CREATE MORE VALUE FROM YOUR NOTES

- In your notes, flag possible test items.

- Experiment with various formats for note taking—the Cornell format, outlines, and concept maps.

- As you review your notes, revise them for clarity.

- "Rehearse" your notes by reciting key points in your own words.

- Create possible test items based on your notes and practice answering them.

LOVE YOUR PROBLEMS

There are three possible responses to any problem:

- Deny it.

- Resist it.

- "Love" it—that is, accept that it exists and find solutions.

To apply this Power Process:

- See problems as neutral feedback about the current limits of your skills.

- State problems clearly and brainstorm solutions.

- Turn solutions into actions.

6 Maximizing Your Memory and Mastering Tests

PREPARE FOR TESTS

- Remember that a grade is only a measure of how you score on a test—not a measure of your intelligence or worth as a human being.

- To begin preparing for tests, create a checklist of the material that you intend to review.

- Create summary notes that integrate material from assignments, class meetings, lab sessions, and handouts.

- Create flash cards based on your notes.

- Create a mock test and "take" it before you take the real test.

- Ask your instructors whether they will release copies of previous tests.

- Do three levels of review—a daily review of new material in each course, a weekly review, and a major review before a scheduled test.

USE THE SIX "R's" OF REMEMBERING

- **Relax** when you study.
- **Reduce** distractions in your study environment.
- **Relate** new material to things that you already know.
- **Restructure** material in meaningful ways.
- **Recite** key points.
- **Repeat** your reviews until you know the material well.

RELEASE TEST STRESS

- Prevent test-taking errors by reading test instructions carefully.

- If you get stuck on a question, reread it, come back to it later, and look for possible answers in other test items.

- Prepare for a test by "overlearning" the material, eating well, and sleeping well.

- Accept your feelings of stress about a test.

- Use stress management techniques, such as deep breathing, relaxation exercises, and aerobic exercise.

- If you feel consistently anxious about tests, see a counselor.

DETACH

- Notice the thoughts and body sensations associated with stress; as you do, release any resistance or self-judgment.

- Put a test into perspective by imagining how important the results will be in a month, a year, or a decade from today.

- Imagine the worst possible outcome of failing a test; it will be something that you can live with.

- Your thoughts, feelings, goals, and behaviors will change over time.

- Remember that you can continue to set and achieve goals—and that you will be okay even if you fail to achieve a goal.

7 Thinking Clearly and Communicating Your Ideas

THINK CREATIVELY AND CRITICALLY

- Practice brainstorming to create many possible ideas.

- Focus intensely on a question for a short time; then take a break while you let go of finding any answers.

- Look for new ideas from a variety of sources.

- Keep track of your ideas by writing them down and reviewing them.

- Read voraciously.

- Write down your ideas, file them for easy reference, and review those files.

- Refine your favorite ideas and follow through with appropriate action.

- Practice critical thinking by asking four questions: Why am I considering this issue? What are the various points of view on this issue? How well is each point of view supported? What if I could combine various points of view or create a new one?

- Be alert to fallacies in logic, such as jumping to conclusions and making personal attacks.

DEVELOP WRITING SKILLS

- List and schedule writing tasks.

- Choose a topic that you can adequately cover in the assigned number of words or length of presentation.

- Write a title and thesis statement—a complete sentence that captures the main point you want to make about your topic.

- Choose a purpose for your paper or presentation—a change in the way your audience members think, feel, or behave.

- Do initial research to get an overview of your topic.

- Create an outline of your paper or presentation.

- Do in-depth research to support your key points, carefully documenting the source of each quotation, summary, or paraphrase.

- Write a first draft without stopping to revise.

- Edit your draft for scope, structure, and style.

- Proofread your paper.

DEVELOP PRESENTATION SKILLS

- Analyze your audience members, remembering that they have a primary question: *Why does this presentation matter to me?*

- Organize your ideas for a presentation into three main sections: introduction, body, and conclusion.

- Create speaking notes and visuals to support your presentation.

- Grab your audience's attention with a compelling fact, quote, or story.

- State your main points early in the presentation.

- Practice your presentation several times—preferably in the place where you will deliver it.

- Deal with nervousness by accepting your feelings and focusing on the content of your presentation rather than your delivery.

- Practice speaking up in class discussions.

FIND A BIGGER PROBLEM

- Our problems seem to follow the same law of physics that gases do: They expand to fill more and more of our time and attention.

- To solve smaller problems in less time and with less energy, take on bigger problems as well.

- The goal of a master student is not to eliminate problems but to take on problems that are big enough to merit our time and energy.

USE YOUR WORD TO TRANSFORM YOUR RELATIONSHIPS

- Before you say that you're upset with someone, see whether you're holding a mental picture about how that person is "supposed" to behave; then be willing to release that picture.

- Make agreements that stretch you toward new possibilities—and then keep your agreements.

- Speak more in terms of possibilities ("I could. . . .") and promises ("I will. . . .") rather than obligations ("I have to. . . .").

- To prevent an overloaded schedule, say no to requests that are not high priorities for you.

- Use "I" messages to communicate you're upset without blaming other people.

- Before you speak, distinguish between your factual *observations* of another person's behavior and your *interpretations* of those behaviors.

THRIVE WITH DIVERSITY AND TEAMS

- Make a conscious attempt to see events from another person's point of view.

- Reflect on your experiences of privilege and prejudice.

- Look for common ground with people who differ from you.

- When speaking with people from other cultures, look for common ground and relate to them as individuals rather than group representatives.

- Reflect on your own experiences of prejudice—and privilege.

- Be willing to accept feedback from people of other cultures.

- Speak out against discrimination.

- Be alert for differences between people from individualist and collectivist cultures.

- When working on teams, be alert for a variety of learning styles, move through the cycle of learning, and apply the Power Processes from this book.

LISTEN EFFECTIVELY

- During conversation, listen without interrupting—then pause for a few seconds before you begin to talk.

- Display openness through your facial expression and posture.

- Send messages that you are listening, such as "Mm-hmm," "Okay," "Yes," and head nods.

- While you listen, notice distracting thoughts and let them go.

- Listen without judging; you can share your own ideas later.

- Listen for the requests and intentions implied by a complaint.

- Allow people to express emotion as they speak.

- Notice nonverbal messages.

- Keep questions to a minimum and avoid giving advice.

- Pause periodically to check how well you understand what other people are saying.

- When people stop speaking, ask: "Is there any more that you want to say?"

- Be willing to change your thinking and behavior as a result of listening.

CHOOSE YOUR CONVERSATIONS

- Conversations shape our attitudes and behaviors from moment to moment.

- Focus on conversations that align with your values and intentions.

- When you find yourself in a negative, draining conversation, change the subject—or politely excuse yourself.

Choosing
Greater Health

TAKE A FEARLESS LOOK AT YOUR HEALTH

- Periodically write discovery statements about your current health habits, including those that relate to eating, exercise, drug use, personal relationships, sleep, and stress management.

- Follow up with intention statements about habits that you'd like to change.

- Act on your intentions daily.

CHOOSE YOUR FUEL

- When planning meals, review the federal government's "food pyramid" guidelines.

- Consider Michael Pollen's summary of nutritional wisdom: "Eat food. Mostly plants. Not too much."

EXERCISE

- Stay physically active throughout the day.

- Look for exercise facilities on campus.

- Find forms of exercise that you enjoy.

- When possible, exercise with other people.

MANAGE STRESS BEFORE IT TURNS INTO DISTRESS

- Focus your attention on the present moment.

- Scan your body for areas of tension and relax them.

- Relax by using guided imagery.

- Notice and release beliefs that make absolute demands of other people and yourself.

- Speak in ways that promote detachment from negative feelings.

- Keep taking constructive action to solve problems, even when you feel angry, sad, or afraid.

- Share your feelings and get professional help when appropriate.

- Remember that a *little* tension before a big event—such as a test or presentation—can boost your alertness and energy level.

- Applying the suggestions in this chapter for sleep, exercise, and nutrition can help you manage stress.

USE ALCOHOL AND OTHER DRUGS RESPONSIBLY

- Make your own choices about the amount of alcohol that you consume, ignoring commercial promotions and peer pressure.

- Pay attention to the consequences of your alcohol and other drug use.

- If you find that you cannot consistently control the amount of drugs that you consume, then get professional help.

PROTECT YOURSELF FROM SEXUALLY TRANSMITTED INFECTION

- Abstain from sex, or have sex exclusively with one person who is free of infection and has no other sex partners.

- Talk openly with your doctor and any sexual partners about sexually transmitted infections and how to prevent them.

SURRENDER

- Recognize problems that are too big for you to handle alone.

- Remember that surrendering means admitting your limits and asking for help—not giving up.

- Look to your religious tradition, spiritual path, or philosophy of life for additional perspectives on the power of surrendering.

- Surrendering can reduce your sense of isolation by inviting other people to become part of your life.

- You can apply all of your energy and skill to solving a problem—and surrender at the same time.

Choosing Your **Major** and Planning Your **Career**

DISCOVER YOUR SKILLS

- **Technical skills** involve a specialized body of knowledge that is applied in a specific job.
- **Transferable skills** involve knowledge that can be applied in several jobs.
- Regularly make an inventory of your skills, including both technical and transferable skills.
- Based on your inventory, plan to deepen your current skills and develop new ones.
- Review the list of transferable skills in this chapter to fuel your career plan.

CHOOSE YOUR MAJOR

- Brainstorm options for your major.
- Consider majors that are consistent with your interests, values, goals, and skills.
- Make a trial choice of major, and then test that choice through experiences such as internships.
- Consider creating your own major and a choosing a complementary minor.
- Remember that many majors can lead you to more than one career.
- Make a trial choice of major as soon as possible.
- Test your trial major with a variety of experiences, such as course work, internships, information interviews, and feedback from other people.
- Remember that it's common for people to change their major—and their career.

PLAN YOUR CAREER

- Begin career planning now.
- When creating a career plan, begin by ruling out the careers that you do *not* want.
- See career planning as a process of ongoing discovery rather than a quest to find the "right" career for you.
- Research the vast range of careers available in today's economy.
- In your career plan, name your preferred skills, your preferred job titles, your job contacts, your preferred employer or clients, and your preferred location.
- Test your choice of a career through internships and other work experiences.
- Revise and refine your career plan frequently.
- To enhance your career prospects, complete your education, create a long-term career plan, and develop skills in complex communication and expert thinking.

I CREATE IT ALL

- When you experience a problem, be willing to see whether it results from any of your own beliefs or behaviors.
- Remember that you have choices about how to respond to any situation.
- Use this Power Process to avoid seeing yourself as a victim of circumstances and the behavior of other people.
- Approach "I create it all" as a way to stimulate your thinking, adopt new ideas, and change habits.

Master Student Essentials—to Go

PURPOSE

- **Clearly define what you** want to experience in all areas of your life and take regular action to get what you want.

- **Apply the three essential elements of success**—discovery, intention, action.

- **Access resources**—campus clubs and organizations, advisors, and school and community services to achieve your purpose for being in school.

LEARNING STYLES

- **You can learn anything** through four activities—concrete experience, reflective observation, abstract conceptualization, and active experimentation.

- **Your preference** for combining those four activities is unique to you.

- When learning anything, expand your preferences by asking: **Why** is this important? What are the key ideas? **How** can I apply this? **What if** I could apply this in a new way?

TIME AND MONEY

- **Take charge of time** by translating desires into goals and action plans.

- **Become more productive** by completing tasks promptly, delegating, saying no, using a calendar, and listing reminders of what you're committed to do in the future.

- **Take charge of money** by aligning your expenses with your income.

READING

- **Question** your text by previewing it, outlining it, and listing what you want to discover.

- **Read** with focused attention, make multiple passes through the text, and find answers to your questions.

- **Review** by reflecting on those answers, reciting them, and returning to them at regular intervals in the future.

NOTES

- **Set the stage** for taking powerful notes by completing assignments on time, getting to class on time, and bringing essential materials.

- **Show up for class** by participating with full attention.

- **Reduce ideas to their essence**, record them in several formats, and review your notes regularly.

MEMORY AND TESTS

- **Detach** from grades by seeing them as measurements of test performance—not measurements of intelligence or self-worth.

- **Prepare for tests** by doing daily reviews, weekly reviews, and major reviews before a scheduled exam.

- **Use stress management techniques** when taking tests.

THINKING AND COMMUNICATING

- **Open up to new ideas** with creative thinking and consider many points of view.

- **Refine ideas** by looking for supporting evidence and avoiding fallacies in logic.

- **Prepare to write** by defining your topic, writing a thesis statement, and listing questions to answer through research.

- **Write a draft and revise it** for scope, structure, and style.

- **Deliver effective presentations** through planning, practicing, and focusing on your content rather than your delivery.

RELATIONSHIPS

- **Release your expectations** about how people "must" behave and respond to how they actually *do* behave.

- **Make powerful agreements** and keep them.

- **Create positive relationships** by accepting differences between people, listening fully to what they say, and asking for what you want in a respectful way.

- **Thrive with diversity** by staying alert to the differences between individualist and collective cultures—and by looking for what you share in common with people from any culture.

- **Lead high-performance teams** by applying your knowledge of learning styles and the Power Processes.

HEALTH

- **Take a detailed and honest look** at your current health habits.

- **Commit to changing** any habits that do not serve your health.

- **Learn a variety of skills** for effective nutrition, exercise, and stress management.

YOUR MAJOR AND CAREER

- **Inventory your skills**, including technical skills and transferable skills.

- **Declare your major** on a trial basis, and then test it through related experiences.

- **Plan your career now** and revise your plan as you gain more self-knowledge and skills.

You're One Click Away . . .

1 GETTING STARTED AND GETTING INVOLVED

More strategies for mastering the art of transition

Online Discovery Wheel

More qualities of a master student

More suggestions for Discovery, Intention, and Action Statements

More information about defining your values and aligning your actions

More ideas for accessing campus and community resources

Sample purpose statements

More profiles of master students

More ways to discover what you want

2 USING YOUR LEARNING STYLES

More information on the four modes of learning

More information on multiple intelligences and VAK styles

More ways to use your current learning styles and develop new ones

More ways to take creative risks

3 TAKING CHARGE OF YOUR TIME AND MONEY

Online goal-setting exercise

Additional ways to become more productive

Online time monitor

More ways to prevent procrastination

More ways to increase your income, decrease your expenses, and pay for school

More ways to "be here now"

4 ACHIEVING YOUR PURPOSE FOR READING

More strategies for powerful previewing

More strategies for reading to answer your questions

More ways to think critically about your reading

More strategies for powerful reviewing

More ways to master challenging material

More ways to see ideas as tools

5 PARTICIPATING IN CLASS AND TAKING NOTES

More ways to set the stage for note taking

More strategies for "showing up" as you take notes

More ways to capture key points and supporting details

More strategies for reducing ideas to their essence

More ways to predict test questions

More formats for note taking

More ways to revise, review, and rehearse your notes

More ways to love your problems

6 MAXIMIZING YOUR MEMORY AND MASTERING TESTS

More information about integrity in test taking

More strategies for test preparation

More memory strategies

More ways to avoid test-taking errors

More strategies for turning tests into feedback

More stress-management strategies

More strategies for succeeding in math courses

More ways to detach

7 THINKING CLEARLY AND COMMUNICATING YOUR IDEAS

More strategies for creative thinking

More strategies for critical thinking

More ways to avoid getting fooled by errors in logic

More ways to make your writing shine

More strategies for effective speaking

More ways to find a bigger problem

8 CREATING POSITIVE RELATIONSHIPS

More ways to make and keep powerful agreements

More ways to thrive in a diverse world

More strategies for deep listening

More ways to say *no* gracefully

More ways to resolve conflict

More ways to deliver an effective "I" message

More examples of the differences between observations and interpretations

More teamwork strategies

More ways to choose your conversations

9 CHOOSING GREATER HEALTH

More healthy ways to fuel your body

More ways to make exercise a regular part of your life

More ways to manage distress

More ways to choose your relationship to alcohol and other drugs

More ways to prevent sexually transmitted infections and unwanted pregnancy

More ways to surrender to big problems and ask for help

10 CHOOSING YOUR MAJOR AND PLANNING YOUR CAREER

More suggestions for choosing what's next in your life

More information about the nature of skills

More examples of transferable skills

More ways to identify your skills

More ways to choose your major

More career planning strategies

More strategies for succeeding in a global economy

Strategies for successful job hunting, including résumé writing and job interviewing

Online Discovery Wheel

Online Lifeline

More ways to master self-responsibility